Women of Faith and Religious Identity in Fin-de-Siècle France

Religion and Politics
Michael Barkun, *Series Editor*

Select Titles in Religion and Politics

Blood and Faith: Christianity in American White Nationalism
  Damon T. Berry

Cultural Conversions: Unexpected Consequences of Christian Missionary Encounters in the Middle East, Africa, and South Asia
  Heather J. Sharkey, ed.

Ecumenism, Memory, and German Nationalism, 1817–1917
  Stan M. Landry

Islamist Opposition in Authoritarian Regimes: The Party of Justice and Development in Morocco
  Eva Wegner

Localizing Islam in Europe: Turkish Islamic Communities in Germany and the Netherlands
  Ahmet Yükleyen

Missionary Politics in Contemporary Europe
  José Pedro Zúquete

Religion and the Rise of Nationalism: A Profile of an East-Central European City
  Robert E. Alvis

Tabernacle of Hate: Seduction into Right-Wing Extremism, Second Edition
  Kerry Noble

Women of Faith
and Religious Identity
in Fin-de-Siècle France

Emily Machen

Syracuse University Press

Copyright © 2019 by Syracuse University Press
Syracuse, New York 13244-5290

First Edition 2019

19 20 21 22 23 24   6 5 4 3 2 1

∞ The paper used in this publication meets the minimum requirements of the American
National Standard for Information Sciences—Permanence of Paper for Printed Library
Materials, ANSI Z39.48-1992.

For a listing of books published and distributed by Syracuse University Press,
visit www.SyracuseUniversityPress.syr.edu.

ISBN: 978-0-8156-3609-0 (hardcover)
      978-0-8156-3615-1 (paperback)
      978-0-8156-5452-0 (e-book)

Library of Congress Cataloging-in-Publication Data

Names: Machen, Emily, author.
Title: Women of faith and religious identity in fin-de-siècle France / Emily Machen.
Description: First [edition]. | Syracuse, NY : Syracuse University Press, 2019. |
    Series: Religion and politics | Includes bibliographical   references and index.
Identifiers: LCCN 2018045393 (print) | LCCN 2018045811 (ebook) |
    ISBN 9780815654520 (E-book) | ISBN 9780815636090 (hardcover : alk. paper) |
    ISBN 9780815636151 (pbk. : alk. paper)
Subjects: LCSH: Women—Religious life—France. | Women and religion—France. |
    Identification (Religion) | Identity (Psychology)—Religious aspects.
Classification: LCC BL625.7 (ebook) | LCC BL625.7 .M325 2019 (print) | DDC
    274.4/081082—dc23
LC record available at https://lccn.loc.gov/2018045393

Manufactured in the United States of America

Contents

Acknowledgments

As an undergraduate, I developed an interest in why people choose to join voluntary associations. The late nineteenth and early twentieth centuries saw a proliferation of organizations aimed at fixing a variety of social problems important to these organizations' members. Some groups genuinely wished to protect the most vulnerable members of society, while others preached hatred, racism, and oppression. I'm fascinated by what motivates some people to devote considerable time and energy toward helping those in need while other people are equally driven by violence, tribalism, and hatred. Often, organizations fail to fit neatly into "good" or "bad" categories but include elements of assistance and oppression at the same time. I grew up in a small, rural community where I saw religious beliefs fundamentally shape the fabric of that community, especially the lives of women. This project has grown out of my interest in understanding what drives people, especially women, to group together for social change and how religion can shape the policies and programs they develop. Unfortunately, my work has not revealed a clear path for overcoming hatred and racism. Like everyone else, women of faith are full of contradictions. The Christian women I study could preach the love of God and hatred for Jews in the same breath. But my research has helped me understand how tribalism, an individual's fierce identification with their particular group, develops and how it can shape politics and identity in powerful ways.

Writing a book often feels like a solitary process with many long hours poring over archival documents and typing alone in front of a computer. Books are never written in true isolation. I'm grateful for the many scholars whose work on women and religion provides context and enrichment for my project. I also owe special thanks to Sue Grayzel, who was my dissertation adviser at the University of Mississippi. She has read and commented on my entire project, but she has also been a kind, supportive, and extremely patient mentor. I have an amazing life, I have a great job, and I've traveled to fascinating places largely because she offered constant encouragement and gave me confidence to try new things when I lacked confidence. Many other people have also contributed to my work and my formation as a scholar. Elisa Camiscioli, Lisa Moses Leff, Leslie Moch, Lynn Sharp, and David Walker commented on various chapters of the book. I was also fortunate to attend classes with Laura Lee Downs and Nancy Green at the École des Hautes Études en Sciences Sociales (EHESS) while I was doing research in Paris. Those classes furnished interesting discussions and a great group of friends who were all researching and writing their own projects.

I've benefited from financial support from a number of sources. The University of Mississippi provided considerable support throughout my time as a graduate student, including funding my first research year in Paris. I received a Chateaubriand Fellowship from the French government that allowed me to spend a second critical year in Paris finishing research and writing a first draft of my work. My current home at the University of Northern Iowa has provided more recent funding to turn a draft into something publishable. The interlibrary loan offices at both the University of Mississippi and the University of Northern Iowa have been overwhelmingly helpful and supportive of my many requests. I appreciate the kind assistance I received in the archives of the Société de l'Histoire du Protestantisme Français, the Action Catholique des Femmes, and the Alliance Israélite Universelle.

My family and friends have also provided extraordinary support throughout my academic career. My dad, Tim Machen, never really understood any of my academic choices but was always supportive of them. My mom, Sherry Machen, has taken care of my dog every time I traveled and provided enormous amounts of home-cooked food that I could take home with me after visiting her. My brother,

Brandon Machen, and I have developed very different careers over the last decade. I've appreciated having him to talk to as we have both navigated our unique professional environments. Finally, Samantha Larimer has been my unfailing friend for the last ten years. It's rare to meet another person who you can always depend on regardless of the situation. Sam has been happy for me when things have gone well, sympathetic when I've experienced setbacks, and always supportive. I'm truly grateful for the friendship she has provided.

Principal Organizations

Action Sociale de la Femme (ASF)
Asile Israélite de Nuit
Association Catholique Internationale des Œuvres
    de Protection de la Jeune Fille (ACI)
Comité de Bienfaisance Israélite
Conférence de Versailles
Conseil National des Femmes Françaises (CNFF)
Devoir des Femmes Françaises
Les Amies de la Jeune Fille (Amies)
Ligue des Femmes Françaises (LFF)
Ligue Patriotique des Françaises (LPDF)
Œuvre Libératrice
Union Française pour le Suffrage des Femmes (UFSF)
Unions Chrétiennes de Jeunes Filles (UCJF)

Women of Faith and Religious
Identity in Fin-de-Siècle France

Introduction

Women and the Spiritual Revival of France

Women have long been important symbols of their religious communities. Prominent women such as Judith, Ruth, and Miriam stand out in the Hebrew Bible, the Christian Bible describes devoted women who followed Jesus and spread the faith after his resurrection, and Mary and various women saints occupy an important place in Catholic iconography.[1] In more modern times, Western societies have come to judge faith communities' compatibility with Western values by how they treat women. Religious women's actions, their dress, and their public visibility often indicate the compatibility of a faith group with Western culture or a faith community's rejection of "modern" values. We see this clearly in recent French debates about wearing the hijab and burqa in public, in concerns about polygamy within some American Mormon sects, and in Catholic debates about family planning and the all-male composition of the clergy. Early twentieth-century France offers an important case study for understanding how women of faith define the place of religion within a society that is increasingly guided by science, technology, and more secular values. Women's religious experiences help explain why religion has continued to exert such powerful influence in countries that seem headed toward religious disaffection.

There is a commonly accepted notion that Americans are more religious than Europeans are and that religion has a greater impact on politics in the United States than it does in Europe. France, in particular, is often presented as a bastion of secular ideals with its strict

1

notion of *laïcité*. Laïcité is a unique understanding of French republicanism that not only insists on separation of church and state but also demands that the state protect individuals from the "claims of religion."[2] Individuals present themselves as devoted French citizens by eliminating outward signs of religiosity and sequestering religion in the private spheres of the home and places of worship. Many observers were therefore shocked when large, well-organized protests erupted throughout France in response to former president François Holland's decision to legalize gay marriage in 2013. The Manif pour Tous movement revealed many things about French society, including the enduring power of Catholicism and Catholics' ability to mobilize to defend their values. France is currently in a period of religious upheaval not unlike one it experienced at the turn of the twentieth century. Some of the players are new, but many of the issues—women's rights, religious freedom vs. separation of church and state, challenges brought by immigration, and the protection of minority groups—are mirrored in both eras. For most nations, even secular ones, religion forms an important component of their culture. Even when church and state are separated, some faith communities become well-accepted parts of the national community while others remain on the fringes or outside of the social mainstream. Whether a faith community is accepted as mainstream or pushed to the social margins often hinges on the community's treatment of women.

The turn of the twentieth century saw the massive mobilization of French laywomen into faith-based organizations aimed at social and religious reform. The same period saw women of faith make significant advances as religious leaders within their communities. As fewer and fewer men actively engaged in religious work, women stepped in to take their places. Women published magazines, founded social programs for the poor, became deacons in their churches, led pilgrimages, spoke at conferences, and served alongside prominent men in a variety of social programs. Where religious and social work occurred, women often forged the path. Male religious leaders were not always thrilled with women's prominent religious positions, but they could not afford to turn away zealous women engaged in God's work. This study explores the faith-based engagement of French Catholic, Protestant, and Jewish women largely through the lens of voluntary associations that these women developed between 1880 and 1920. I argue that women's faith-based work promoted democratic, egalitarian practices within religious communities and the French nation. It allowed women to protect the place of religion in French society by presenting their communities as modern, progressive, and patriotic. Through faith-based work, women shaped France's ever-changing cultural and religious identities in ways that protected institutions that promoted their goals and provided them with a public platform unavailable in other areas of French society.

Women's Associations

Women's faith-based engagement was most noticeable and most dramatic within the Catholic community. The twentieth century saw hundreds of thousands of Catholic women engaged in very public efforts to defend their faith, save souls, and facilitate social change. Jeanne Chenu, the wife of a prominent conservative judge, founded the first of these twentieth-century organizations, the Action Sociale de la Femme (ASF), in 1900. Chenu created the ASF in response to the Dreyfus Affair, the unjust treason conviction of a Jewish army officer that divided the French nation. Chenu's biographer called the affair an "emotional shock" that made her determined to act. The year after the Dreyfus Affair ended, Chenu began looking for ways to relieve some of the social, political, and religious tensions that divided France. She gave her new organization the mission of educating women about the causes of social problems and their responsibility to solve those problems.[3] By 1904, the ASF had about 5,000 members.[4] A year after the ASF's creation, Jeanne Lestra founded the Ligue des Femmes Françaises (LFF). Lestra's goals for the LFF were more militantly Catholic and initially more political than those of the ASF. Lestra founded the LFF to raise money to fund Catholic and conservative political candidates for the 1902 elections. She hoped that a conservative win would help stem the tide of anticlerical legislation. The LFF had strong ties with the Jesuits, legitimist politicians, and right-wing nationalists such as Paul Déroulède and Jules Lemaître. With the defeat of most conservative politicians in 1902, the LFF reoriented its action away from politics and toward religious and social work, although it remained a very conservative organization.[5]

Within a year of the creation of the LFF, a split in that organization led a committee of women in Paris to create the Ligue Patriotique des Françaises (LPDF). The LPDF quickly became the largest and most influential French Catholic women's league, and by 1910, it had 500,000 members across France.[6] The LPDF, largely under the direction of Marie Frossard, had strong ties to the Jesuits as well as Jacques Piou's more moderate, right-wing political party, the Action Libérale Populaire. Like the LFF, the LPDF financially supported conservative political candidates. It engaged in a wide variety of social work aimed at re-Christianizing society and materially and morally supporting the poor.[7] It did not reject the legitimacy of the Third Republic but worked within the republican framework to make France more Catholic.

My project focuses primarily on the ASF, LFF, and LPDF. I have also included the Association Catholique Internationale des Œuvres de Protection de la Jeune Fille (ACI), an international immigrant aid organization founded in 1897 with a French branch created in 1898. The ACI combatted the "white slave trade" (the traffic in women) by assisting young women traveling to cities to look for work. These four organizations provide a holistic picture of Catholic women's goals, activities, and beliefs as well as their responses to feminism and social problems. They all printed their own journals, had affiliated branches all over France, and maintained significant ties with Catholic women's organizations around the world.

Protestant and Jewish women also formed or joined numerous faith-based social and religious associations. The small size of these communities allowed me to include all women's organizations that I uncovered as well as women's leadership roles within churches, synagogues, and some mixed organizations of men and women. At the turn of the twentieth century, the Protestant community numbered about 600,000 and the Jewish community numbered about 80,000.[8]

The Protestant community divided primarily into Lutheran and Reformed (Calvinist) churches with small numbers of Mennonites, Quakers, and Baptists in the mix. André Encrevé notes that the differences between these denominations was not that great. They all saw themselves as belonging to the same Protestant family.[9] Most French Jews identified with the conservative brand of Judaism associated with France's consistories, the bodies created by Napoleon I to oversee the direction of French Judaism. However, France's first Reformed community was established in 1905, and immigrants from Eastern Europe created Orthodox and Hasidic communities as well. A small Zionist movement also attracted some French Jews and "opened up new avenues for discussion of the nature of Judaism and the place of Jews in French society."[10]

Protestant women created organizations such as the Unions Chrétiennes de Jeunes Filles (UCJF), the French counterpart to the Young Women's Christian Association, and Les Amies de la Jeune Fille (Amies), an organization that assisted young immigrant girls, and they formed numerous girls' hostels. They also created the Conférence de Versailles, an interfaith organization with a Protestant base that brought women together to discuss social issues. Jewish women participated in the Comité de Bienfaisance Israélite de Paris, which offered a variety of services to poor Jewish families. They taught courses for the Université Populaire Israélite, and they created the Toit Familial, a home for girls working away from their families. Paula Hyman, in her work on Alsatian Jews, notes that French Jewish leadership also depended on women to transmit Jewish culture to children and maintain traditions in families.[11] The same was true for Catholics and Protestants.

A significant part of my source base comes from publications produced by women's faith-based organizations. Published sources indicate the public image that each organization wished to create. Through publications, women advertised their activities, recruited new members, indicated the services they offered to other women and children, and explained their religious and political goals. Women's publications had multiple audiences. The organizations' members read magazines and newspapers, but women writers also aimed their messages at their broader religious communities, including male religious leaders, and the French state. Police reporters monitoring religious organizations often read religious publications. Women used their publications to craft a modern, progressive image of themselves and their communities. Published documents reveal the ways in which women of faith wished to reshape their faith communities and ensure that those communities remained a central part of France's changing religious identity.

Published documents are key sources of information for projects focusing on image and identity. There are, of course, limitations to these kinds of sources. They rarely provide readers' responses to the information presented. Likewise, women's efforts to create a particular image sometimes concealed conflicts or disagreements among members as well as underlying goals that they did not feel they could freely print. Where possible, I have supplemented published documents with archival ones. The LPDF has an extensive archival collection that includes correspondence between women members and the Church hierarchy, minutes of LPDF meetings, and correspondence with Catholic women leaders abroad. The Paris police archives also provide a rich source of information about how police reporters, and to some extent the French state, viewed Catholic women's public activities. Archives for Protestant and Jewish organizations were harder to come by. In order to broaden my source base for these women's activities, I combed through minutes of church meetings, general Protestant and Jewish newspapers, and statutes published by churches and synagogues after the 1905 separation of church and state. These sources provided critical information about women's roles within churches and synagogues, debates within each community about women's rights and responsibilities, and how each community viewed women's public actions.

The women who directed faith-based organizations and engaged in faith-based action were the most active and most prominent members of their communities. Women leaders had enormous energy and a driving desire to shape their societies. They frequently entered the public sphere through philanthropic or charitable work and moved into organizations with more active political and social agendas. Women brought a variety of talents and educational backgrounds. Marie Frossard (1863–1954), one of the most dedicated and active members of the Catholic community, never married but devoted her life to various Catholic endeavors. She began her apostolic mission assisting poor, working women and children before serving as general secretary of the LPDF and editing its magazine, the *Echo de la Ligue Patriotique des Françaises*.[12] The Baronne de Brigode (1831–1912), the first president of the LPDF, began her social engagement with programs that assisted poor, young mothers. Vicontesse Marthe de Vélard, president of the LPDF from 1910 to 1933, had a degree in nursing, and Germaine Féron-Vrau (1867–1929), also an LPDF member, was the editor in chief of *La croix du nord*, a prominent Catholic newspaper.[13]

In the Protestant community, Sarah Monod, daughter of Adolphe Monod, a prominent pastor and professor at the University of Montauban, served as part of an ambulance team during the Franco-Prussian War. She continued to assist populations devastated by the war after its end. She later directed the French section of the Union Internationale des Amies de la Jeune Fille and became active in the Unions Chrétiennes de Jeunes Filles. Monod coedited the Protestant journal *L'ami de la jeunesse*, and she helped found the moderate feminist journal, *La femme*, the magazine of the Conseil National des Femmes Françaises (CNFF). She served as president of the CNFF from 1901 until she died in 1912.[14] Marguerite de Witt-Schlumberger, also Protestant, codeveloped a program that assisted women recently released from prison and campaigned vigorously against regulated prostitution and the traffic in women. She was also very active in various feminist movements such as the CNFF and the Union Française pour le Suffrage des Femmes (UFSF).[15] In the Jewish community, Clarisse Simon (1855–1950) followed a similar path. She engaged in numerous projects aimed at assisting women and children. She served on hospital boards, campaigned against human trafficking, and founded the Toit Familial, a home for young, working Jewish women. Gabrielle Alphen-Salvador (1856–1920), widowed early and left with a fortune, created her own hospital and financed an association aimed at assisting the sick. She then "launched a crusade to develop hygienic practices and professionalize nursing." She worked with her Protestant counterparts in the moderate feminist CNFF, and she actively opposed human trafficking and regulated prostitution. Like many of their contemporaries, Monod, Simon, and Alphen-Salvador moved easily between religious and secular organizations.[16]

Women leaders tended to be well connected to male political and religious leaders within their communities. Geneviève Reille (1844–1910), the second president of the LPDF, had two sons who served in the French parliament. Not content to let her sons direct France's political future, she used her position in the LPDF to legitimize Catholic women's engagement in politics.[17] Julie Siegfried, the daughter of a Protestant pastor, married industrialist and social activist Jules Siegfried. She frequently worked with prominent men in the Protestant community, including Wilfred Monod, a leader in the social Christianity movement. With Sarah Monod, Siegfried helped organize the Conférence de Versailles, a moderate feminist organization, and she served as president of the CNFF. She also served on the directing committee of the Protestant Association for the Practical Study of Social Questions.[18] Women leaders were intensely religious and felt called to express their faith by assisting poor women and children, lobbying the government for more fair legislation, and demanding more rights for women. These women became an important part of the public face and voice of their communities, especially as male religious leadership declined. They shaped those communities to be more open to women's religious and political leadership, and they presented their communities as progressive, staunchly patriotic, and central to French culture.

The Secularization Debate

Changes in women's faith-based activism were prompted largely by fears about growing religious indifference in French society. Women in all three faith communities believed that secularization was a driving force in France, and they acted on this belief. Signs of secularization seemed to be everywhere. Fewer and fewer men attended church and synagogue services, the working class had become more intensely anticlerical, and religious teachings no longer seemed to hold sway over people's lives as they had in the past.[19] Evidence of secularization manifested in increasing numbers of civil marriages and burials and fewer baptisms. Church attendance decreased, especially among men, and the urban working class seemed particularly susceptible to religious indifference.[20] In 1883, philosopher and historian Ernst Renan declared "there are no longer masses of believers, a large part of the people no longer believe in the supernatural and one can foresee the day when this type of belief will disappear. . . ."[21] Evidence seemed to support his claim.

Leaders from all three religious communities frequently complained about churches devoid of men and families no longer guided by religious precepts. In some areas, such the region around Nantes, religious observance among Catholic men and women remained high, but by the end of the nineteenth century, "more than half of France was considered 'tepid' in its religious duty." Around Chartres, only 2 percent of men attended mass, and many rural parishes had no men receiving communion at all.[22] Hugh McLeod writes that "the number of such parishes [with few men] increased considerably during the later years of the century, reaching its highest point during the first decade of the twentieth century."[23] Things were hardly better for Protestants. In 1907, a Protestant pastor in Nîmes complained that people hardly ever came to church any more. The situation was especially bad among men, as a 1909 report from one Protestant synod confirmed. The report noted that there were only 500 men practicing in the synod's member churches compared to 5,000 women.[24] Even among those people who remained Protestant, a new liberal current questioned the validity of miracles and rejected a literal interpretation of the Bible, a heresy as bad as atheism to many conservatives.[25]

Jews believed their crisis of faith was at least as bad, and maybe worse, than Catholics and Protestants. Over the course of the nineteenth century, French Jews found themselves gradually accepted as full citizens of the French nation. In order to fit in with their Christian neighbors, Jews were sometimes obliged to give up their religious traditions.[26] McLeod notes that "observance of the Sabbath was a major problem, since many Jews worked for gentile employers, and even Jews who owned their own businesses often felt that they had to follow the same hours of work as their competitors. There were also many urban Jews who felt that, if they were going to win acceptance, they would have to adapt to local custom. So the men cut their hair, shaved off their beards and removed their skull caps. Married women took off their wigs."[27] The education of children proved another area in which Jews had to alter religious practices in order to accommodate Christian society. French public schools required children to attend classes on Saturday. Sending children to Saturday classes violated the Sabbath requirement not to work, but many parents viewed it as necessary to provide opportunities for their children.[28]

In addition to the general trend toward religious apathy that seemed to plague France, French republican politicians adopted laïcité as one of their primary projects. Laïcité, a unique French version of secularism, became one of the cornerstones of a shifting French religious identity in the first part of the twentieth century. This French secularism not only protected freedom of conscience, but also protected people from what republicans saw as harmful effects of religion by preventing religious persecution or harassment and "prohibiting the use of religious funds for secular purposes."[29] Bronwyn Winter notes that, for contemporary France, "citizens of the [French] Republic have a right to freedom (as defined by the state), but this right is not optional to take or leave. To be a citizen of the Republic, one is paradoxically, *obliged* to be free."[30] This can mean being free from constraints imposed by religion that seem contrary to human rights and equality. By the 1880s the French Third Republic's parliament was full of anticlericals, many of them Protestants or Jews, who wished to protect religious freedom but keep religion and government separated. They took particular aim at the Catholic Church partly because of its traditional support for monarchy and partly because "the Church assumed that the spiritual world was superior while republicans assumed that human reason could fully know the world."[31] Between

1880 and 1890 the state secularized cemeteries, enacted a divorce law, and eliminated obligatory Sunday rest.[32]

Women were at the heart of the Third Republic's efforts to reform the place of religion in French society. Concerns about the Catholic Church's hold on women had existed since at least the mid-nineteenth century. In his famous 1859 publication, *La Femme*, French historian Jules Michelet argued that priests controlled bourgeois women and thus challenged husbands' dominance in the family. Michelet's essay remained popular throughout the nineteenth century and was followed by other similar works, including Emile Zola's novel *A Priest in the House* (1874). Zola created a world in which women, influenced by priests, managed to "sap the republican convictions of men."[33] One of the most important measures taken by the state in the 1880s was the creation of a free, obligatory, and secular state-run school system in France to draw students away from Catholic schools. Schools designed to teach children secular, republican values became the heart of French democracy and republicanism. The education laws of the 1880s affected boys and girls. Jean-Marie Mayeur and Madeleine Rebérioux suggest "the most revolutionary innovation in secondary education was the creation of *lycées* and *collèges* for girls."[34] Within this new girls' school system, the teaching of morals was still compulsory but teaching religion was optional. Jules Ferry, the architect of the secular French school system, declared "he who has the women has everything: first because he has the children, and second because he has the husbands."[35]

Ferry and other republican leaders (many of them liberal Protestants) who oversaw the creation of this new school system hoped to mold good republican wives for republican men and to "end the Church's influence over middle-class girls."[36] Camille Sée was the young republican deputy who put forth the bill establishing secondary education for women. He believed that until women's education extended to the secondary level, women would remain superstitious and under the power of the clergy. Clerical influence was especially dangerous because although women could not vote, they could influence the votes of their husbands, thereby giving the Catholic Church the power to threaten the Republic.[37]

For women and men living in the early twentieth century, secularization was an undeniable fact—a disturbing trend that had to be opposed at all cost. Women mobilized en masse against the religious disaffection they believed pervaded their society. Among modern historians, this narrative of secularization has been called into question. Much debate has occurred among historians about what secularization means, how it should be defined, and whether it occurred at all. It is true that by the 1890s the majority of the population had stopped going to mass on a regular basis. However, 90 percent of the adult population in France had been baptized as infants, most women wished for a church wedding, 80 percent of marriages still occurred in the Church, and just before death, people generally received the last rights.[38] Religious attachments clearly persisted in a variety of forms despite the rapidly changing religious environment that characterized the late nineteenth and early twentieth centuries.

Rather than a linear process toward secularization, historians have increasingly argued for more expansive ways of understanding the ebb and flow of religious sentiment. An example can be found in Carol Harrison's work on "romantic Catholics." These Catholics, born in the years immediately following the French Revolution of 1789, wished to reinvigorate Catholicism to make it more "hopeful" and "forward-looking."[39] "Romantic Catholics" helped revive and renew a Church torn apart by revolution and state-sponsored violence. A similar process of renewal occurred in the post–World War I years, when a new generation of Catholic thinkers worked to reimagine Catholicism as "being thoroughly compatible with 'modernity.'"[40] Harrison warns that "this recurrence of 'renewals' should lead us to question the assumptions about decline, resistance, and revival that undergird modern religious history." She argues that "the frequency with which French Catholics have experienced renewal suggests an ongoing dynamic between the secular and religious rather than an inexorable progress toward a secular goal." According to Harrison, "There is no end point to this process . . . and we should not expect it to result in the victory of either the secular or of the religious."[41]

Revival and religiosity took many forms over the course of the nineteenth century. Thomas Kselman has traced the continued vitality of folk traditions and superstitious beliefs as well as the importance of the Catholic Church and Catholic symbols in people's understanding of death.[42] Kselman suggests that a continued attachment to religious symbols as people approach death "might be interpreted as evidence for changes in the way religion is imagined and lived, but not necessarily as 'dechristianisation.'"[43] The decades between 1880 and 1910 also saw a rising interest in Spiritism. Spiritist practices included the belief in reincarnation, the ability to communicate with the spirits of the dead, magnetic healing, cabala, theosophy, and a variety of other practices generally considered outside the religious mainstream.[44]

The ebb and flow of religious fervor did not affect everyone equally, and pronounced differences occurred between the religious responses of men and women. Sarah Curtis discovered that as early as the 1790s, "Catholic women were at the forefront of a grassroots religious revival in France . . . energized by the persecution of priests who refused to take the loyalty oath, the de-Christianization campaign during the Terror, and the closure and ransacking of churches."[45] Her study of women missionaries likewise reveals that the Catholic Church was revitalized "from the ground up" in the postrevolutionary years by "hundreds of women who founded new, active, and apostolic religious orders in the wake of the French Revolution."[46] Ralph Gibson acknowledges that men's participation in the Catholic Church declined after the middle of the nineteenth century, leaving women as a very important base of the Church's support.[47] This left the way open for women to step into some leadership positions men had abandoned. Rebecca Rogers has also demonstrated that the nineteenth century saw a "strong rebirth of religious activities, primarily among women," as evidenced by the hundreds of thousands of women who entered or were associated with religious orders or congregations.[48] Likewise, Ruth Harris, in her study of the religious shrine at Lourdes, argues that "the extravagant gestures and rituals during pilgrimage typified a Church increasingly reliant on women."[49] These repeated contests between secular and religious forces opened new opportunities for women to employ their faith for the "salvation" of their communities and the French nation. This led to a dynamic, fluid, and constantly evolving religious identity for France that each generation contributed to in its own way.

Christopher Clark provides the most useful framework for understanding the interplay between the secularization and religious revival that characterized early twentieth-century France and sparked the massive mobilization of women into religious activism. Clark reminds readers that processes of secularization and religious revival can occur at the same time. Over the course of the nineteenth century, "church properties were seized and sold off; ecclesiastical privileges were removed; clerical authorities came under pressure to retreat from their positions in education and charitable provision. . . ." However, the same period saw a "proliferation and elaboration of popular devotions, church buildings, religious foundations and associations, and confessionally motivated newspapers and journals." Clark suggests that secularization campaigns and religious revival fuel each other. As governments worked to undermine the influence of the Catholic Church, the Church "acquired the means to mobilize its support base."[50] Whatever the outcomes of this debate among historians, secularization was a powerful, motivating idea for individuals living in turn-of-the-century France. Early twentieth-century church/state conflicts and general fears about declining religiosity facilitated the massive mobilization of women into faith-based organizations and other forms of religious engagement. This, in turn, opened considerable new opportunities for women's leadership in their faith communities.

Feminization

Tied to debates about secularization are questions concerning the "feminization of religion" in the nineteenth and twentieth centuries. As with the concept of secularization, the "feminization thesis" is fraught with complications. Many historians have grappled with this idea, defining feminization in a variety of ways. Claude Langlois's pioneering study of French female congregations reveals that the number of women joining female congregations exceeded the number of men joining the clergy over the course of the nineteenth century. He points to this as well as to an increase in certain forms of female devotion as evidence of a "feminization of Catholicism" that transformed the Catholic community.[51] Ralph Gibson also forcefully argues that nineteenth- and early twentieth-century Catholicism in France was "very largely" a feminine affair. He cites statistics indicating the numbers of women attending mass and Easter services as well as the growth of massive Catholic women's organizations including the LPDF and LFF.[52] Caroline Ford, in her work on gender and religion in modern France, focuses less on numbers of women involved in religious activism. Instead, she emphasizes how perceptions of men's and women's religiosity altered. Ford defines feminization as "a reflection of a perceived rejection of Catholicism by men, which threw women's religiosity into sharp relief."[53] Similarly, Ruth Harris argues that from its inception, the religious shrine at Lourdes "put women and young girls into the limelight, as visionaries, enthusiastic witnesses and as the first worshippers at the shrine."[54]

Other historians have questioned the usefulness of thinking about a feminization of religion at all. Patrick Pasture notes that there is no agreement among historians about the definition of feminization. Feminization can refer to increasing participation of women in religious organizations and religious rites, shifts in piety toward emotion and sentimentalism, or changes in "Christian culture" in which piety is gendered as feminine and therefore a worrisome quality in men.[55] Bernhard Schneider argues that feminization can be a useful concept if it is limited and defined in very specific ways. He acknowledges that Caritas in early nineteenth-century Germany "displayed a strikingly frequent 'feminine face,'" but male clerics still controlled many charitable organizations. He suggests that it may be useful to talk about a feminization of charity but not necessarily a feminization of religion.[56] Similarly, Michael O'Sullivan acknowledges the difficulty of applying the feminization thesis broadly. In the case of interwar Germany, "the Catholic community encompassed a diverse mix of men and women

. . . Men remained the public carriers of Catholic identity . . . while young women ambiguously sought active roles in public ritual; alternative expressions of faith; and long-term careers beyond Catholic motherhood and feminine domesticity."[57]

It is clear that the concept of feminized religion opened up new avenues for studying and valorizing women's involvement in European and American religious life. The notion of feminized religious life has encouraged historians to explore women's religious activities and consider them as positive sources of female empowerment rather than as examples of female backwardness. That said, the problems with defining feminization limit its usefulness in illuminating women's positions in their religious communities. My work clearly demonstrates that women increasingly become the public face and voice of their communities. They took on new positions previously held by men, and religious work offered them leadership opportunities not available in any other area of French society. Women's activities were sometimes shaped by female culture and expectations about appropriate behavior for women. However, just because women filled men's positions did not always mean the nature of these positions changed. Women who became deacons or voters or even pastors may or may not have acted differently or significantly differently from their male counterparts. So one might argue that religion was feminized, but one might equally argue that women were masculinized as they entered new positions.

Caroline Ford's definition of feminization as the perception of men's rejection of religion may provide the most helpful framework for thinking about feminization.[58] Rather than employing feminization as a master narrative to explain broad trends in France or Europe, Ford's definition focuses on how people at various moments have perceived changes in religious life. Historians have clearly demonstrated that certain forms of religious expression remained the purview of men. New organizations and movements at the turn of the century drew men into religious life.[59] However, at least in early twentieth-century France, there was real concern that granting women new leadership positions or allowing women to fill positions previously held by men would encourage men to further abandon religious engagement.

A conservative writer for a Jewish newspaper argued that including women in Jewish prayer services would weaken Judaism further by causing more men to leave since someone else was available to take their place.[60] Anthony Steinhoff found similar concerns in his study of churches in Alsace and Lorraine. In the decades leading up to World War I, Protestant churches in that region considered granting women parish suffrage, much like their French counterparts. Opponents feared that "granting women the right to vote would lead to the feminization of the church" with women "gradually displacing men in the organs of church governance."[61] My work supports scholarship that reveals women's increasing importance as public religious leaders in the early twentieth century. However, the idea of feminization may be most useful in highlighting fears within these early twentieth-century communities about the consequences female religious leadership could have for male religious engagement.

Legacy of Charity

Women's religious engagement was clearly not new in early twentieth-century France. French women had been joining convents and creating charitable organizations for centuries. As early as 1633, Les Filles de Charité began providing a space for celibate women who were not nuns to gain a certain degree of independence and empowerment from male authorities through Catholic charitable work.[62] Nineteenth-century Catholic women's religious orders played a crucial role in opening new professional opportunities for women and revitalizing the Church. By 1850, there were more women in religious orders than male priests or male members of religious congregations. Three decades later, 130,000 women in France had joined either convents or congregations, with most involved in hospitals, teaching, or social work. The number of women involved in congregations declined after 1880 with the Ferry Laws' establishment of free secular schools and the state's closure of most congregations. However, Claude Langlois argues that women's work in religious congregations helped prepare public opinion to see women enter a variety of professions. These religious orders gave women access to positions of responsibility and professional opportunities that they would not have had otherwise. Although nuns had to follow a strict set of rules, obey superiors, and remain celibate, they also opened the way for women to advance in certain professions, especially education and nursing.[63]

Catholic religious congregations opened important spiritual and intellectual opportunities for single women and provided them with independence to engage in public life in ways impossible for most lay-women.[64] This was especially true in France's colonies, where Catholic women missionaries had much greater freedom than either laywomen or nuns in France. Sarah Curtis notes that few nineteenth-century French laywomen had the freedom to "travel outside of France, nego-tiate with colonial agents," or "challenge church power and evangelize among non-Christians," but a handful of nuns working in France's colonies did all of these things. Through their colonial missionary work, "nuns carved out a space to pursue new and often controversial agendas, including evangelization on a global scale."[65] The Catholic Church was in no position to reject the services of these women. With male religiosity on the decline, female congregations maintained important links between Catholicism and the popular classes.[66]

Nuns were not the only nineteenth-century women carving out new spaces for women's activity. Nineteenth-century laywomen who did not wish to join religious congregations created charitable soci-eties, sponsored schools, provided bread and soup for the poor, and collected straw to donate to prisons. Hazel Mills argues that women's charitable groups had "real involvement with formal structures of local government" through their cooperation or conflict with local authorities. "For certain groups of bourgeois women," Mills sug-gests, "the images of femininity and female virtue propagated by the French Catholic Church, . . . offered an access to legitimate public and political activity."[67] Sarah Curtis has likewise noted that mid-nineteenth-century Catholic women's lay associations, working with female religious orders, were instrumental to Church efforts to re-Christianize the poor. These organizations "waged war against pov-erty and social revolution," and they helped "renew parish structures."

Women who joined charitable organizations "used them to bend the bonds of domesticity without challenging its ideology, while gaining a sense of personal and religious self-worth."[68]

Female congregations and charitable organizations left an important legacy for the twentieth-century women's groups that followed. They helped legitimize women's movement away from the home and into public service. They created more spaces for women to engage with the wider world, work with male religious and secular leaders, and shape state policies. Marie-Emmanuelle Chessel insists on the importance of building ideas over time in the history of women's social action. Earlier organizations influence those that follow. Even when programs or organizations stop functioning, their ideas are often incorporated into subsequent groups.[69] Chessel's notion of idea-building provides an important framework for comparing organizations created by different generations of women. When moving from one era to another, it is critical to recognize the legacy and contributions of earlier women's groups.

Twentieth-century faith-based women's organizations did not abandon more traditional philanthropic or charitable endeavors. However, women leaders in twentieth-century movements came to believe that charity was no longer sufficient to deal with the problems France faced. Rather than focusing on handouts to the poor and work with local governments, twentieth-century women leaders wished to transform the social conditions that created poverty. Magali Della Sudda, Bruno Dumons, and Anne Cova have done the most to reveal Catholic women's motivations and new forms of action. Their work demonstrates the interplay between Catholic women's desire to preserve Catholic traditions, especially in the area of gender, and forces pushing Catholic women toward a new understanding of women's social and political roles. Anne Cova's study *Au service de l'église, de la patrie et de la famille* highlights the central role that women's "maternal mission" continued to play in Catholic women's social action. Organizations like the ASF, LPDF, and LFF all emphasized the "educational mission of mother-teachers." To be good teachers for their children, women had to be educated in areas such as home management and childcare as well as instructed in finding good reading material for themselves and their families. However, women leaders also increasingly pressed for legislation to protect motherhood.[70]

Catholic women's movement toward political involvement, noted by Cova, has been further explored by Della Sudda and Dumons in their histories of the LPDF and LFF, respectively. Both emphasize the importance of these organizations in bringing conservative Catholic women into political engagement. Della Sudda traces the means by which Catholic women's organizations carved a space for conservative women to engage in collective action, employ modern techniques of mobilization, and expand the scope of feminine activities.[71] Similarly, Dumons marks the creation of twentieth-century Catholic women's organizations as "a rupture in their own universe." Women leaders and members employed political methods that had been reserved for elite men. They came to understand the force that "women could exercise over the scene of masculine politics." Although they were not paid, Dumons argues that women leaders turned their LFF positions into a true "métier" that "mobilized their time and their money" and contributed to the "political professionalization" of women.[72]

Protestant and Jewish women also mobilized in similar ways to defend the interests of women and their faith communities. Protestant women, in particular, gained more significant rights and leadership opportunities than any other faith group. By 1905, the year church and state were separated in France, Protestant and Jewish women had gained the right to vote in elections held within their communities. Many Protestant women had also gained the right to be elected to presbytery and synod committees.[73] Protestants and Jews not only expanded women's religious leadership opportunities, but also actively supported secular feminist goals including women's suffrage. In one of the few studies of French Protestant women, Florence Rochefort suggests that Protestant communities' perceived loss of influence at the turn of the century pushed them toward promoting gender equality.[74] She traces the early development of feminism among Protestant women in the late nineteenth century, focusing on the experiences of early feminists such as Eugénie Niboyet and Jenny d'Héricourt.[75]

There are no studies specifically mapping Jewish women's path toward social and political engagement. However, Yolande Cohen has explored the central role Protestant and Jewish women played in the development of the moderate feminist CNFF. Cohen argues that, in addition to promoting women's rights, the CNFF "played an important role in defining the scope and type of welfare policies affecting mothers and children in France in the first half of the twentieth century." Moreover, female-run Protestant and Jewish philanthropies "helped shape a progressive republican agenda in the 1910s and 1920s and to form a style of state maternalism."[76]

Women's twentieth-century religious activism provided them with social, religious, and political influence unattainable through any other French institutions. Florence Rochefort warns against automatically linking the secularization of a society with the advancement of women's rights. Efforts by the French Third Republic to undermine the power of the Catholic Church in late nineteenth- and early twentieth-century France did not involve expanding women's political rights. The same secular French republicans who promoted France's particular brand of laïcité were often adamantly opposed to women's equality.[77] Women's influence within their religious communities therefore expanded more quickly than their rights as citizens of the nation. Their faith-based organizations gave them a voice denied to them in other venues of French society. Twentieth-century women's activism contributed to a steady progression toward women's equality both in religious communities and within French society. Women's organizations provided women with a respectable path toward more public, political engagement. Shortages of men's and women's enthusiasm for religious activism pushed their communities toward greater equality for women in both secular and religious realms.

Modernization

Early twentieth-century women leaders modernized their faith communities and the French nation by embracing new techniques in communication, reinterpreting traditional religious teachings, demanding greater equality for women, and mobilizing globally to enact change. Historians frequently talk about modernization and modern methods of action, but these terms can be tricky to define. What counts as modern varies depending on the era being studied and the historian doing the research. Both Rita Felski and Christopher Clark remind us that the terms modern, modernity, and modernization are themselves frequently value-laden: "to be modern is to be on the side of progress, reason, and democracy" rather than aligned with "disorder, despair and anarchy."[78] In *The Concept of Modernism*, Astradur Eysteinsson tackles the simplistic definition of modernism as simply a "rage against prevalent traditions" or an opposition to tradition.[79] Nineteenth-century liberals and anticlericals frequently used this definition in their battles against the Catholic Church. They characterized Catholics as reactionary, backward looking, and in opposition to modern society. Although historians have moved away from such a simplistic view, Christopher Clark argues that this "antinomy between modernity and 'tradition' still informs the way we think" about European religious history. Religious revival is often presented as a "detour, a distraction, from the 'norm' of an irreversible process of secularization." This is true despite the "modern" aspects of nineteenth- and twentieth-century Catholic action, including "mass-circulation media, voluntary associations, demonstrative forms of mass action, the expansion of schooling among deprived social groups, and the increasingly prominent involvement of women in positions of responsibility."[80] Every generation adopts practices and ideas that are efficient and effective at bringing about the changes they wish to achieve. These may be completely new ideas or practices or they may be recycled and repurposed from previous generations. In either case, the users see them as essential to being accepted as progressive and effective in their contemporary societies.

Modernizing, especially in the case of women of faith, did not mean rejecting tradition. In his study of nineteenth-century French Jewish communities, Jay Berkovitz has usefully noted that the "terms and concepts" of a religious tradition often remain central to a faith community's discussion about modernization.[81] This was true for all

three faith communities in the early twentieth century, especially for
Catholics. Catholic women, in particular, did not have the luxury,
or necessarily the desire, to reject tradition. Rather, they wished to
update their traditions by using new methods and ways of thinking
to protect their faith. Female congregations had created a model for
balancing tradition with innovation in the nineteenth century. Claude
Langlois suggests that the success of female congregations was due
partly to their ability to "adapt to all situations but to also integrate
themselves into the traditions of daily life."[82] In the case of the LPDF,
Magali Della Sudda has convincingly argued that mobilization against
secularization shifted women away from charity and toward modern
political action. It made them militants of social action who wanted to
reconquer the French nation and the French government with conservative values.[83] Likewise, Marie-Emmanuelle Chessel argues that the
French Consumers League, which had a strong Catholic base, looked
for ways to "evolve categories of thought and action in their universe."
They shifted women from housekeepers to consumers, militants, and
public speakers, and they helped "redefine femininity."[84] Maintaining
certain traditions, like the supremacy of Catholicism in French society, rested at the heart of Catholic women's goals. Forcefully rejecting
traditional roles for men and women would have been too radical for
their communities to accept. These women did not necessarily set out
to reject tradition, but to link their traditions to contemporary practices and changing social norms. The same was true for Protestant
and Jewish women. Rather than rejecting traditions, women helped to
reform those traditions in ways that expanded their religious influence
and kept their communities at the heart of France's evolving religious
identity.

Stephen Schloesser, in his work on Jazz Age Catholicism, provides
a useful and more expansive way to understand modernity. He suggests that modernity can simply mean an "embrace of temporal progress over unchanging tradition."[85] Schloesser's definition furnishes the
most useful way to think about modernization and women's religious
activism. Women religious activists used new technology for travel
and communication, took advantage of the new opportunities for

women in the public sphere, called for women's legal rights, organized globally, and promoted democratic and egalitarian ideas.[86] Women clung to traditions that were important to them and their communities, but they demonstrated a willingness to see those traditions altered to respond to changing social, political, and religious trends. They helped their communities reinterpret traditional religious teachings that governed women's place in the family, the faith, and the nation. Women did not see their faith as static and unchanging but as alive and dynamic, able to meet the challenges of their contemporary world.

My work builds on previous scholarship by mapping the path Catholic, Protestant, and Jewish women took toward greater political and social engagement as well as greater equality within their faith communities. This path developed differently for women in each faith group. Comparing the religious activism of all three groups provides a framework for understanding the advantages and challenges that religious work offers to women. Women's religious activism pushed all three faith communities toward greater acceptance of women's social and religious equality but not to the same extent or at the same pace. Catholic women walked a very fine line between promoting women's traditional roles as mothers and moving women into politics and religious leadership. Catholic women leaders rarely argued for women's rights as individuals. Instead, they presented their activism as a way to protect home, family, children, and tradition. The position of the Vatican, especially on women's suffrage, severely constrained the types of rights Catholic women could demand and the rhetoric they could use. No discussion occurred about allowing women to become priests or creating other official positions within the Catholic hierarchy. Women had to subtly carve out other types of religious leadership, like leading pilgrimages, giving talks at conferences, publishing religious magazines, and engaging in social activism. Despite these limitations, women gradually moved the Catholic community toward support for women's suffrage, and they created a very visible place for women as unofficial public leaders of French Catholicism.

For Protestants and Jews, the situation was different. Protestant women made by far the largest gains toward religious equality. They became deacons in their churches and gained the right to vote for and serve on church leadership councils, and a few served as pastors during the First World War. Jewish women received voting rights within their community and were admitted to traditionally male-dominated prayer groups in certain situations. Both the Protestant and Jewish communities were largely favorable to women's equality in politics, education, and professional work. The Jewish community, in particular, frequently praised the secular, professional accomplishments of its women. Protestant and Jewish women furnished most of the leadership for France's moderate feminist movements. Exploring women's experiences in all three communities provides a much more complete picture of how religion promotes and restricts women's advancement and how national political and social questions influence women's religious engagement.

My work is partly the story of women's advancement, but it is equally a story about the cultural transformation of France and its three largest faith communities. Too often, scholarship about women's religious engagement focuses solely on the impact religion has on women's lives. However, women are part of communities and as women's religious positions change, the culture of their communities also transforms. The Catholic, Protestant, and Jewish communities all coped with perceived religious disaffection, shortages of male leaders, and conflicts with the French state. Women increasingly became the face and voice of their communities as they stepped in to fill positions vacated by men. Accepting women's expanded religious mission required all three faith groups to reinterpret religious texts and update traditional practices. Through women's organizations, social work, and church leadership, women modernized and democratized their faith communities. Women's religious activism also pushed France toward becoming a more democratic, equitable society. The state alone, even if it had the political will, could not have completely emancipated women. Laws and civil rights are only effective if people embrace them. Religious communities' support for women's suffrage, access to education and jobs, and engagement in the public sphere was critically important to redressing women's subordinate position to men.

Finally, women's religious engagement shaped the national image of their communities and reshaped France's religious identity. Julie Kalman reminds readers that the French have not traditionally "agreed on a model of nationhood." Rather, French society has been a "terrain for intensely competing discourses of nationhood as French men and women sought to define themselves and assert a meaning for French-ness."[87] Women's faith-based activism and faith communities' engage-ment with women's rights ensured that religion remained part of the public debate about what religious future France should have. Rather than having religion relegated only to the private sphere or individual conscience or disappear altogether, women helped keep religion visible in French society. Women activists printed journals, held mass meet-ings, organized pilgrimages, petitioned politicians, funded political campaigns, created vast networks of social programs, and drew con-siderable attention from the French police. These women became the visible presence of religion in French society. Through women and the question of women's rights, the Catholic, Protestant, and Jewish com-munities demonstrated that religion was still a vital force in France and could play a positive role in directing the French nation. Women pre-sented their faith communities as integral, inseparable parts of French culture. As France struggled to redefine itself in the early part of the twentieth century, women, either as symbols or as activists, ensured that their faith communities occupied a place as unyielding patriots in France's national narrative.

Religious Identity and the Challenge of Feminism

"She's called the Papesse of Protestantism. She is very small . . . [and] dresses like a Quaker always with a black bonnet, a long jacket and a round skirt. . . . She protests when people call her a feminist, but without thinking she fights the arguments of anti-feminists. . . . She alone possesses the means to assemble and govern . . . feminism in its entirety."[1] Jane Misme, editor for the feminist journal *La française*, wrote this description of Sarah Monod in July 1899. Monod was a leader in the moderate feminist movement in France, where she worked in the good company of many of her Protestant coreligionists. However, Monod was also a tireless laborer in Protestant religious organizations and faith-based social programs. Monod's experiences illustrate the convergence of religion and feminism occurring within the French Protestant, Catholic, and Jewish communities. The predominance of the "woman question" in France required these communities to reconsider women's place in the nation and in their faith groups.[2] It forced them to take a position on the question of women's suffrage.

The engagement of France's three religious communities with the question of women's rights shaped the French nation in two key ways. First, it was centrally important to religious communities' struggle to keep religion visible and relevant in French society and to carve out a space for themselves as part of France's religious landscape. For Catholic women, the reluctance to support suffrage but the desire to mobilize for religious work pushed them into large Catholic women's organizations that made their presence felt on both the national and international stage. Meanwhile, support for women's civil rights allowed the Protestant and Jewish communities to present a progressive, democratic public image of themselves that facilitated their efforts to make Protestantism and Judaism foundational blocks of France's religious identity. Second, religious communities' engagement with feminism promoted egalitarianism for women and a modernization of their status in France.

The Catholic Church in France throughout the late nineteenth and early twentieth centuries was known for its reactionary, antidemocratic, and anti-egalitarian positions. It was not a likely candidate for the promotion of egalitarian values, especially though women's rights. For the most part, following the teachings of the very conservative Pope Pius X, the Catholic community rejected women's suffrage, and conservative Catholic women often refused to participate in secular feminist or social programs. Secular "feminist principles," as Odile Sarti suggests, "contradicted too many tenets of the Church to be acceptable to most Catholics." Catholics feared that "open access to education and careers would make women more ambitious, heighten their desire for independence, and make them unwilling to shoulder their marital and social responsibilities." Happiness, the Church taught, "resulted from sacrifice and abnegation, not from emancipation or the pursuit of individual rights."[3]

The Church hierarchy's resistance to secular feminist work for women made the religious sphere even more important for devout Catholic women who accepted the Church's teachings. It helped cluster women into a few very large Catholic women's organizations. Despite their conservative rhetoric, Catholic women were not as uniformly conservative and reactionary as is sometimes assumed. Their organizations could be fairly progressive. They educated women about how to work within a parliamentary, democratic system and taught women modern methods to reach people with their messages. The size of Catholic women's organizations gave women a powerful platform from which to push for Catholic-inspired, but also woman-centered, reform in France. By 1910, the Ligue Patriotique des Françaises (LPDF), the largest women's organization in France, had 500,000 members, and its conferences could draw crowds that far exceeded anything seen in secular feminist circles.[4] These organizations helped make Catholic women collectively a very important part of the political and spiritual defenses of the Church as well as visible symbols of religion in French society. They forced the Church to pay more attention to women and women's issues. In the process, they helped to gradually infuse the Catholic community, if not necessarily the Catholic hierarchy, with a more egalitarian spirit.

The question of women's rights was equally important to the Protestant and Jewish communities' efforts to keep themselves relevant in a rapidly secularizing society and to facilitate their own political goals. As Patrick Cabanel notes, the integration of Protestants and Jews accelerated in the second half of the nineteenth century, as did their participation in the creation of a "*société laïque*," which proponents understood to be non-Catholic.[5] The Protestant and Jewish communities wanted to solidify France's identity as a nation of liberty, equality, and justice that accepted all of its citizens regardless of faith background. They also wished to present themselves as faith communities founded on principles of justice and liberty and thereby compatible with the values of the secular Third Republic.

Support for women's rights became an important avenue to achieve these goals. Supporting a greater degree of civil equality for women helped strengthen the image of these communities as progressive faiths. Men and women in both communities often linked their support for women's rights to the "naturally" progressive nature of Protestantism and Judaism. Rabbi Emile Lévy argued that all Jewish history and teachings tended toward the "enhancement of the condition of women" and aimed at placing women on an "equal footing with all members of humankind."[6] These communities used the issue of women's rights to demonstrate their staunch commitment to equality and democracy, principles upon which the Third Republic was founded and that they wished to protect. Although Protestants and Jews had been adopted later by the nation, unlike their reactionary Catholic siblings, they were good, devoted children of France. Protestant and Jewish men were not the only worthy citizens of the nation;

Protestant and Jewish women were also enlightened patriots who could be trusted to help direct the future of France. Through these messages, Protestants and Jews affirmed their right to full citizenship and their right to be equal members of the Republic. At the same time, they reinforced the importance of democratic and egalitarian ideals within the nation, and they demonstrated that religion could still play a positive role in France.

Feminism and French Society

By the 1890s "suffragism was well-established in France," according to Steven Hause and Anne Kenney, although "it still commanded the energies of relatively few women." These women suffragists tended to cluster in Paris and were "divided into competing organizations, and isolated from other feminists. Suffragists remained a minority of the women's movement which itself could claim the support of only a small minority of French women."[7] Reasons for the weakness of the French suffrage movement are multiple and varied. Many Protestant and Jewish women did join suffragist organizations, but they were small minorities in primarily Catholic France. Catholic women, for the most part, refused to join secular suffrage associations or even publicly promote women's suffrage until after World War I. This happened partly because Pius X rejected women's suffrage, partly because Catholics feared it would lead to a further breakdown in the family, and partly because Catholic women did not want to work with Protestants and Jews.[8] In any case, the absence of most Catholic women from the suffrage movement until the interwar years assured that suffrage organizations remained small.

Despite the small scale of the suffrage movement, French women in the early twentieth century did not remain cloistered in the home or allow men to direct their lives. Evelyne Diebolt affirms that by the early twentieth century, women had become determined "not to let themselves be excluded from social and political life."[9] The women's movement in France encompassed a broad range of initiatives that included suffrage, but also addressed educational reform, prison reform, antiprostitution efforts, and workplace reform. All of these initiatives had in common their desire to improve the condition of women and girls and make sure that they were safe, protected, and healthy.

Feminism came in many different forms in France, which makes it difficult to provide an exact definition. The French themselves did not agree. Feminism could include a demand for suffrage, but it did not have to. Karen Offen notes that continental European feminists, such as those in France, often rejected the individualistic Anglo-American model of feminism. They favored a more "relational" form of feminism that emphasized women's distinctiveness from men and their ability to contribute to the betterment of society because of their specific womanly qualities. Offen argues that "by the early twentieth century . . . most French feminists had rejected competitive individualism as anti-French." Rather, they adopted a feminism more closely allied with "republican nationalism" that "continued to emphasize sexual difference, a sexual division of labor, motherhood and education for motherhood, and state subsidies for mothers." They also called for "enhanced legal, educational, and economic rights and the vote for women." French feminists of many varieties "advocated putting France's welfare and a reconstituted family ahead of individualistic or personal needs."[10] This was definitely the case for many women in all three of France's religious communities.

French women had plenty of reasons to involve themselves in the social and political life of their nation. The inability to vote was only one of many legal and social barriers women faced to achieving equality. Laurence Klejman and Florence Rochefort note that the Napoleonic code "deprived [women] of a social identity." It gave them the status of "civil minors" after they married and instructed them to obey their husbands. Women had little voice in either politics or the family, and they were not authorized to engage in legal action without the agreement of their husbands. The code also denied married women rights to their salaries until 1907. The constitution of the Third Republic maintained these legal and economic inequalities, despite the Republic's rhetoric emphasizing natural rights and equality. Klejman and Rochefort suggest that a sustained feminist movement developed over the course of the nineteenth century as French women took ideas from the American and French revolutions and the abolitionist movement. The improvement of girls' education after 1880, which gradually opened professional opportunities to women, also made them more aware of the discrimination they faced. The expanded class of educated, financially independent women began to challenge the sources of their discrimination.[11]

Educated women's desire to improve their own situation and that of their poorer, working-class counterparts contributed to the flourishing of women's organizations in the late nineteenth and early twentieth centuries. Women tried to educate themselves about the roots of social problems and develop sustainable solutions to those problems. Anne Cova notes that "the first decade of the twentieth century was rich in the organization of congresses, in the creation of new groups and in the appearance of new publications." Three international women's congresses took place in France in 1900: one Catholic and antisuffragist, one largely Protestant and moderately feminist, and one more militantly feminist. The following year saw the creation of the Conseil National des Femmes Françaises (CNFF), which advocated for women's suffrage but also devoted itself to charity, educational work, labor issues, and improving public health.[12] The CNFF became the largest feminist organization in France, joining a list of many others including the Ligue Françaises pour le Droit des Femmes and the Union Française pour le Suffrage des Femmes (UFSF).[13] Protestant women also founded the Conférence de Versailles, which brought women from a variety of backgrounds together each year to discuss women's efforts to deal with social problems.

Upper- and middle-class French women became increasingly concerned about social problems they perceived in their society, especially those faced by poor women and children. Christine Bard notes that many feminists wanted to "preserve the family" while at the same time creating conditions that allowed women as individuals to thrive. French feminists were a diverse group involved in a variety of different causes that ranged from suffragism to syndicalism to hygiene and morals.[14] Upper- and middle-class women became involved in a range of organizations that combated poverty, prostitution, the "white slave trade," alcoholism, immorality, and a variety of other social ills. The primary goal of moderate feminist organizations such as the Con-férence de Versailles was not to promote suffrage but to help its members tackle social problems. Likewise, Yolande Cohen convincingly argues that the CNFF "played an important role in defining the scope and type of welfare policies affecting mothers and children." Protestant and Jewish women in particular, "who were already active in several philanthropies, sought to build a network of women's associations to influence republican family policies." The CNFF promoted both "equality and distinct gender roles."[15] Whether they accepted suffrage or not, women leaders increasingly wanted to create a society that offered more protection to women and children.

The division between religious and secular women's organizations was often fairly fluid, at least for Protestants and Jews. Both the CNFF and the UFSF had strong Protestant and Jewish leadership. Protestants Sarah Monod and later Julie Siegfried presided over the CNFF and Marguerite de Witt-Schlumberger became president of the UFSF in 1913. Mmes Weill and Alpen-Salvador, both Jews, held prominent roles in the CNFF, and Cecile Brunschvicg, also Jewish, served as the secretary-general for the UFSF after 1910. Christine Bard notes that all of these women were "known and respected for their competence in the social domain."[16]

The trend throughout the West seemed to be moving toward granting women greater equality with men, even in France, where the suffrage movement remained small. After 1880, French women saw some improvement in their legal situation. Between 1886 and 1901, women gained the right to open savings accounts by themselves, serve as witnesses in civil court cases, control their own wages, and have some joint control over family property with their husbands. James McMillan also suggests that the 1884 divorce law helped to "undermine the absolute authority of the husband in the household."[17] During the same period, education expanded, especially secular education for girls at the secondary level. Professional employment opportunities for middle-class women gradually increased as well.[18] In addition, Mary Louise Roberts suggests that a small group of urban, middle-class women "became the object of public scrutiny" simply through the lifestyles they chose. Some of these women remained single, others "entered nontraditional marriages," and several became feminist activists, lawyers, doctors, journalists, and actresses. They challenged gender norms by "living unconventional lives" and by doing work coded as masculine. These women's "disruptive acts" caused some observers to conclude that "conventional femininity . . . was in crisis."[19] Religious communities' engagement with the "woman question" developed in the context of a broader effort by French women, as well as European and American women, to shape their societies and improve the lives of women and children. This trend toward rethinking women's opportunities was especially important for the Protestant and Jewish communities who wished to put themselves at the front of the movement toward greater equality in French society.

The Suffrage Debate

The development of competing forms of feminism and the engagement of many women in feminist and social programs propelled all three religious communities to decide what kind of feminism they would accept. Religious groups came to see political benefits for their entire communities in encouraging women to participate in different kinds of feminist work. Sometimes this included suffrage and sometimes not. As Lynn Abrams notes, most women could not simply reject the ideology of domesticity. It held too much power in French society. Rather, women had to "struggle—not always with total success—to find a language which resolved the tensions between domestic ideology and the notion of women having rights."[20] Moreover, the development of a women's movement aimed broadly at improving conditions for women and children shaped the kinds of programs created by Catholic, Protestant, and Jewish women. It also shaped the rights and responsibilities women received within their faith communities.

French Catholics entered the twentieth century facing what they saw as severe social, religious, and political problems. In the decades leading up to World War I, France had experienced increasing numbers of civil marriages and burials, fewer baptisms, and decreased church attendance, especially among men.[21] The Church wished to protect as many traditions as possible, including its gendered practice of relegating women to positions subordinate to men. Pope Pius X reminded women that the Bible designated them as companions for men. He warned that those who wanted to give women the same rights and "social functions" as men taught contrary to the Church.[22] As the suffrage movement gained momentum, Catholic women had to ask themselves whether they "were more Catholic or more feminist." The vast majority decided that "they were more Catholic." Militant feminist campaigns for women's political equality challenged Church notions of "divinely ordained" social hierarchies. Similarly, Anne Cova suggests that an alliance between Catholic women and secular feminist groups in the early twentieth century would have been very difficult, especially in the wake of the Dreyfus Affair, as Protestants and Jews had generally supported Dreyfus. The largely Protestant leadership of the CNFF and its ties to international Protestantism led Catholic women such as Adéle Moreau to complain that it was a "huge Protestant machine."[23]

Yet Catholics could not simply ignore suffragism and militant feminism. Although Pope Pius X condemned women's suffrage, a small minority of Catholic women openly claimed it, and French society, including other faith groups, frequently discussed its merits. By 1900, feminism and suffragism had become frequent topics of discussion within Catholic women's magazines. Men and women debated the appropriate Catholic response to increasing demands by women around the world for more rights. For those who believed God had arranged society according to hierarchy and difference, militant feminism demanding full equality with men was a moot point. In a speech to a Catholic women's conference, Emile Ollivier, a member of the Académie Française, argued that modern feminists erred in believing that only women's inferior education had kept them from attaining the same success outside of the home as men. For him, the idea that women had capabilities equal to men contradicted religious teachings, science, and practical experiences. Ollivier claimed that Christianity had done much to liberate women. It had given men and women the same responsibilities of fidelity in marriage and had curbed the "brutalities of men." However, it had also "established the theoretical subordination of women," with men clearly dominant. Ollivier affirmed that no woman ever had a genius that surpassed that of men in her field. Rather, women had been created especially for the responsibilities of motherhood.[24]

Like much of the Catholic community, women LPDF members publicly rejected women's suffrage and rarely collaborated with non-Catholic women. In 1906, the LPDF declared that women's suffrage would create a "new breach" in the "constitution of the family and a deviation in the role of women as it was understood by Christian civilization." Other women agreed, expressing concerns that women might vote badly and arguing that women should use their influence alone to combat Freemasons.[25]

That said, rejecting suffrage within the French Catholic community was far from universal. Magali Della Sudda argues that in the face of danger, some men encouraged women to engage in politics to defend the Church; this mobilization against secularization shifted women away from charity toward becoming "modern political women."[26] The tension within the Catholic community concerning women's suffrage reveals a growing independence of thought among some Catholic men and women and the gradual infusion of more egalitarian ideas into the Catholic community. Marie Maugeret and her small Féminisme Chrétienne movement had been demanding women's suffrage since the late nineteenth century. Jeanne Chenu's organization, the Action Sociale de la Femme (ASF), began printing articles and holding conferences discussing the positive merits of women's suffrage well before the Vatican's approval in 1919. As early as 1903, Anatole LeRoy-Beaulieu argued before a group of ASF members that women needed the vote to combat state encroachments on Catholic liberties, especially in the area of education. The ASF, he argued, "was given the important mission of raising the level and role of the French woman," and "teaching women to love and practice liberty." Women had to become citizens not only for themselves but primarily so that they could protect the faith and religious liberty. Political liberty for women was the precondition for all other liberties.[27]

LeRoy-Beaulieu's article demonstrates the complex nature of Catholic ideas concerning liberty and women. His arguments for granting women suffrage encompassed both traditional and progressive elements. On the one hand, he believed women had to have political rights to defend traditional female purviews such as children, the family, and religion. On the other, by arguing that women should be citizens and have their voices heard, he recognized the independent personhood of women. His objective was to protect Catholic values and rights, but he and the ASF promoted progressive ideas about women's individual rights in the process.

The ASF was not the only Catholic women's organization to consider women's political rights well before the Vatican gave them the green light. After 1911, even the very conservative LPDF began holding study groups on women and politics, which Steven Hause suggests moved that organization toward an acceptance of women's suffrage. Once Pope Benedict XV expressed support for women's suffrage in 1919, Catholic women in the ASF, LPDF, and LFF all quickly jumped on board. They created a new organization with over a million members aimed largely at demanding the vote for women.[28] The rapid growth of the Catholic women's suffrage movement in the 1920s suggests that Catholic women had been considering the positive effects of suffrage among themselves for some time.

The Protestant and Jewish communities' contribution to the struggle for women's civil rights was much more straightforward and has been fairly well documented. Florence Rochefort, Yolande Cohen, Christine Bard, and Steven Hause have all noted the strong participation of Protestant and Jewish women in both secular and religious feminist associations. Rochefort concedes that there was no natural connection between Protestantism and feminism in France. Rather, a relationship developed between the two over the course of the nineteenth century.[29] Protestant and Jewish defenders of women's rights frequently drew on their own interpretation of biblical texts or God's will to justify their positions. They presented Protestant and Jewish theology as progressive and egalitarian while advancing the position of women. Hélène du Pasquier, a writer for the *Journal de la jeune fille*, a Protestant journal directed at girls, declared that Christ had created spiritual equality between men and women. Jesus had sanctioned women's work outside the home by teaching that "the nation, humanity [and] the kingdom of God" could take precedence over the family. Du Pasquier affirmed that for women to be successful in public life, they had to have the right to vote and a voice in government decisions. Since women had equal responsibilities to the nation, they deserved equal rights. She reminded readers that feminism had been born among Christians, and it was in the heart of evangelical churches that the principles of feminism, such as the right to vote, had first been put into practice.[30] In the same spirit of theological modernism, Wilfred Monod, a prominent Protestant pastor, argued that there was no legitimate reason to deny women the right to vote. The Apostle Paul had written to "our ancestors the Galatians" that there was "no longer Jew nor Greek, nor slave nor free, neither men nor women" because everyone was united in Christ.[31]

The Jewish community generally responded favorably to granting more civil rights to women as well. Writers linked Judaism's "progressive" spirit to feminism's political goals. In 1906, Rabbi Emile Lévy gave a sermon affirming that Judaism, "the religion of progress and light," supported the extension of educational and career opportunities to women, which he saw as an "act of justice and humanity." He referred to feminism as a "movement of regeneration and progress . . . which had as its goal the emancipation of women and the revendication of [their] rights." Lévy noted that "the tendency of our era," emphasizing the "inviolable respect of the person," had been "justly extended to women."[32] Another writer affirmed that if people "rejected all of the old prejudices that kept women in a state of inferiority, minority, and incapacity," they would be "forced to admit that nothing authorized the confiscation of certain natural rights. . . ." This writer praised laws such as the 1907 decision granting women the right to control their wages, and he encouraged the Jewish community to uphold these laws and make sure they were applied.[33]

Equality and Justice

Despite their varied reasons and degrees of support for women's suffrage, all three communities managed to promote equality and justice as fundamental values of French culture. Catholic women's growing support for suffrage and civil liberties suggests that egalitarian ideas were infused into the Catholic community in France through women and women's issues. Catholic women and men continued to support conservative goals of re-Catholicizing the nation and protecting Catholic education. However, they also used the republican language of liberties and acknowledged women's right and ability to engage in civic action and even vote. Even Pius X, known for his staunchly conservative political and religious positions, acknowledged to a group of women in 1909 that women had responsibilities that exceeded those in the family.[34] Catholics continued to shy away from emphasizing individual rights, especially for women, but the Catholic community increasingly expected men and women to undertake more equal social, political, and religious duties.

Catholic women's consideration of suffrage also suggests that women were privately questioning the teachings of the Vatican on issues like women's rights. This indicates independence of thought among women rather than blind acceptance of Vatican doctrine. Women as individuals had certainly questioned Church authority in the past, but now women's faith-based organizations provided lay-women with a group environment in which they could question the teachings of the Church hierarchy. This might not have had much effect on the hierarchy, but it did move the French Catholic community toward acceptance of greater equality among men and women. Faith-based organizations facilitated more independence of thought among women concerning religious teachings, which suggests limits to the Vatican's hold on the hearts and minds of believers. Thus, the Catholic community's engagement with women's suffrage infused the French Catholic community with a more modern, egalitarian spirit. This does not mean that French Catholics suddenly accepted full equality between men and women and rejected traditional Church teachings. Catholic women remained very conservative. But they made progress toward promoting a more equal position between men and women both in the Church and in French society.

Catholic women's organizations engaged women in the modernization of France and the Church. Women took advantage of laws passed in the 1880s that provided freedom of the press and freedom of organization. Although they wanted to protect Catholic and French traditions, they did not want those traditions to remain static. They accepted that men and women might have some different social and religious responsibilities, but they increasingly challenged (sometimes inadvertently) women's subordinate position to men. Catholic women leaders understood that the world was changing, and they needed to adapt. One contributor to the ASF warned women "not to recoil from innovations" because as society changed, so did the needs of its people. As a result, the Church needed to be an innovator rather than static and unchanging.[35] Rather than waiting to be protected by men, women armed themselves with a new confidence and determination. They became an important part of the Church's circle of defense—the physical, visible presence of the Church in France. This made Catholic women a growing force within the Church as well as in French society despite their limited ability to promote suffrage. Twentieth-century organizations were more visible and more political than earlier charitable ones. They printed mass circulation newspapers, organized nationally and internationally, held public mass meetings, and aspired to shape politics at national and international levels. In modernizing and promoting equality within the Catholic community, women helped to promote the same values in the nation as well.

For the Protestant and Jewish communities, promoting equality through women's rights built on a long tradition of struggling for democracy in France.³⁶ The Dreyfus Affair, along with the rise of a new nationalist, antidemocratic, and anti-Semitic far right in the 1880s, had shaken both communities' confidence in the stability of France's democratic traditions and its commitment to individual rights.³⁷ Both the Protestant and Jewish communities wished to protect the Republic and solidify France's identity as a nation that equally accepted all of its citizens regardless of their faith background.³⁸ They did this partly through supporting women's rights, including suffrage.

Protestants and Jews often spoke of women's suffrage as an act of progress and justice for women that would allow women to work more fully toward achieving a just society. Wilfred Monod, a theologian and a leader in the social Christianity movement, was an ardent supporter of women's rights. He referred to men's continued supremacy over women as a legacy of a less civilized era when brute force created dominance. In place of this, he argued that natural cooperation should exist between men and women not only biologically but also morally, spiritually, and intellectually. He rejected the notion that women should not vote because they did not serve in the military, noting instead that they gave birth to children, an equally risky service to the nation.³⁹ Another Protestant writer noted that the "Protestant mentality" favored "the complete emancipation of women." He argued that no one could deny women had the same interests to safeguard as men both in the nation and in the Church. Like men, women were victims of bad laws and beneficiaries of good reforms. Women were part of *la patrie*, and they lived and suffered with it. As such, he believed that women had the right to help direct the nation.⁴⁰

Jewish women who participated in feminist organizations such as the UFSF, the organization that published *La française*, also had considerable support from Jewish leaders in their quest for civil rights. Grand Rabbi M. Netter extolled what he called "the reasonable feminism of *La Française.*"⁴¹ Emile Cahen, a writer for the very conservative journal *Archives israélite*, praised the UFSF's quest for civil rights and supported its request that women be admitted into administrative commissions. He also advocated for women to receive "equal pay for equal work [and] equality in intellectual culture." Cahen expressed pride in the important part that Jewish women or "women of Jewish origin," including Mme Léon Brunschwig, Suzanne Grinberg, Mme Legrand-Falco, and Valentine Thomson, played in France's feminist movement.[42] Pierre Birnbaum notes that for Jews in the nineteenth century, "public space and private space became separate and distinct entities." Jews wished to create a nation that "would be composed exclusively of 'citizens' whose private values no longer mattered in the public sphere."[43] For both Protestants and Jews, support for women's rights reinforced the democratic, egalitarian values of the Republic at a time when France desperately needed those values fortified.

Feminism's Contribution to the Faith Community

For all three faith communities, supporting an expanded public role for women had positive implications for the status and reputation of their faith communities. This is not to say that these communities only promoted women's rights for cynical reasons. However, supporting an expanded public position for women allowed each community to define itself as a fundamental and acceptable part of French culture, French religious tradition, and French republican and democratic ideals.

Regardless of their position on women's suffrage, Catholic women were instrumental in keeping religion visible in French culture and promoting it as an important force in French and European society. The ASF, LFF, and LPDF created a tightly woven network of organizations throughout France that brought hundreds of thousands of Catholic women into social, religious, and, to some extent, political work. This kept women actively and publicly practicing in the faith, and it provided group support for people who wanted to be Catholic activists. These organizations made it acceptable to be a publicly religious person in a state that increasingly valued secularism. By 1902, the ASF's lectures had become popular enough that it rented a lecture hall seating 1,000, and by 1904, the organization had provincial branches and links with similar groups in 200 towns throughout France with about 5,000 members.[44] The success of the LPDF was even more spectacular. By 1910, with around 500,000 members, the LPDF declared that it had founded "124 libraries, 121 patronages, 7 vacation colonies, 24 day care centers, 42 homemaking schools, 18 study circles, 14 dowry funds, 45 workshops, 43 information centers, 11 mutual aid societies."[45]

The ASF and the LPDF also had strong ties with international Catholic women's organizations, which allowed them to promote Catholic values not only in France but throughout Europe and other parts of the world as well.[46] This kept religion active and visible on a national as well as international plane. In 1905, the ASF created a secretariat for international affairs headed by Mme Gautier-Lacaze, who, according to the ASF's journal, "understood most of the major languages of Europe," and could therefore coordinate correspondence between diverse linguistic groups.[47] The ASF shared information, exchanged bulletins, and reported about the actions of their international counterparts, including the Catholic Women's League in London, the Consumers League in the United States, and the Catholic Women's League in Germany, among others. In 1910, the ASF had eighty international correspondents sending information about women's activities throughout the world.[48] The LPDF engaged in similar international work. The primary goals of both organizations were to combat anticlerical politics, re-Catholicize the world, and improve the lives of the poor. This meant bringing individuals back to the Catholic faith but also reintegrating Catholicism and Catholic leadership into political, social, and educational institutions. It also meant bringing women out of the home and engaging them in social work in an effort to save individual souls, protect the Church, and strengthen the French nation.

The Protestant and Jewish communities' engagement with the question of women's suffrage also incorporated political goals that extended to their entire communities. Protestants and Jews used support for women's rights to demonstrate the progressive, democratic character of their communities and the compatibility of their faiths with the secular Third Republic. As noted earlier, the trend in France seemed to be moving in the direction of granting women more rights and a more equal place in society. Women's suffrage was in the realm of possibility. The Protestant and Jewish communities put themselves at the head of this trend toward women's rights.

Supporting feminism and women's suffrage allowed the Protestant and Jewish communities to emphasize their attachment to the ideals of liberty, equality, and justice—the ideals of the Enlightenment, the French Revolution, and the Third Republic. They presented themselves as devoted patriots and republicans promoting values compatible with those of the Third Republic, unlike their Catholic counterparts. Ferdinand Buisson, a liberal Protestant feminist supporter and director of primary education for the French government, felt similarly. He argued that women's rights needed to be understood not as something exceptional but as part of the larger notion of rights and liberty in France. Buisson believed that there was no way to justify making women pay taxes but refusing to give them the right to vote.[49] Buisson's ideas were especially important because they emphasized principles of rights and liberty in France. He linked women's rights to the protection of rights for everyone.

Supporting women's civil rights also allowed the Protestant and Jewish communities to emphasize their dedication to achieving a just society and to present themselves as modern and progressive.[50] Paula Hyman notes that by the mid-nineteenth century, emphasizing Judaism's progressive position toward women had become an important part of Jews' "claim to Western norms of civilization."[51] In France, in particular, it became a way for the community to carve out a space for Judaism as a religion supportive of secular democracy and, therefore, useful to France. In 1908, Gabrielle Lipman, a self-proclaimed "moderate feminist" involved with the prosuffrage Conférence de Versailles, spoke to the Université Populaire de la Rue de Jarenet. Judaism, Lipman argued, had resolved the feminist problem by "respecting the rights of the woman and treating her as equal to men," while at the same time "taking into consideration her own nature." She noted that from the beginning of the Bible, women had been "called to aid and support men," and men had frequently consulted them in all sorts of important affairs. Jacob, for instance, only made his decision about his relationship with Laban after consulting Leah and Rachel. Miriam and the other women of Israel had played a considerable part in the exodus from Egypt. Lipman suggested that Judaism had "created an equilibrium directed by good sense and recommended by fairness."[52] Nadia Malinovich notes that as French Jews "created new forms of Jewish cultural life" in the first part of the twentieth century, they "attempted to work out a new kind of French-Jewish synthesis in step with the changing cultural and social realities of the day."[53]

Supporting women's rights also aided the Jewish community in its struggle against anti-Semitism, which by the late nineteenth century was on the rise in France. French Jewish history had been marked by persecution, and even during the late nineteenth and early twentieth centuries, Jews faced a barrage of anti-Semitic attacks. In 1886, Edouard Drumont published *La France juive*, which became "the first best-seller on anti-Semitism in France." *La France juive*, followed by Drumont's magazine *La libre parole*, accused Jews of trying to destroy Catholicism and controlling the French financial system for their own personal gain, among other things. At about the same time, anti-Jewish attacks increased in the Catholic daily newspaper *La Croix*.[54] The French Jewish community had worked hard throughout the nineteenth century to show their patriotism and "Frenchness" in hopes of reducing anti-Semitism. However, the frequent anti-Semitic articles published in the Catholic and nationalist presses revealed the potential fragility of Jews' position in France.[55]

Anti-Semites sometimes pointed to "the treatment of women within Jewish tradition" to emphasize the irreconcilable differences between Jews and European society.[56] As a result, the feminist question in the Jewish community quickly moved beyond the debate about whether women should vote and came to focus on whether Judaism oppressed or ignored women. L. Suffète, a writer for *L'univers israélite*, declared that "the doctrines and traditions of Judaism" that assigned women a large place in Jewish life as well as a "spirit of justice and fairness" had encouraged him to support more rights for women.[57] In the context of rising anti-Semitism in France, writers who dealt with the feminist question tried to present Judaism in the best possible light for those inside and outside the community. They affirmed that Judaism had always respected the rights of women. The feminist question provided Jewish leaders with an opportunity to defend the Jewish faith as progressive and modernizing. Jewish writers and religious leaders endeavored to create a positive identity for Judaism as inherently progressive and open to appropriate changes in women's roles. At the same time, they tried to solidify these values as part of the foundational political identity of France.

Florence Rochefort notes that "in the face of a Catholic traditionalism which had long rejected individualism and the principles of 1789, feminism and Protestantism of the nineteenth century placed themselves together in a post-revolutionary modernity, both stakeholders in the process of laicization."[58] This was true for Judaism as well. The engagement with women's rights allowed both communities to demonstrate that religion could still be relevant and beneficial to the French nation. This relationship between Protestantism, Judaism, and feminism was strengthened in the early part of the twentieth century as Protestants and Jews looked for ways to create a positive image of their communities that would illustrate the relevance of those communities to the nation. Support for women's rights allowed them to create a progressive, democratic public image and reinforce the importance of democracy and equality in the French nation. This was good for women, but it also helped to solidify the idea that people regardless of faith merited equal treatment in France.

Importance of Faith Communities for Women

Many of the goals women and their religious communities wished to achieve might have been accomplished more easily if women, especially Protestants and Jews, had banded together in secular feminist organizations. This raises questions about why women remained so attached to their religious organizations. Catholic women's organizations like the ASF, LFF, and LPDF offered an alternative way for women to engage in public life and shape the identity and the future of the French nation. As will be shown in subsequent chapters, it also allowed them to develop a real sense of their own importance to the salvation of the nation and the Church. Suffrage work, as Marie Maugeret, one of the few Catholic suffragists, discovered, was a thankless task, but religious work came with much praise and status. Although Catholic women continued to elevate women's role in the home, they also believed that they had to engage more fully in reshaping France into a nation that accepted Catholic values. The ASF aimed to "teach women their role in society, make them understand how their actions could be exercised in the family, education, the professions and public life." It also wanted to help women defend the "principles upon which our French life has always rested."[59] Women came to see themselves as the keepers of the faith and French tradition. For France to continue to be prosperous and blessed by God, it had to be Catholic. However, the nation was being tempted by secular, godless trends, and Catholic women had to pull it back from the brink of self-destruction. In doing so, they pushed themselves toward more modern, more egalitarian forms of action.

Given the Protestant and Jewish communities' overall progressive position on women's rights, continued participation within their faith communities offered Protestant and Jewish women a number of advantages as well. Maintaining close ties with their faith communities allowed Protestant and Jewish women to legitimize their secular feminist work and retain a degree of respectability that they might have lost without a connection to religion. Women of faith who engaged in secular feminist and suffragist activities rejected any accusations of selfishness by grounding their work in Judeo-Christian values. They argued that rights for women would further a commitment to justice in France. It would also allow women to fight more effectively for the protection of the poor and disadvantaged. Julie Siegfried, a prominent member of the Protestant and moderate feminist communities, gave a speech to the Congrès International des Femmes in 1913 where she argued that women, who directed the education of children, had a right to participate in the organization of public life. She considered the right to vote as an act of justice that should be accorded to women. She suggested that with the right to vote, women could more fully work to overcome the suffering of others "to form a *Cité Nouvelle* of peace and love" that would come when people learned how to act with justice.[60]

Religious communities provided women involved in feminist pursuits with a network of support that they could draw on as they made their demands for more rights. These women were not fighting alone. Rather, they had the spiritual and moral backing of important men and other women within their faith groups. Support for women's rights and suffrage in the secular sphere also gave women an opportunity to demand greater religious rights. It forced communities as a whole to consider or reconsider the kinds of rights women should have within their churches and synagogues. At the same time that Protestants and Jews were debating women's rights on a national level, they were also considering allowing women to vote in church elections, serve on synod and presbytery councils, and even be pastors. Protestant women, and to a lesser extent Jewish women, gained administrative and leadership rights within their faith communities much more quickly than they did on a national level, which also made participation in faith-based organizations and churches appealing to them.

Conclusion

The engagement of Catholics, Protestants, and Jews with women's suffrage in the early twentieth century was directly related to each community's political goals. Despite the efforts of the Third Republic to undermine the power of the Catholic Church, the activities of hundreds of thousands of Catholic women ensured that Catholicism would remain a central part of France's cultural landscape. Women's organizations offered women an opportunity to think more independently about what role they should have in France and within the Catholic community. For Protestants and Jews, support for women's rights proved that their faiths were entirely compatible with a secular, modern state and were useful in promoting democratic and egalitarian ideals. These communities wanted to assure France's future as a nation that accorded equal worth to all its citizens regardless of religious background. They endeavored to found the reputation of their communities on the pillars of liberty, equality, and justice. Women's rights, including suffrage, played a powerful role in that process. Women became symbols of the progressive, modern spirit that rested at the heart of these communities—the same spirit they wished to see infuse the nation.

2

The Development of Women's "Ministries" in France

In a 1906 sermon, Emile Lévy, the Grand Rabbi of Bayonne, pro-claimed, "at the most critical hours and the most somber periods of our history, the women of Israel have shown the most attachment to the beliefs of our fathers." These women "gave their husbands and children an example of stoic, invincible fidelity to their faith and a contempt for death. This influence that the Jewish woman possessed in the past, she must conserve in the present for the glory of her sex and for the salvation of our religion."[1] Lévy's sermon exemplifies the position of Catholics, Protestants, and Jews toward women's religious responsibilities in the early twentieth century. All three communities worried about the increasing secularization of French society. They came to depend on women to bring people back to the faith, gain new converts, and ensure the transmission of religious values across generations.[2] None of these communities was willing to grant women leadership positions completely equal with men. However, they did accept women as spiritual equals who were capable of understanding and transmitting religious teachings.

Faith communities' engagement with the question of women's religious ministries was driven by a desire to preserve religion as a vital force in French society. Each community struggled to carve out a place for itself as part of France's religious identity amid the religious upheavals of the early twentieth century. Women and women's issues became a means to position their communities as foundational blocks of the nation. For Catholics this meant motivating as many women as possible to engage in re-Christianizing France by expanding their public mission as apostles of the faith. For Protestants and Jews, it meant expanding women's spiritual vocation as well as demonstrating the progressive, egalitarian character of Protestant and Jewish theology. In all three cases, either directly or indirectly, faith communities' decisions about women's ministries helped promote a greater degree of equality for women in both the religious and secular spheres.

Missing Men and Women's Ministries

By the turn of the century, Catholics, Protestants, and Jews all worried about declining religiosity, especially declining numbers of men participating in their faiths. For Catholics, the 1905 separation of church and state pushed them further toward the political right, and confirmed their "self-image as an embattled minority, fighting a desperate rearguard action against the forces of evil."[3] Catholic women, with the support of the Church hierarchy, were determined to revitalize the Catholic faith and demonstrate the centrality of Catholicism to the well-being of the nation. In 1904, the Bishop of Marseille sent a letter to the Ligue Patriotique des Françaises (LPDF) reminding women that God had used women like Joan of Arc to save France in the past. God would use women again to pull France, the "eldest daughter of the Church," out of the grip of the Freemasons. The bishop declared that if Catholics "united in action, in sacrifice, and in prayer," they would triumph quickly over the enemy who wished to divide them.[4] By acknowledging that the fate of France and the Church rested largely in women's hands, this bishop tacitly conceded the failure of men to adequately protect the Church. Leaders in the LPDF were more explicit about the problems the Church faced. One LPDF member noted in 1909 that since most men did not engage in winning people back to the faith, the 400,000 members of the LPDF would have to turn the masses back toward God.[5]

Similar dynamics shaped the Protestant and Jewish communities. A writer for the Protestant magazine *L'ami chrétien des familles* noted that an overall decline in church attendance had caused some churches to close entirely. In the churches that still existed, men were "conspicuous for their absence," leaving women and young girls to form the "majority, often almost the totality of the audience." In the town of Anduze, average attendance at Sunday services was 300 to 350 but only about fifty of those attendees were men. One Anduzien writer commented that men suffered from indifference, skepticism, and a lack of faith. Worse, men often feared that they would be ridiculed for attending church.[6] Jewish writers similarly complained that many Jewish men neglected their obligations to pray, noting that when the hour of services came for the Sabbath or holidays, men went to walk in gardens or parks or near the sea. One commenter noted that men never considered the "mistake" they made by "deserting the house of God" where there no longer remained the necessary ten faithful men for prayers. In many communities, the temple remained deserted not only during vacations but for the whole year.[7] Many Jewish religious services—certain prayers, chanting from the Torah, reciting the Kaddish—required a quorum. In the French conservative form of Judaism, this meant the presence of at least ten men. However, synagogues, especially those in the provinces, often had difficulty drawing the requisite ten men even for Saturday services and during religious holidays. Catholic, Protestant, and Jewish leaders from all over France discussed solutions to these grave problems. As the Bishop of Marseille suggested, many of those solutions rested on the willingness of women to take up the religious torch that men had abandoned.

Women Revitalize Religion

Although France's religious future seemed imperiled to many, the situation was not all bad. As men neglected their religious duties, women stepped up to keep their faith communities alive and vibrant. French Catholic women believed that early twentieth-century France was at a crossroads.[8] An anonymous Catholic woman writing in 1902 affirmed that under the present conditions, Catholic women could not remain indifferent to the "life of France," which she feared risked dying. Women had an "important responsibility" to "save France and to work toward uplifting the nation." She encouraged women to "enlighten the indifferent, the free thinkers, [and] the hypnotized" to the notion that France could be nothing other than Catholic. If not Catholic, it would no longer be France since, as she declared, the "French soul is a Catholic soul."[9] French and Catholic identities were closely intertwined in the minds of Catholics, and if France lost its Catholic faith, it would no longer be France. Unless France repented of its sins against the Church and God, the nation risked God's wrath, spiritual disorientation, and the veritable loss of a true French identity.

Catholic women accepted this call and placed themselves at the head of efforts to keep Catholicism as a powerful force in French society. Women were determined to become warriors for God and the Church, and they saw themselves as ideally suited to battle spiritually for the salvation of the nation. Laywomen increasingly refused to remain in the shadows of religious philanthropy. They preferred instead to take a more organized, more public, and more militant approach to the re-Christianization of the nation. The Bishop of Marseille pointed to Joan of Arc as women's model, but Joan of Arc was a decidedly unfeminine version of a woman. She had rejected traditional femininity in order to follow God's orders and save France. This notion of women as warriors was reflected in the militant language women used to describe their work. Women might not have been able to fight for France on a battlefield like Joan of Arc, but they could emulate her through their spiritual warfare for the salvation of the nation. As one Ligue des Femmes Françaises (LFF) member put it, a "war" had been declared on God by "sectarians who never ceased to insult him." It was up to women of the LFF to reform the "the appalling state in which France found itself. . . ."[10] Similarly, Mlle de Noaillait, a leader in the LPDF, declared that women carried the "weapons" of prayer, devotion, and love. Nothing their adversaries tried to do would succeed. The "salvation of France," she declared, was in women's hands.[11]

The depiction of women as saviors of France was not just hollow talk on the part of the clergy or on the part of women. It led to a real increase in women's active spiritual engagement in France and thus acted as a revitalizing factor for French Catholicism. It is true that not all of the several hundred thousand women members of various Catholic organizations were equally engaged (some undoubtedly only paid dues to the organization and nothing more). However, many were involved in various forms of religious work. Religious retreats held in various French cities managed to draw hundreds of women each year.[12] In 1908, 12,000 LPDF members took part in pilgrimages to Notre-Dame de Paimpont and Bois-Renou. The morning of the pilgrimage to Bois-Renou, a reporter noted that while waiting for members to arrive, Mlle de Sallier du Pin gave "a speech that vibrated with faith and patriotism" to LPDF members who had already arrived.[13] Even in 1916, in the midst of WWI, the LPDF attracted about 800 people to a three-day conference at Lourdes. The pope sent a telegram praising these women and blessing their work.[14] Pilgrimages represented traditional aspects of Catholic religious life. Ruth Harris notes that nineteenth-century pilgrimages to Lourdes were animated by "aristocratic women and members of new female orders who joined with activist priests to promote a vision of pilgrimage that brought rich and poor together in Catholic solidarity." The organization of pilgrimages by Catholic women gave them a different quality and a new importance. These kinds of movements "valued and gave status to women, acknowledging many of the tasks that they did in private, as they consoled, fed and nursed."[15] Pilgrimages were no longer the domain of priests alone; they also represented laywomen's efforts to work for the re-Christianization of France.

The Protestant community also decried religious indifference among men, but like their Catholic counterparts, leaders took note of the devotion and spiritual successes of women. Pastor Charles Babut declared, "God, who has used many instruments to advance his reign, has found it good, in these last times, to employ the most weak of all, the woman."[16] He noted that even among Protestants' "numerous conquests over Catholicism," none were more blessed and more fruitful in spiritual results than those created by Protestant women. He cited numerous moral projects in which women had taken a leading position, such as campaigns against slavery and prostitution and programs aimed at aiding people in prisons. Babut suggested that beyond these few examples existed a more general movement among Christian women to be "engaged in the active service of the Lord," which included women's participation in interior and exterior missionary projects.[17]

Protestants recognized that women could be more successful than men in certain types of spiritual outreach. Women needed an expanded spiritual mission supported by the community. A woman missionary in France noted that in some areas of France, the Gospel exercised no influence over the lives of either men or women. This rampant lack of belief convinced her that women had an important role to play as evangelists. She worked in a poor region where many women and children were victims of their alcoholic husbands and fathers. These women, "exhausted with the struggle to maintain their own courage and the effort to provide bread for their children," often lacked the energy or the will to go to church. As a result, they needed women evangelists who could go into their homes and "enter into the details and difficulties of their lives."[18] No clear consensus existed in 1909 about whether women should be pastors, but many Protestants were quickly moving in that direction. Women could already be missionaries and the distinction between missionary and pastor was not clear. In any case, the community by and large accepted the idea that women could understand and teach the Gospel equally with men.

The situation for Jews differed slightly from their Catholic and Protestant counterparts. Jews do not proselytize, so the Jewish community did not need to mobilize women for religious outreach in quite the same ways. Jewish women tended to be more active in faith-based social work than in direct spiritual renewal. However, Jewish leaders frequently tasked women with revitalizing Judaism among Jews, especially in families. More than one writer affirmed that the survival of French Judaism depended on the devotion of families and their willingness to practice Jewish law at home. Many believed that women held the keys to the community's survival. Rabbi Emile Lévy gave two sermons in 1906 insisting on women's roles as "guardians of religion" and fortifiers of "peace, union, and harmony" in the home. As Lévy put it, in the home more than in the temple, Judaism drew strength to resist "the most terrible storms that had assailed it throughout its long and tragic history." Women served as the "priestess of the foyer [and] the guardian of religion" by creating an atmosphere of "dignity, purity, and holiness." As mothers, women fulfilled their religious mission by "cultivating religious sentiments" in their children. He warned that the "salvation of Judaism" rested in women's hands. Like Lévy, the Rabbi M. J.-H. Dreyfuss also emphasized the religious influence women exerted in the home. Dreyfuss defended Judaism's emphasis on men's predominance in public ceremonies, arguing that while women in ancient times did not go with their husbands and fathers each day to visit the Temple, they made the home a sanctuary. The responsibilities of women as wives and mothers constituted a religious calling in themselves, and he referred to women as the "priestess of the home" in all ages and all civilizations. When religion permeated every aspect of the home and every moment of the day, it was because of the faithfulness of mothers. In this way, women in ancient times had made the home an "annex of the house of prayers."[19]

Gabrielle Bauer, one of the few Jewish women to engage in the debate about women's religious responsibilities, agreed with the men in her community. She also described women as the "priestesses" of the family, which she saw as the "indestructible sanctuary of Judaism." Bauer put a special emphasis on women's responsibility to teach their daughters about Judaism. Mothers had to make them proud to be Jews, to teach them to practice Judaism with intelligence, and to make them capable of fulfilling their own future roles as Jewish wives and mothers with dignity. As Jews prepared to celebrate Passover, the deliverance of Jews from Egypt, she reminded women that they could also "deliver modern Jews from religious indifference."[20] Rather than giving women official leadership positions, Jewish leaders tried to elevate women's spiritual position in the home to equal or exceed that of men in the synagogue.

Women and Spiritual Equality

The desperate need for women to revitalize their faiths contributed to a growing acceptance of equality in women's spiritual missions, especially within the Catholic and Protestant communities. Both communities had long acknowledged women as equal with men on the level of the soul—everyone could go to heaven and be accepted by God. These communities increasingly came to accept women's equal abilities to understand, interpret, and spread the religious messages of their respective communities.

Although there was no discussion among Catholics about making women priests, the Catholic hierarchy provided considerable support for an expanded religious mission for women. Catholic women began to undertake what they described as more "priestly" work through their participation in women's leagues. In an effort to prepare themselves to undertake projects of social and religious uplift, a number of women's organizations, especially the LPDF, began organizing religious retreats designed to "fortify the Christian life," which had been "attacked on multiple sides." Religious retreats brought women together, often in monasteries, for a few days of religious meditation, reflection, and instruction. The LPDF designed its retreats to serve as "schools of apostleship," to instruct women about their special responsibilities as LPDF members. The Vicomtesse de Vélard, president of the LPDF, believed that religious retreats could contribute to the creation of an elite group of women "composed of true apostles who, filled with light," could "radiate that light around them" in an effort to prevent the faith in French souls from being stifled by the rising wave of immorality and unbelief.[21]

The creation of religious retreats allowed women to circumvent restrictions on their access to the priesthood by creating their own centers for ministerial growth. The retreats also affirmed that women other than nuns had the right and the responsibility to receive training for religious vocation. Religious retreats served as one way in which Catholic women's leagues worked to create a parallel army of laywomen trained to battle for French souls in ways similar to priests.

The insistence on Catholic laywomen's work as apostles proved to be one of the most innovative aspects of the new focus on women's responsibilities to the Church. Many Catholic leaders and scholars, both men and women, discussed the "apostolic mission" of women in an effort to define it and encourage women to undertake more active "apostolic" responsibilities. One writer suggested that women's religious work, especially their work with children, provided women with an opportunity "to become a bit of a priest" themselves. The writer declared that women "guided by the spirit of God" could participate in the "ministry of the priest, to console and aid the holy Church in a time when the ministers of the altar were more and more rare."[22]

The LPDF expected all members to be apostles in one way or another, but it created leadership positions for especially active members, *dizainières*, who visited the homes of women in their neighborhoods to encourage religious devotion. At an LPDF conference in 1909, Mlle de Noaillat defined the apostolic mission of the dizainières. She encouraged them to develop relationships with the women they visited and find out about their lives and their children. Once people began to trust the dizainières, they would be able to give counsel or maybe a slight reproach, such as encouraging women to attend church, have their children baptized, or send their children to private Catholic schools.[23] Even police reporters who kept tabs on some of the larger organizations such as the LPDF commented about the proselytization undertaken by Catholic women. A 1904 Paris police report noted that the goal of the LPDF was to "bring the unbelievers to the Church." The reporter verified that the LPDF had made many sacrifices to achieve this goal, but failed to explain what methods the women employed.[24] Although women continued to limit their contact to other women and children, their rhetoric and that of male religious leaders attached them more fully to the male-centered power of Christ's apostles rather than only the motherly influence of the Virgin Mary.

Women's religious organizations also created much stronger ties between laywomen and high-ranking members of the clergy. Women's greater visibility as potential saviors of France and the Church drew attention all the way to the Vatican. Even the very conservative Pope Pius X, who staunchly rejected women's suffrage and condemned the idea of equality between men and women, praised the work of Catholic women's leagues. He even invited delegations from these leagues to the Vatican. In a 1908 meeting between Pius X and leaders of the

LPDF, he compared them to the "holy women" in the Gospels. He declared that through their attachment to the Holy See, their devotion to the nation, and their courage to "brave the dangers necessary to maintain the faith," they resembled Mary Magdalene and the "Holy Women" who were the first "apostles" of the resurrection.[25] One of the reasons the Church denied and still denies women access to the priesthood is that Jesus chose no women when he picked his twelve apostles. Pius X did not link women with male apostles in this speech, but he did recognize their ability to be apostles and their importance in that position.

The Catholic Church has never created a completely equal spiritual mission for men and women. However, the early twentieth century saw women close the gap between the spiritual importance given to priests and that accorded to laywomen. They built on the advances made by nineteenth-century women, especially those in female congregations who had already been pushing the limits of acceptable public action for women.[26] A subtle change occurred in the rhetoric surrounding women's actions, although there was no effort to fundamentally reevaluate biblical or church teachings. Women sought out ways to expand their spiritual work despite the conservative rhetoric used by the Church. They did not necessarily directly challenge the gendered traditions of the church, but they modernized those traditions in order to expand their spiritual mission. The language describing women as militant warriors and apostles who could save France gave women a real sense of their own importance. It also helped link them to more masculine kinds of action. Christ, a man, had come to save the world, and he had chosen twelve men to serve as his primary apostles. However, at this moment of crisis in France, with men failing in their responsibilities, women could also become saviors of the nation in Christ's image. This contributed to a shift in the identity of the Church itself. The image of the Church's apostles and spiritual warriors as presented in the press and at Catholic conferences had come to include an important feminine element.

The French Protestant community came closer than any other community to granting women full religious equality with men. The most significant obstacle to women's spiritual equality among Protestants was the writings of the Apostle Paul. In the Bible, Paul had demanded women's silence in churches and had forbidden women from taking leadership over men or teaching men. Paul's teachings seemed to exclude women from pastorships. Some Protestants accepted Paul's words as an immutable barrier against public ministries for women and as a sign of women's perpetual subordination to men. Others were more willing to look for alternative biblical models for women's actions.

One writer for the Protestant magazine *L'église libre* suggested that Luke's writings could serve as a "Gospel for women" and, by association, as a model that Protestants could use to expand women's religious vocation. Luke provided many examples of Christ's caring and respectful attitude toward women as well as women's own supportive role in Christ's ministry. Luke mentioned the group of women who followed Christ and aided him as he preached, as well as the prophetess Anna, who, in her devotion to God, never left the temple (Luke 2:36–38). This author emphasized Christ's recognition of women's faith and his equal acceptance of them as Christians.[27] Similarly, E. Borel-Brun, a writer for the *Journal de la jeune fille* (a magazine of the French version of the YWCA), referred to the story about Jesus' conversation with a disreputable Samaritan woman. She argued that Christ had undermined prejudice by speaking with a woman who was not Jewish or viewed as respectable by her contemporaries. Although Jesus's disciples had been surprised by his conversation with the woman, she became a messenger to the Samaritans in a way the disciples had failed to do. In this instance, Borel-Brun argued that the woman had become more of an apostle than the apostles themselves.[28] Others argued that Jesus had liberated women from oppression and made men and women spiritually equal.[29]

If Christ had accepted the work of men and women equally during his time on earth, then many in the Protestant community would see that as a sign that men and women had the same spiritual mission and abilities. Pastor Charles Babut argued that the success of Protestant women's various "ministries" suggested that these ministries must be the will of God. Protestants needed only to rethink Paul's teachings to reflect God's acceptance of men's and women's work. Babut pointed out that although Paul seemed to oppose women speaking in churches, Paul had also written that in Christ there was neither slave nor free, neither man nor woman.[30] Other pastors saw Paul's support for the deaconess Phoebe as the acceptance of a religious vocation for women. At a pastors' conference in 1904, Pastor Hoffet suggested that while individuals received different "gifts and ministries," no difference existed in the possibility to develop those gifts and employ them. He declared that when Paul had made restrictions against women teaching men and speaking in church, he had taken into account the situation and culture of his time. Paul had left open the possibility for greater religious activities for women by teaching that "in Christ there is neither man nor woman."[31]

Evaluated in this way, Paul's teachings, and the Bible in general, seemed malleable and opened to interpretation. These writers presented the Bible as able to adapt to changes in the modern world, including women's roles in churches. Many Protestants grew to believe that excluding women from developing a greater religious "ministry" was depriving churches of valuable workers. By emphasizing the public religious roles that women had played during the life of Christ, these writers provided a foundation for the Protestant community's efforts to expand women's vocations and recognize their spiritual abilities as equal to men. They also presented an image of Protestantism that was inherently progressive and egalitarian.

The Jewish community, like their Catholic counterparts, never considered making women rabbis. However, other religious positions were up for debate. The early twentieth century saw the Jewish community engage in a heated discussion about whether women could be counted as part of the minyan, the quorum of ten people needed for public prayers. In many ways, this debate mirrored that of the Protestant community. It focused on interpreting or reinterpreting Biblical texts and the degree to which Jews should maintain traditional practices or modernize to meet the changing needs of the community. The minyan debate played out both in the Jewish press and in rabbinical council meetings. Jewish leaders considered women's position in terms of justice, Jewish theology, and practical considerations for the community.

Writers in favor of including women in the minyan argued that the Jewish community owed women the right to participate because it was just and reasonable. They used language reflecting their republican leanings, which linked them with values of the French state. In 1901, a frequent contributor to *L'univers israélite* chided the Jewish community for refusing to remedy the "shocking inequalities" created by Jewish law between men and women. He accepted that women's domestic responsibilities might prevent them from fulfilling "certain pious responsibilities," but he rejected the notion that men and women should have different rights within the faith.[32]

Other writers assured readers that Judaism included enough theological flexibility to accept an expansion in women's participation. Mathieu Wolff, an ardent supporter of women's rights, noted that women had traditionally been assigned religious duties that could be accomplished in the home "at moments of the day that would not constrain her from any of her domestic occupations." However, Wolff suggested women's domestic responsibilities no longer confined them to the home as they had in the past, thereby opening up greater possibilities for participation. In light of this, he argued that women should be accorded the same religious rights as men to "elect the officials of our religion, to become officials themselves, to form the *minyan* [and] *quorum*, in brief, all the rights said to be masculine." In the context of current circumstances, he declared that "it would be absurd to reject any help, and it would be even more mad to disregard [the help] of women."[33]

French rabbis found overturning tradition more difficult than Jewish writers. However, the shortage of religiously practicing men propelled some rabbis to look for ways to reinterpret Jewish teachings to allow women to engage more fully in the synagogue. In 1908, the Association of French Rabbis met to discuss these particular issues. Rabbi M. Sèches, after noting that synagogues in the provinces had particular problems forming a minyan of ten men, asked the group to consider reducing the number of men required for a minyan to seven and including three women. In contrast, Rabbi M. Haguenauer insisted that the community keep the tradition of ten men for both public services. However, for private services, especially those held in homes in mourning, he conceded that three women might be included to make the requisite ten. After a long discussion, the group decided to study the issue further and reopen discussions at the next congress.[34]

Other members of the Jewish community flatly rejected the idea of changing the minyan on the grounds that change undermined the foundation of Judaism. In the month immediately following the rabbinical conference, a writer for *L'univers israélite* spoke sharply against the idea of reducing the number of men needed to form a minyan as well as admitting women. He argued that the issue of the minyan called into question the identity of the Jewish religion itself. He reminded readers that public religious ceremonies served as an "act of sanctification, a profession of collective faith, a public proclamation of the unity of God and the moral law." However, even this writer avoided presenting his position as antifeminist. He declared that the "emancipation of women" had nothing to do with the question of the minyan. He was not necessarily opposed to emancipating women in other areas, but he balked at seeing yet another Jewish tradition destroyed. He explained that reducing the minyan to seven not only contradicted scripture; it also meant accepting the absence of three men who should have been in service. In his view, every woman who participated in a minyan caused a man to leave. Of all the Jewish religious institutions that had constituted the religious life of communities in the past, only public religious services had been preserved. He cautioned Jews to protect this aspect of Judaism as part of the traditions of the community.[35]

The Rabbinical Congress of 1910 opened in the midst of this rather heated debate about how to reform the minyan. One of the central speakers at the conference, Rabbi M. Lehmann, warned the group that the minyan had to be reformed. The reforms had to take into account not only "the thoughts of revered masters in different eras and diverse countries" but also "our own sentiments, the sentiments of our era."[36] After considerable debate, the Congress decided to make very moderate changes to the minyan. The rabbis agreed to continue requiring the presence of ten men as tradition demanded. But, in cases of emergency and on the advice of a rabbi, the minyan could be composed of ten men or women having religious majority. There was no great enthusiasm surrounding this decision, and it was not a profeminist decision. Rather, the council simply recognized the impossibility of accepting only men all the time since so few men participated in religious services.[37]

Although the Jewish community resisted including women in traditionally male positions, it enthusiastically recognized women's secular achievements. By the early 1920s, *Archives israélite* frequently printed announcements of the scholarly and professional successes of French Jewish women. When the Academie Française awarded Lily Javal a 500-franc prize for her book *La quenouille du bonheur* in 1921, *Archives israélite* announced the prize to its readers.[38] That same year it applauded three women for earning teaching certificates in philosophy, humanities, and math. In 1928, it recognized Dr. G. J. Tedesco, a physician, for being named assistant electroradiologist at the hospital where she worked.[39] These are only a few of the many such announcements that appeared throughout the journal, indicating the pride the community took in the secular accomplishments of its women.

Women's Ministries and French Religious Identity

Women were central to all three communities' efforts to keep religion relevant in people's lives and carve out a space for their communities as foundational blocks of the French nation. Catholics' position as the spiritual leaders of France had eroded over the nineteenth century and had been further undermined by the separation of church and state in 1905. Catholics could no longer take their privileged position for granted. Rather, they had to prove their worth and importance to the nation and remind France of its spiritual roots. Women were central to this process. In contrast, the Protestant and Jewish communities emphasized the liberty and justice toward women embedded in their faiths, the same principles they wished to safeguard as foundations of the French nation.[40]

Many Catholics saw women as the last bastion of spirituality in a nation drowning in immorality and unbelief. Women themselves had high expectations for what they could achieve. One speaker at an LPDF conference affirmed that the organization was counting on its female leaders to create a future in which the LPDF would have a million members, small children would "bless the name of God, immoral papers would no longer have any influence," and every Sunday men and women would go to church.[41] Men accepted and encouraged these goals. In a 1909 article for the *Association des mères chrétiennes*, the priest P. LeJeune suggested that women would find ways to reach people spiritually that men would never have found, and they would do so with the help of God.[42]

Catholic women's organizations frequently held large conferences designed to enlighten women about religious problems and their responsibilities to remedy them. Each year, these conferences drew hundreds of people. Between 1900 and 1914, the Action Sociale de la Femme (ASF) organized conferences on topics such as "the state against the family," liberty of education, and the necessity for Catholics to oppose the proposed law separating church and state.[43] Police reporters kept close tabs on the LPDF because of their perceived reactionary and antigovernmental programs. One such report noted that a 1909 LPDF conference encouraging mothers to take a stronger stand against the suppression of religious education drew about 1,000 women and children and 200 men.[44] A similar LFF conference in 1911 drew 500 women in Lyon to hear the association's president, Mme la Comtesse de Saint-Laurent, discuss martyrs who had given their lives as witnesses for Christ. She encouraged women "not to refuse our Savior Jesus Christ the double witness of an active faith and an openly Christian life."[45]

Catholic women spent enormous amounts of time and money supporting the Catholic and conservative press. They hoped that by ensuring that men had access to "good" Catholic and conservative newspapers such as *La croix*, *La libre parole*, and *La lantern*, they could influence the political decisions men made and counter the anti-Catholic, communist, and socialist propaganda printed in other journals. Women in the LPDF took the lead in the Press Project. Its committees placed "good" journals at reduced prices in barbershops, wine cellars, and restaurants with the concurrence of the owners of these establishments.[46] Women hoped that this would encourage men to buy Catholic and conservative newspapers rather than newspapers produced by their opponents and thus turn the political and religious tide in France. An LPDF committee at Cambrai, the most successful Press Project by 1908, distributed 40,000 newspapers each month at a reduced price. Other regional committees throughout France set up similar programs. The section at Avallon sent magazines such as *Le soleil*, *La libre parole*, *La croix*, and *Le nouvelliste* to a nearby village, where it hoped to counter the influence of Freemasons. This committee affirmed that its program was successful, although it gave no specific numbers of magazines distributed.[47]

Catholic women's organizations managed to draw thousands of women into new and more active spiritual missions. In so doing, they succeeded in both reinforcing the importance religion held in France and making religion relevant to people's modern lives. They kept religion as a visible, public part of French society through their conferences, journals, and pilgrimages. Unlike Protestants and Jews, Catholics had no desire to link themselves to the Third Republic, which they believed persecuted them. Rather, they wished to demonstrate the centrality of Catholicism to the nation, not its current political structures. Expanding the spiritual mission of women and valorizing that mission encouraged more women to contribute their time and energy to Catholic causes. It made women believe in the importance of their religious activism. Even though they did not receive access to the priesthood, many women believed that they could save France. Women's acceptance of such an important task and the hierarchy's continual praise for their efforts helped religion remain a relevant, important part of their lives. Catholic women made themselves a central part of the public image and the public spiritual defense of the

Catholic community in France. In the process, they created a more equal spiritual position between Catholic women and men.

The Protestant community clearly wished to present Protestantism as compatible with the values of the Third Republic, and it did this partly by emphasizing its progressive theology toward women. However, there were some sticky points that remained. As with Catholics, spreading their faith and encouraging people to convert was important to the Protestant community. However, Protestants worked hard to ensure that efforts to convert people did not undermine their reputation as supporters of religious liberty. Unlike Catholics, Protestants never presumed that their faith should have a special place in France. They only wanted an equal place. Protestants framed their spiritual outreach as compatible with religious liberty. The right to spread the Protestant faith freely affirmed Protestants' position as equal members of the nation.[48] However, Protestants wished to distinguish their proselytization from Catholics' efforts to force Catholicism on the nation.

Examples of this carefully crafted message appear in advertisements for some of the many girls' foyers created by Protestant women. These foyers provided housing for women and girls working away from their families. They all had a Protestant Christian base and made efforts to provide religious instruction to the girls who stayed in them. However, Protestants were anxious to affirm that they did not force their faith on anyone. Writers describing these foyers often presented them as religiously neutral. Directors of the Foyer de l'Ouvrière presented it as a shelter that admitted girls of "irreproachable conduct" regardless of nationality or religion.[49] Similarly, the Foyer de l'Étudiant welcomed all young women without asking about their faith background, and it practiced the "absolute respect of consciences." That said, women leaders presented themselves as "disciples of Christ" and they "worked openly" for God.[50] The balance between stated religious neutrality and a desire to gain converts was not always easy to achieve. While Catholics wished to remake France as a Catholic state, Protestants were careful to present at least some their religious projects as neutral areas that respected the religious traditions of others. Protestants were more than happy to convert people. However, they wanted to present conversions as entirely dependent upon the free will of the converted person, not as an effort to impose Protestantism on the nation as a whole, especially by means of the government. They wished to protect their image as devoted adherents to the secular, republican ideology of the Third Republic. With some difficulty, Protestant women played a part in reconciling these contradictions by using their social programs to affirm the importance of liberty of conscience and their respect for the beliefs and traditions of others.

The refusal to grant women full access to the minyan contradicted Jews' other efforts to use women's issues to present their community as modern, progressive, and democratic. Real tension existed within the Jewish community between promoting justice and theological flexibility and maintaining Jewish traditions. However, restricting women's access to the minyan in some ways supported Jews' over- all goal of affirming their image as integrated, accepted members of French society who were not distinguished by their faith. Jewish lead- ers in Italy increasingly promoted the idea that the Jewish community would be saved from irreligion not primarily through participation in public rituals or synagogue attendance but by a fortification of Jewish traditions in the home.[51] A similar situation occurred in France, as it became the task of Jewish mothers to save the Jewish community from secularization while at the same time helping to solidify Jews' position as equally accepted citizens.

The Jewish community's emphasis on the salvation of Judaism coming from the home rather than more public expressions of the faith corresponded with Jews' efforts to present themselves as fully assimilated, loyal, republican citizens. Jews essentially shifted the emphasis on religious practice away from the public sphere to the home. In the wake of the Dreyfus Affair, "French republicanism came to mean the evacuation of difference from the public sphere."[52] Pierre Birnbaum notes that the Third Republic "encouraged Jews to assimi- late as completely as possible into a society of truly equal citizens . . . Jews suddenly became *israélites*, identical, as far as public life was con- cerned, to their fellow citizens." Jews were "loyal allies" in efforts to consolidate the Republic, they "fully subscribed to the universalistic values of the Republic, and they worked to promote unity within the French nation."[53] The emphasis on domestic religiosity as the salvation of the faith at least partly exonerated men from saving Judaism through their public adherence to rituals, something that would have made their Jewishness more evident to their non-Jewish associates. The emphasis on the home and the continued exclusion of women from public rites of the faith meant that the promotion of Judaism for both men and women could become a more private affair that allowed men and women to present themselves publicly as fully assimilated French citizens. Women could save the faith by keeping religious practices in the home and teaching their children to be good Jews while protecting Jews from anti-Semitic violence by allowing all Jews to present a secular public face.

Conclusion

Women and spirituality held a central part in all three communities' discussions about how to keep religion relevant in people's lives and how to carve out a place for their faiths within the context of a rapidly secularizing France. The new emphasis on women's ability to save the nation and their communities forced each faith group to reexamine women's spiritual vocation. All three communities accepted the equality of women's souls before God, but they now had to consider whether or not God had given women and men different spiritual missions and spiritual abilities. The ways the Catholic, Protestant, and Jewish communities defined women's spiritual mission reflected the image or reputation they wished to create for themselves. It also reflected women's own determination to assume more "masculine" spiritual vocations. The secularization of men had the effect of creating greater fluidity between what could be considered masculine or feminine missions.

Of the three religious groups, Catholic women had the most success in using spirituality to revitalize the Catholic community and keep Catholicism as a visible, important part of French society. Catholic women's organizations offered hundreds of thousands of women new opportunities to work for the salvation of the nation and the protection of the Catholic Church. The value and importance given to women's spiritual work made Catholic action especially appealing to women. It elevated their belief in the importance of their work and in what they could accomplish. It helped make religion an even more relevant part of women's lives because they could potentially achieve so much through religious action.

Catholic women were not content to let men or other women determine the future of the nation. Rather, they used their position as keepers of French spirituality to engage in the process of remaking Catholic France. The perceived crisis posed by secularization opened up new opportunities for women. The need for their spiritual leadership gradually made them more confident in their roles as public religious leaders. A writer for the ASF suggested that in their efforts to inspire in people "healthy, energetic, moral principles," women had ceased to be timid and no longer doubted themselves and their cause.[54] Women's work in spiritual revival allowed them to shape the spiritual destiny and identity of France, reestablish their communities as spiritual leaders, and expand their own apostolic missions.

Women's spiritual vocation also offered the Protestant community an effective way to show its importance to the nation and its worthiness to be included as part of France's religious identity. Discussions about women's spiritual equality allowed the Protestant community to emphasize its commitment to the ideals of liberty, equality, and democracy. This again allowed the community to link itself closely with the values of the Third Republic and prove the value of the Protestant community to the nation. Gender thus helped to reinforce the centrality of justice and liberty to Protestant identity. It demonstrated the usefulness of Protestantism to a democratic and progressive France. It also encouraged the community to recognize women's spiritual abilities as equal to men. Finally, as the next chapter will show, it allowed women to take on greater spiritual leadership positions within the community.

Although the Jewish community also accorded women the ability to save the Jewish faith, the spiritual leadership opportunities available to Jewish women differed from those of their Christian counterparts.

As shown in chapter one, the Jewish community was very open to women's rights in the secular arena. Like Protestants, Jewish leaders used women's issues to present the community as progressive, democratic, and egalitarian. Support for women's rights in the secular realm became an important way for Jews to create a progressive public image of their community that was also closely linked with the values of the Third Republic. However, Jewish women did not form any large women's organizations that could have pressed for greater influence within the community. Likewise, Jewish leaders proved resistant to opening opportunities for women's greater participation in the public rites of the Jewish faith. Leaders argued that the salvation of Judaism would come from the private sphere. Jewish women were encouraged to maintain Jewish traditions in the home. This reluctance to admit women into the public participation of the faith reflected a desire on the part of Jewish leaders to maintain Jewish traditions. However, it also facilitated the goals that Jews had for their members as citizens of the French nation by keeping religion in the private sphere.

For women in all three communities, spiritual work allowed them to further the goals of their communities, themselves as women, and the nation. Through prayer, proselytization, and the transmission of religious values across generations, women seized power to save their communities and the French nation from unbelief, promote morality, and gain new converts to increase the ranks of the saved. Catholic and Protestant women also gained status as public spiritual leaders. Religious work allowed women in all three communities to shape the religious destiny of the French nation and carve out a place for themselves within France's changing religious landscape.

3

Political Engagement, Community Voting Rights, and Women's Pastorate

In 1907, a writer for the Jewish newspaper *L'univers israélite* congratulated women who had voted for the first time in elections for the Paris Consistory, a Jewish council with administrative responsibilities over Jewish institutions. Women had only recently received the right to vote in the Jewish community's elections. This writer referenced the oft-cited phrase "men make laws and women create morals," but he suggested that women's contributions to the creation of consistorial rules would be positive for the Paris community.[1] By the early twentieth century, and especially after the separation of church and state in 1905, the Catholic, Protestant, and Jewish communities all began looking for ways to broaden women's participation in the political protection and administration of their faith groups. The shortage of practicing men and a recognition of women's spiritual importance opened up new opportunities for women to engage in more official religious and political leadership. Protestants and Jews granted women suffrage in elections for church and community leaders, and some women were elected to leadership posts themselves. The Catholic community refused to admit women or laymen into the administration of churches, but women nonetheless used their faith-based associations to carve out significant new leadership roles for themselves in the political defense of the Church.

By granting women greater administrative and political leadership opportunities, the Catholic, Protestant, and Jewish communities maintained religion as a visible public force in French society and as

72

an attractive opportunity for women's public engagement. Through women, these communities demonstrated the value of their faiths to the nation, and they helped to carve out a place for their communities as part of the religious identity of France. Catholic women were instrumental in keeping religion at the forefront of French politics. They demonstrated the powerful hold that Catholicism still had over the French nation by mobilizing large numbers of people for political action. Their political fundraising, petitions to politicians, political conferences, and magazine articles kept religion and especially Catholicism at the center of the French debate about identity. This public demonstration resulted in growing attention from the police. These women ensured that religion would not be crushed under the weight of secularization or fade into the private sphere of the home. Rather, they demanded that the nation recognize its Catholic heritage and ensured that Catholicism would continue to occupy a central place in French culture.

For the Protestant and Jewish communities, granting women community suffrage and administrative rights helped to reinforce their identity as progressive, democratic, and egalitarian. When Protestants and Jews explained their decision to grant women religious voting rights or the right to serve on presbytery and synod councils, they emphasized the justice of these decisions and their desire to promote liberty. Greater equality in women's religious rights allowed Protestants and Jews to link themselves closely to the ideals of the French Third Republic, thus proving their value to the nation. Through their engagement with the "woman question," the Protestant and Jewish communities demonstrated that their faiths were acceptable moral foundations upon which the Third Republic could solidly rest.

For all three communities, expanding women's administrative rights and political responsibilities helped keep religion an attractive option for women's public engagement. These responsibilities discouraged women from abandoning the faith like many men. All three communities valorized women's work, credited them with the power to shape France and their religious communities, and made them feel useful and appreciated. Changes in women's political and administrative responsibilities within their religious communities moved both the French nation and these faith groups toward becoming more democratic and egalitarian.

Catholic Women, Feminism, and the Political Defense of the Catholic Church

"For or against God, that's the true electoral program for this year. We are in the midst of persecution, our dearest beliefs are trampled down and defending them is our duty. Give generously so that generosity will bring about the day where liberty and peace will be rendered to Christians."[2]

Women leaders of the Ligue des Femmes Françaises (LFF) published this small announcement in the *Echo de Paris* in 1906. It typifies Catholic women's new involvement in French politics in the early twentieth century. The French Catholic community failed to accord women greater official leadership positions in the administration of their churches in the years before World War I. There were no church elections in which they could vote or pastoral positions they could hold. Nonetheless, women refused to sit idly in the midst of what they saw as "persecution" against the Church. Although Catholic women generally refused to promote women's suffrage until after World War I, they found important ways to influence French politics. Their organizations in no way excluded them from the political life of the nation. If anything, organized religious work affirmed the critical role they had to play in political life. One writer for the *Bulletin de l'Action Sociale de la Femme* suggested that women's financial contributions would allow good men with limited means to run successfully for office, and that money could act as a woman's vote.[3] Women sent petitions to politicians, created political propaganda, educated other women about political issues, and funded the campaigns of pro-Catholic political candidates. This gave women in Catholic organizations the opportunity to become leaders in the political defense of Catholicism. It also allowed them to create a new civic status for themselves in line with their goals for their faith and for themselves. Catholic women's organizations gave women a collective political voice and a platform from which to influence the French political system in an era when women could not vote.

Catholic women's leagues such as the LFF and the Ligue Patriotique des Françaises (LPDF) came into existence because women wished to carve out a space for Catholicism in France's changing religious environment. In the wake of a 1901 law closing most religious congregations of monks and nuns, Catholics were desperate to promote the election of pro-Catholic candidates or at least candidates not hostile to Catholicism.[4] The LFF and the LPDF, founded in 1901 and 1902, respectively, came into existence to help create a pro-Catholic parliament from the 1902 parliamentary elections. Members of the clergy recognized women's potential influence while simultaneously denying women's right to suffrage. In the months leading up to the 1902 parliamentary elections, one priest asked for and received financial support from the LFF to fund a propaganda campaign against the Freemason candidate running for election in his region. This priest noted that a strongly Catholic candidate had no chance of winning, but he hoped that a "nationalist" candidate not hostile to Catholicism would win, rather than a Freemason.[5] Male Catholic leaders encouraged women's political action largely out of desperation to protect France's identity as a Catholic nation in the face of "attacks" by the Third Republic. In the process, they helped make religion attractive to women who believed in their potential to shape France through faith-based political work.

Despite the best efforts of Catholic women, right-wing candidates suffered a disastrous defeat in the 1902 elections at the hands of a coalition of republican parties. The victory of the left-leaning republican coalition radicalized the government's religious policies further.[6] As the government moved toward the separation of church and state in 1905, Catholic women once again mobilized, bitterly opposing the separation law. In February 1905, the Congrès Jeanne d'Arc, an organization that grouped together several Catholic women's organizations including the LPDF and the LFF, sent out a petition opposing the separation law. The petition declared that women protested "energetically" against "hindrances of all sorts brought against the exercise of the Church." The petition demanded that the nation, rather than Parliament, vote on the issue through a referendum.[7] In the minds of Catholic women, the proposed law put at stake the "souls of children and the right to pray" in churches. By July 1905, the *Bulletin du devoir des femmes françaises*, a more radical, right-wing organization, claimed that women had collected 3,853,238 signatures and sent them to the deputies of each region.[8]

Catholic women failed to prevent the separation of church and state. However, they succeeded in involving hundreds of thousands of people in the struggle to keep Catholicism as an important part of French religious identity. The bitterness that Catholics felt in the wake of the separation law remained for years after its passage. The separation bill mandated that churches and synagogues create religious associations of laypeople to oversee the use and maintenance of religious buildings and direct the faith in accordance with the traditions of each community. These associations opened new opportunities for Protestant and Jewish women to participate in the administration of churches and synagogues, but this was not the case for Catholics. In protest against the law, Pius X refused to allow Catholics to create these associations, which meant that avenue of participation did not exist for Catholic women.[9] Catholics' conflict with the French state over the creation of these associations continued until the 1920s, when the French government and the Vatican, under a new pope, managed to reach a compromise.[10] Nonetheless, the political battles of the early twentieth century energized the political work of Catholic women and gave it added legitimacy. Despite their failures, Catholic women remained committed to their new political participation and to their duty to protect the Church from political attacks.[11]

Catholic women's engagement in faith-based politics drew them into the democratic process and made them increasingly conscious of themselves as citizens with rights and liberties. It engaged them with a language of egalitarianism and liberty even as they defended conservative values. Catholic women justified their participation in politics strictly on the grounds of religious defense, which they contrasted with feminism's "individualistic" efforts to deny differences between men and women. Nonetheless, they believed in the power of their influence, and they used republican language demanding that their "liberties" be respected. The Baronne Geneviève Reille, president of the LPDF, affirmed that her organization acted only as "convinced Catholics" dedicated to defending "our liberties" and especially the liberty of education. The LPDF simply wished to group people together who wanted to contribute their zeal into "remaking France Christian."[12] Faith-based women's organizations allowed Catholic women to shape the religious identity of the French nation, making it more Catholic. At the same time, women themselves were shaped by the democratic, egalitarian ideals of the Republic that they drew upon to defend their conservative values.

Catholic women tended to downplay the political nature of their organizations. However, their new role as part of the public political defense of the Catholic Church was evident to police reporters assigned to keep tabs on various women's organizations. The amount of time and energy the police took to watch over these women's organizations indicates women's success in maintaining Catholicism's power in France. In 1910, a police reporter affirmed that the LPDF revealed its "political character" through its creation of a fund in of favor of the Catholic press. It used this fund to subsidize "clerical and reactionary papers" and to make these papers freely available to electors during election periods.[13] A follow-up report in May 1913 noted that the LPDF was a "feminine annex" to the Action Libérale Populaire, a conservative political party directed by Catholic men, to which it provided important subsidies.[14] That same year, another officer discovered that the central committee of the LPDF had instructed all of its departmental presidents about how to prepare for the 1914 elections. The committee asked members to collect the names of cabaret and hotel owners to whom the LPDF might effectively send Catholic, conservative, and nationalist journals to be distributed to patrons. The LPDF leadership warned members to act carefully and to write "good, doubtful, or suspect" beside each cabaret owner's name depending on how reliable they would be for the LPDF's purposes.[15] The LPDF may have been reluctant to openly label its work political, but police reporters had no doubts that women increasingly engaged in shaping the political landscape of France. These reports suggest the critical role women held as part of the public face and voice of the Catholic community.

Women's success in the political realm and the benefits they reaped for Catholic men gradually encouraged men to accept and even expect women's political participation. Catholic men gratefully acknowledged women's support for Catholic politicians and praised the high standards and nobility that women brought to political battles. In May 1902, just after the parliamentary elections, Jacques Piou, a leader in the Action Libérale Populaire and a close associate to the LPDF, thanked women for the "devoted support" they had offered to him and his "former colleagues in the Chamber [of Deputies]." Although he lost his seat in this election, he praised LPDF women for giving Catholic men "nerves for war." Women had set an example for men who had previously been inactive in campaigns for Catholic candidates. Piou lauded women's political involvement, declaring that it would be unthinkable for the political force that women offered to remain untapped, especially in a nation that called on everyone "to express their opinion."[16]

The following year, an author for the *Bulletin catholique semaine religieuses du Diocèse de Montauban* wrote similar praise. He cautioned that in "ordinary times," women "should not occupy themselves with politics." However, an "open war" had been declared against religion that threatened children's lives and insisted on education that countered their beliefs. He warned that women "would abdicate all their responsibilities if they did not defend what [was] most dear to them in the world." He complained that men had largely abdicated their religious responsibilities. As a consequence, women had to draw on their piety and devotion to find the courage to tackle current problems.[17] The anticlerical policies enacted by the French state served as a motivator for even conservative Catholics to rethink women's civic responsibilities. This acceptance alone was a step for Catholics toward closing the equality gap between men and women at least in the secular realm. It is also an example of the modernization women were enacting within the Catholic Church.

Women's engagement in the political sphere altered the public image of the Church and how the Catholic community incorporated women into its identity. While rejecting "radical" feminism and shying away from suffrage, Catholic men and women gradually accepted women's responsibilities as "citizens" to influence the political direction of France. Women became an important part of the public, political defense of the Church. Women's Catholic activism offered an alternative ideology to secular feminism that expanded women's public, political engagement as well as their religious duties. It encouraged them to guide the nation toward a path of redemption and renewed faith. As police reports suggest, it also made them increasingly visible representatives of the Church in France. The power accorded to women to save France, the belief in what they could accomplish, and the appreciation they received from their community kept Catholic activism attractive to women. It also discouraged them from leaving faith-based work for secular pursuits and gradually pushed women to demand suffrage.

Protestant Women, Church Administration, and the Pastorate

"Friday at 4:00 pm! . . . Are we on vacation? The halls are empty and dead. The Synod was it just a dream? No traces of delegates . . . Yet, a confused noise reveals some sort of presence in the Hall of Acts. Entering. What a scene! The moderator standing—bell in hand—barely containing the general excitement. Speakers enroll *en masse* waiting with impatience for their turn. Frazzled secretaries blacken page after page. And the audience? Like the Synod, it's vibrant and agitated; the feminine element—barely suppressing its excitement—is often called to order . . . What is the cause of this commotion? What is the question to be debated? The problem to be raised? . . . The eligibility of women (to be elected to presbytery councils)."[18]

In July 1911, an anonymous reporter gave this lively account of a session held by the Reformed Synod of Montauban discussing the

eligibility of women to serve on presbytery councils. The synod ultimately decided to allow each member church to make its own decision
in this matter rather than imposing a uniform rule on all churches.
The Montauban debate mirrored debates held in many other synods
throughout France regarding the appropriate place for women in the
administration of Protestant churches. Many churches did not have
enough devoted men to deal with the administrative questions that
arose in their congregations. E. Barnaud, a writer for the *L'éclaireur:
Journal populaire évangelique*, estimated that men made up only about
a quarter of most congregations. Given that not all men showed up to
vote, an eighth of the congregation often elected pastors, deacons, and
delegates to synods. Barnaud knew of one church with 200 members
in which the delegates to conferences and synods were elected by fifteen voters.[19]

The issue of women voting and holding church-related administrative positions was more complicated than the problem of shortages
of men. Protestants tied it to their efforts to present their communities
as progressive, democratic, and especially well-suited to form part of
the Third Republic's foundation. Barnaud presented women's church
suffrage as a justice that the community had to accord to women. He
argued that only a lingering spirit of paganism in churches had contributed to the denial of women's due rights. The moment had come to
repair the errors of the past by inviting "our sisters to take their legitimate place in the family of God to which they, like men, belong."[20]

In the midst of France's efforts to construct an identity based
largely on laïcité and anticlericalism directed against Catholics, the
debate over women's church suffrage and electability took a predomi-
nant place in many Protestant synod discussions. The debate began
in 1899 when the Union des Églises Évangeliques Libres de France
allowed each member church to decide whether women should vote
in church elections. The question quickly spread to other churches
and other denominations, revolving largely around the principles of
justice and progress so dear to the Protestant community.[21] In 1900,
M. Mailhet argued before his synod (Synode Particulier des Alpes et
du Jura—Église Réformée de France) that "from all points of view,"

it seemed "natural and legitimate to accord women the right to vote in the administration of churches." He challenged those who used the Apostle Paul's teachings to oppose women's church suffrage and argued that "the spirit of the Gospel [was] stronger than that the text itself." After his talk, the synod voted to put together a study group tasked with developing a plan for women's voting rights.[22]

As Mailhet's speech suggests, advocates for women's religious administrative rights used the same arguments as those demanding expanded spiritual and civic missions for women. They founded their arguments on the ideals of justice and liberty, ideals that character-ized the Protestant community. Rather than presenting Protestant theology as static and entrenched in tradition, Mailhet created a pro-gressive, flexible image of Protestantism that could adapt to modern trends. A writer for *Le protestant liberal* concurred with Mailhet, argu-ing that men had already "generously abandoned women with projects of welfare and uplift." He saw no reason to limit women to these pro-grams. Women who sat on church councils would undoubtedly show ineptitudes, but these ineptitudes would be no different than those of their male counterparts. He suggested that many men would do well to keep quiet. They should listen to women like Josephine Butler and Emilie de Morsier, both leaders in campaigns against regulated prostitution and the "white slave trade." In the Protestant milieu, he concluded, there was no reason to worry about women's influence. Protestants were the "children of Liberty" and it was "the light of Liberty" that would judge them.[23]

The year after the Églises Évangeliques Libres de France granted women voting rights, other synods across France also took up the issue, coming to various conclusions. Many agreed that women should vote.[24] In some cases, reluctance to grant women immediate voting rights stemmed from Protestants' unclear relationship with the state. Some Protestants worried that they did not have the legal right to grant women suffrage in churches. Technically, under the Concordat created by Napoleon Bonaparte in 1801, Protestant churches had to receive authorization from the French government before they made significant changes in doctrine or organization. By the late nineteenth century, governing structures of Protestant churches had become incredibly complicated, with authority divided among a variety of different institutions. At the most local level, each church was governed by a presbytery council that included the pastor and men elected by the male members of the congregation to deal with daily problems facing the church, such as the direction of its social programs or the regulation of its budget. Small groups of churches made up Consistories that acted as representatives between the churches and the government.

Each year, churches elected representatives to serve at regional synods that brought together churches within a particular denomination in a particular region to discuss theological issues and other problems and questions facing their congregations. Deputies from regional synods periodically held national synods, which acted as a sort of parliament for churches, primarily to discuss issues raised in regional synods and issues affecting churches all over France, such as women's suffrage in church elections. However, before the separation of church and state, both the regional and national synods were unofficial, which meant that they were legal but were not supported by the state, so they had no authority to enforce their decisions in churches. Under the Concordat system, for a synod to be official and have real power of enforcement, it had to be called, or at least sanctioned, by the state. This only happened once in 1872 when Adolphe Thiers signed a decree convoking a general synod of Reformed churches in an effort to repair the split that had occurred between evangelicals and liberals within the Reformed community over doctrinal issues. This synod failed to repair the divisions within the Reformed church and none of its decrees were enforced. Rather, it ended up solidifying the split between the two groups, which the state agreed to recognize. Despite the unofficial nature of synods, churches willingly sent representatives, and they saw synods as a legitimate way to work through problems that churches experienced, even if they were not obligated to accept the synod's decisions.[25]

By the 1870s and 1880s, the state took little interest in the workings of Protestant churches, preferring to meddle as little as possible in Protestant affairs.[26] Nonetheless, in theory the state still exercised considerable control over churches, which left churches confused about whether they could legally grant women the right to vote in church elections without state approval. The ERF Synode Particulier de la Basse-Ardèche voted that women had an "incontestable right" to vote in parish elections. As such, the synod gave women the right to vote, although it specified that this vote should be tried unofficially until legal questions concerning the church's relationship with the state could be resolved.[27] The ERF Synode de Générac "expressed the wish" to allow women to vote in church elections, but until the legal questions could be resolved, it decided to limit women's participation to an unofficial vote.[28]

This uncertainty, especially in the context of France's religious turmoil, raised further questions for some about the appropriateness of tackling touchy questions such as women's church suffrage. One author noted that as long as churches remained linked with the state, the state would have to agree to such a change. Although he hoped to achieve a separation of church and state in the near future, he feared that raising the question of women's church suffrage might further complicate matters.[29] In June 1901, a regional Églises Réformées Évangéliques synod decided that since church and state were united, churches did not have the liberty to grant women the right to vote. This decision could only be approved in an official synod, called or recognized by the government. However, the regional synod invited presbytery councils in its region to find legal ways to allow women to express their opinions on issues facing their churches.[30]

The separation of church and state in 1905 removed all barriers to churches' decisions about women's rights. The vast majority of churches responded by granting women church suffrage and some even allowed women to serve on presbytery councils. The state demanded that each church create *associations cultuelles* (religious associations) in the wake of the separation. The statutes of these associations explain the process by which churches would be administered. They provide valuable information about the rights given to women in various congregations. Of the 716 associations created between 1905 and 1907, 558 (78 percent) explicitly granted women voting rights in parish elections. Another 147 (20 percent) did not specifically state whether women could vote, although many of these churches probably granted women suffrage. Some of these churches granted men and women equal rights, suggesting that women could vote. A handful of other churches allowed certain categories of women, such as heads of households, to vote, and only four churches (.56 percent) specifically prevented all women from voting in church elections.

As churches created their associations cultuelles, many not only granted women the right to vote but also allowed them to serve on presbytery councils and in some cases synods. Of the 716 available association statutes, seventy-nine churches (11 percent) explicitly allowed women to serve on the presbytery council. Another 166 (23.2 percent) did not exclude women from serving on the councils. The admission of women into church councils was not just rhetorical; many churches elected women to these councils. Methodists tended to be particularly progressive in electing women as members of church councils, and many of the statutes for their associations list women as council members. The Methodists were not alone, and in 1907, *Le témoignage: Journal de l'église de la confession d'Augsbourg* (Lutheran) announced that members of a presbytery council in the Midi region had voted for a council composed entirely of women.[31] The willingness to grant women more equal positions in churches was not just the purview of a few liberal Protestants. Rather, it extended to most of the community.

The debate about women's leadership within Protestant churches intensified during the First World War. Pastors volunteering for wartime service led to severe shortages of pastors on the home front. In 1915, one synod in the Charentes region noted that ten of its fifteen pastors had been mobilized for war. Retired pastors filled some of those positions, but many churches were still without a male pastor. Fortunately, the region's women stepped in to fill the positions left by men. The synod gratefully acknowledged pastors' wives and other women who, "inspired by the love of the *Patrie* and by authentic Christian sentiments," had assured the continued functioning of their parishes.[32]

In fact, throughout France, many women completely took over the direction of their churches and parishes, assuming the responsibilities usually assigned to pastors. In late 1916 or early 1917, Marguerite de Witt-Schlumberger, a respected Protestant leader, published a small pamphlet describing the work of nineteen Protestant women who had taken over the direction of their parishes. These women performed most pastors' tasks, even preaching on Sundays to their churches. One woman whose husband had been mobilized wrote that she directed Sunday school, visited the sick and poor, helped care for refugees, and visited hospitals. She served as a nurse for the Red Cross, which allowed her to visit military men at the request of their families. In addition, she took over the direction of Sunday services, a task that had been especially difficult for her. She wrote, "It cost me enormously to begin this wartime ministry, and I had to defeat strong emotions to hold church services in town before audiences of 60 to 80 people, sometimes with several superior [military] officers in the front pew."[33]

Many other women undertook similar tasks. The importance of women in the functioning of their communities propelled Protestants to consider ordaining women, especially since many women were already serving unofficially as pastors. The debate about ordaining women as pastors mirrored debates about women's spiritual vocations and church suffrage. It also revealed the limits of the Protestant community's egalitarian values. Protestants discussed whether they could reconcile the Apostle Paul's teachings with women's pastoral work, whether women were physically and mentally suited to serve as pastors, and whether pastoral work was an act of justice that needed to be accorded to women. Some in the community argued that women would make excellent pastors, while others felt that it was too great a rejection of biblical teachings. One wife of a mobilized pastor argued that women in the early days of Christianity had received authorization from the Holy Spirit to preach. She declared that if the Apostle Paul were alive, he would surely call on women to "rise up with haste" and proclaim the Gospel in the little time left before the coming of Christ.[34] Another writer asserted that judging women as unqualified to be pastors before giving them a chance was simply to remain enslaved to "the concepts of the past."[35]

The Fédération Protestante de France (FPF), a loose federation that included most Protestant denominations, did not entirely agree. In May 1916, it rejected the idea of ordaining women but did ask member churches to look for ways to expand women's ministerial work.[36] Most Protestant churches in France ultimately declined to ordain women as pastors, and not until the 1960s did women in most denominations gain the right to be pastors.[37] However, there were a few exceptions. In 1927 and 1929, respectively, both the Reformed and Lutheran churches in Alsace and Lorraine began allowing women to serve as pastors to deal with the shortage of male pastors caused by the war. Berthe Bertsch began her ministry in the Reformed Church of Alsace and Lorraine in 1927 and was officially ordained in 1930. A second woman, Madeleine Blocher-Saillens, became the first female Baptist pastor after she took over her late husband's parish in Paris in 1929. Although these were exceptional cases, they were early important steps in the direction of full religious equality for women.[38]

More significantly, early in the interwar years, the Lutheran and Reformed communities created theological training programs for women and developed the positions of *femme-évangéliste* or *diaconesse-évangéliste* for women who completed religious training.[39] These theological study programs were particularly important for women's advancement in the Protestant community. Theological training was the factor that distinguished pastors from Protestant laypeople. Education gave pastors the legitimacy to preach and direct parishes even though everyone had the responsibility to read and interpret the Bible for themselves. Providing women with theological education brought them a step closer to having the same legitimacy as men to be pastors and lead their communities.[40] The positions of femme-évangéliste and diaconesse-évangéliste also allowed women to take on more official pastoral tasks, such as spiritual counseling, visits to the sick, and direction of religious services in the absence of a male pastor.[41]

Although Protestant women did not achieve complete equality with men, many received considerable new rights in the administration of their churches. Not all Protestants welcomed the changes in women's religious rights, but most acknowledged that women's faith and devotion to their churches merited recognition. In the context of declining numbers of men in churches, excluding women from administrative duties no longer made sense. Many Protestants came to believe that denying Christian women suffrage in church elections was unjust. It failed to recognize women's status as good Christians and capable individuals, and it undermined Protestants' reputation as defenders of justice and liberty. Giving women administrative rights solidified the reputation of the Protestant community as progressive and democratic. It helped them prove their value to the nation and the suitability of Protestantism to act as a foundational block of the Republic even in an environment of laïcité and anticlericalism. It also made women a much more prominent part of the public face and voice of their communities.

Jewish Women and Community Voting

Philip Nord, in his book *The Republican Moment*, argues that the mid-nineteenth century was a formative moment in the making of French Jewish identity. The community as a whole grew wealthier, became more "French," and also became more republican. Nord writes, "Jews, in search of a new identity edged toward . . . a conception of Jewish selfhood that embraced the republic as a secular incarnation of values embedded in Jewish tradition." Nord suggests that, rather than simply assimilating into existing French culture, Jews shaped the society into which they were assimilating.[42] Lisa Moses Leff concurs, suggesting that "assimilated French Jews affirmed their Jewish identities even as they became French. Integration did not, in fact, erase Jewish identity. Even though the acquisition of citizenship, the dissolution of the traditional communal bodies, and increased contact with gentile Frenchmen represented cataclysmic changes, French Jews reaffirmed their Jewishness in new terms meaningful in French culture."[43]

As with the Protestant community, women's issues became an important avenue through which the Jewish community expressed its republicanism and demonstrated the importance of Judaism to the nation. In 1870, the Grand Rabbi Lazare Isidor proclaimed that the "spirit of exclusion" was "alien to Judaism."[44] Although he was not speaking about women, by the early twentieth century, the Jewish "spirit of inclusion" was being extended to women. Jewish leaders remained wary of admitting women into religious rites such as the minyan. But the Jewish community showed itself to be very progressive in extending new religious rights to women when those rights did not conflict with Jewish law. This allowed them to more fully recognize the importance of women to the community, and helped solidify the community's republican character.

The debate over women's position within Judaism played out as the Jewish community reorganized itself to deal with the separation of church and state in December 1905. Like their Protestant counterparts, Jewish congregations created associations cultuelles of laypeople to oversee the administration of synagogues, seminaries, and charitable programs.[45] Members of various synagogues paid a small fee to join the associations cultuelles. As members, they voted for a directing board in charge of "raising and distributing charity money," holding elections, building and renovating synagogues and other community buildings, choosing rabbis, and generally overseeing the practice of the Jewish faith.[46]

Like the Protestant community, the Jewish community had to decide whether or how women would participate in these associations. Many communities decided to give women voting rights. The decision to grant women suffrage in community elections seems to have been relatively uncontroversial. Not many people contributed to the debate, at least in the Jewish press. The few who did had fairly polarized ideas. Mathieu Wolff, a writer for L'univers israélite, hoped that allowing women to vote would be a step toward admitting them into other religious leadership positions. He suggested that women's voting rights would be accepted easily by both orthodox and liberal Jews, since it would not break or infringe upon any principle of Judaism nor on any part of Jewish tradition. Rather, Wolff suggested that it would involve women more fully in the faith.[47]

On the opposite side of the debate, Hippolyte Prague, the very conservative editor for *Archives israélite*, opposed any change in Jewish traditions. Prague saw the introduction of voting rights to the "feminine element" as a "small revolution" in synagogues. Religiously speaking, Prague acknowledged that granting women suffrage did not raise many problems. Deborah had been a judge in Israel, and other women had been prophets. Despite this, he had serious misgivings about women voting that mirrored his concerns about women entering all other aspects of public participation in Judaism. Prague feared that women's "temperament" made them more susceptible than men to indecisiveness and seduction by "sophisms." He worried that women would "develop a taste for the public affairs of the religion." Worse, women might "profit from the indifference of Jews of the stronger sex" and demand risky reforms that would disrupt the traditions of the synagogue. He encouraged people to consider the unintended consequences that might result from giving women a voice in running synagogues. He warned that women might break with the spirit of Judaism and its traditions if they used their right to vote to lead the Jewish faith in a new direction.[48]

The Jewish community seems to have sided with Wolff on this issue, which is not very surprising since even Prague admitted that women voting did not contradict any Jewish traditions. No evidence is available about discussions that might have occurred within rabbinical councils concerning women's voting rights, which suggests that it was not a terribly controversial issue. Out of a total of sixty-four association statutes sent to the minister of the interior between 1906 and 1907, thirty specifically allowed women to vote, two allowed women to vote and serve on administrative councils, twenty-nine did not specifically state whether women could vote or serve on the council, and only five specifically excluded women from voting and serving on councils.[49]

Women's voices are absent in debates about whether they be allowed to vote in their associations' elections. But some women took the opportunity to vote once their communities made it available to them. Hippolyte Prague noted that a number of women's names appeared in the membership columns of the new associations, affirming that women welcomed the opportunity to participate more actively in the life of the Paris community. Of the 1,400 members of the Paris association, he counted 150 women, a fairly strong showing in his opinion since women now made up more than a tenth of the association's membership.[50]

Although 150 women out of a total of 1,400 members may seem rather small, other writers also noted the new participation of women in elections. In November 1907, the Paris Consistory, the lead institution of French Judaism, held its first elections after the separation of church and state. Women voted for the first time. A writer for *L'univers israélite* suggested that many women had taken advantage of this new right. The author congratulated women who had accepted the responsibility to vote. He reminded readers that the Midrasch credited women's "merit and virtue" for Israel's exodus from Egypt. Hippolyte Prague's fears that women might introduce radical reforms did not come to pass. Instead, the elections produced a "homogenous consistory well composed [of] men of great knowledge, of good will, and proven devotion, faithful to the good traditions of the faith . . ."[51]

Like Protestants, the French Jewish community wanted to present itself as a modern, progressive, moral base for the Republic. As Philip Nord notes, Jewish leaders argued that "a responsible citizenship . . . was inconceivable without religion." Judaism, which, as one writer noted, "recognizes no 'infallible authority,' no 'pontiff or sovereign,'" was a perfect republican religion.[52] Women's issues, especially in the aftermath of the Dreyfus Affair, became a central part of the Jewish community's efforts to be progressive, fair, and democratic and to present such an image to the rest of the nation. As noted earlier, France seemed to be moving in the direction of granting women more rights and the Jewish community wanted to make sure that it was engaged in this modern project as well. Voting allowed the community to find a balance between its dual goals of promoting a greater degree of equality for women and protecting religious traditions that remained in practice.

Conclusion

The anticlerical laws passed in the early twentieth century combined with the general trend toward secularization shattered France's traditional religious identity by challenging Catholic dominance. Catholics, Protestants, and Jews all had to prove their worth to the nation. They did so partly through women. Catholics' encouragement of women's political action and the importance they gave to that action helped make religion an attractive option for women's public engagement. The constant positive reinforcement women received kept religion as a relevant part of their lives. In turn, politically active women ensured that Catholicism remained a powerful, visible force in French society. Women became an important part of the public, political defense of the Church. No longer was it only a few exceptional women like Joan of Arc who could occasionally engage in the political or military defense of France. Catholic women modernized the tradition of Joan of Arc by attaching it to their mass mobilization of women for the political defense of the Church. Women's conferences, magazines, and petitions, along with the attention they received from police reporters, made them a central part of the public face and voice of the French Catholic community. When the community imagined its political defenders, it could no longer only imagine men. Rather, women had inserted themselves into the identity of the Church's political defenses as well.

For the Protestant and Jewish communities, the inclusion of women into the administration of the faith helped make these communities more progressive and democratic and presented a public image that also reflected democratic, egalitarian values. The desire to create a more just position for women within their faith groups also mirrored each community's desire to solidify France's identity as a nation that accepted and respected everyone equally, including religious minorities. Promoting women's religious rights helped present Protestantism and Judaism as faiths that could serve as moral foundations of the nation without conflicting with the democratic, secular values of the

Republic. Expanding women's administrative rights, especially in the case of the Protestant community, also helped to keep women engaged in their communities, which prevented religious disaffection among women.

For women in all three communities, religious institutions offered a space in which they could acquire influence and power to shape the direction of their communities and the future of the nation. Women's religious work and women's issues also helped modernize their faith groups and democratize France. Women's civil equality happened in steps, and their move toward religious equality, even if incomplete, was one of those steps. Debating women's rights and expanding women's faith-based administrative and political work forced a significant part of the French nation to acknowledge women's political and administrative abilities. It accustomed them to seeing women engage in politics and voting or even serving on church councils. These were all important elements in gradually preparing the nation to accept full equality between men and women in law.

4

Faith for Social Progress

Women, Social Action, and the Modernization of France

In 1913, the Countess Keranflec'h-Kernezne spoke to a group of Catholic women about the importance of Farm Women's Circles. As she described them, Farm Women's Circles were professional associations that helped stop "the rural exodus by increasing resources in the countryside, spreading practical ideas about the rational education of children," and improving "the moral and material situation of the [rural] population." She wished to see such circles provide lectures four or five times a year on topics important to farm women, such as how to establish a dairy, make butter and cheese, care for sick farm animals, and package agricultural products for market sale.[1] These farm circles, as well as the farm syndicates and agriculturally focused schools that Keranflec'h-Kernezne proposed, were not simply important for farm women. At issue was the continued prosperity, strength, and identity of the French nation, all of which would be reinforced by creating stability for poor families and "modernizing" them through education.

Keranflec'h-Kernezne's engagement with rural renewal projects exemplifies Catholic, Protestant, and Jewish women's new social engagement in the early twentieth century. Religious women had been involved in philanthropy for centuries, but the early twentieth century saw them developing new kinds of programs for the poor. Faith-based organizations developed women's syndicates, work assistance, and educational programs designed to make long-term improvements in the material and moral conditions of the working class. In the context of France's church/state battles and the general decline in attachment

93

to religious traditions, women's social work took on added importance. By developing programs for the poor that incorporated methods and ideas popular in the early twentieth century, Catholic, Protestant, and Jewish women demonstrated the positive effects that religion could have on people's lives. They also presented their communities as modern, progressive, and forward thinking, thus compatible with the "progressive" nature of the Third Republic and modernizing trends shaping French society.[2] Through faith-based social work, women demonstrated the usefulness and necessity of religion in the modern world to cope with modern social problems. Finally, in the absence of political rights, women's faith-based organizations provided them with avenues through which they could shape the direction of the nation by engaging in national debates about agriculture, immigration, and women's working conditions.

Women of faith were by no means the only group interested in social reform in turn-of-the-century France. As Judith Stone notes, the "social question" had become an "important political issue" by about 1890 and preoccupied the French nation up to the First World War. The period between 1895 and 1909 saw the development of a "new vision of social peace which centered on reform legislation as the means to create an environment where workers could attain security."[3] A number of factors contributed to a new French social consciousness, including the emergence of an increasingly organized and militant working class demanding change in sometimes violent ways. The growing militancy of working-class movements made ensuring social peace a top priority of republican politicians who led France's reform movement, as well as women, doctors, and social scientists who joined their efforts.[4]

France was not alone in its desire to enact legislation to assure social stability. The late nineteenth and early twentieth centuries saw similar attempts at reform and social legislation across Europe and the United States. Governments, individuals, and myriad private organizations all developed legislation and social programs to improve health and welfare, especially for women and children.[5] Rachel Fuchs notes that "well-baby centers and free milk dispensaries spread to many countries." British organizations "developed programs to educate mothers in methods of efficient 'scientific,' hygienic infant care," and the Russians created "day nurseries and boarding institutions for infants of widowed, deserted or working mothers as part of an effort to reduce infant mortality."[6] Meanwhile, in 1877 the Swiss pioneered laws mandating eight weeks of maternity leave for women, and by 1883 Germany and Austria-Hungary had mandated "paid maternity leaves of three weeks after delivery for insured women."[7] France was only exceptional in that its reformers were more preoccupied with the threat posed by depopulation than their European or American counterparts.[8] France began experiencing demographic decline earlier than other European countries. By the end of the nineteenth century, it had the lowest birth rate in the world, with deaths actually exceeding births in some years. France's humiliating defeat in the Franco-Prussian War increased warnings about a possible population catastrophe. French reformers therefore gave special attention to women as "regenerators of a degenerating race."[9]

Creating social legislation, especially legislation that affected men's employment, was controversial throughout the West, but legislation and social programs directed toward women and children appealed to many different groups. Mary Lynn Stewart argues that "promises of lower infant mortality and better child care, and hence of more and healthier young men for the military draft, appealed to nationalists preoccupied with revenge; rhetoric about the housewife as guarantor of family cohesion attracted Social Catholics, and moderate republicans concerned about social order, and oratory about the 'superior interests' of babies, husbands and families was agreeable to politicians of all political persuasions."[10]

French efforts to construct legislation and social aid programs that could limit worker militancy and create a more just and healthy society were neither coordinated nor harmonious. Rather, many groups, including businessmen, politicians, physicians, and women, proposed competing and sometimes contradictory strategies to achieve social peace.[11] Unlike the United States, where only a handful of men showed an interest in child health, Alisa Klaus notes that "the French movement to prevent infant mortality" was led primarily by men and especially by prominent politicians and doctors.[12]

Klaus suggests that this domination of welfare debates by men and especially politicians severely limited women's ability to influence policy decisions.[13] Women played an important part in charitable institutions, but Klaus believes that this failed to translate into real influence over health and welfare policies. Moreover, women virtually never sat on "official commissions to investigate maternal and infant health . . . and very few positions in public or private welfare agencies of any kind were open to women."[14] Rather, women's work was usually voluntary, unpaid, and poorly recognized by male politicians and doctors. Klaus suggests that women were unable to attain real influence in welfare debates due to political and religious divisions among women's organizations and a lack of access to political and professional power. She also notes that "French women faced more rigid and powerful male-dominated health and social welfare institutions than American women."[15]

Klaus presents a rather bleak picture of women's involvement in the development of social welfare, but women of faith did not remain passive and voiceless. They refused to present themselves as victims of domineering men who shut them out of productive activity outside the home. Even though the rhetoric of the nineteenth and early twentieth centuries sometimes relegated women to the home, that relegation was never absolute. Women used the language of "feminine maternal qualities" to further their access to nontraditional roles. By the 1830s the French government had begun hiring women as inspectors of nursery schools and eventually women's prisons and girls' reform schools. Politicians argued that women's maternal abilities suited them for these kinds of positions and made them more effective than men.[16] Inspectresses also pointed to their own maternal qualities to justify their access to such positions. Pauline Kergomard, a Protestant and the "first woman elected by fellow educators to the Higher Council of Public Instruction," argued that "women's inspection of schools was a natural 'extension' of the maternal role." Furthermore, she suggested that "inspectresses could handle 'the most intimate educational questions' affecting female pupils and teachers, questions that men could not and should not address."[17] Linda Clark argues that the position of inspectresses put women "into contact with an adult public of women teachers and male officials" rather than just students. It also gave women an opportunity to show that they had the ability to "do the same rigorous work as men." Many women took pride in successfully accomplishing difficult assignments that adversaries believed would discourage them. The struggle to prove their worth and defend their right to their jobs led some women, such as Kergomard, to join the ranks of the feminist movement and demand the right to vote.[18]

Women might not have had full access to political or professional positions by the early twentieth century, but they were not powerless or entirely submissive to men. In addition to advocating for women's access to jobs like inspectresses of social programs, feminist groups and women's organizations "helped instigate social programs for children and mothers by shaping public opinion and influencing legislation."[19] This was equally true for faith-based women's organizations. Although women could not vote, the large organizations women formed and the programs they developed gave them a platform from which they could influence French society and push forward their goals for themselves, their religious communities, and the French nation. Women of faith held conferences, printed newspapers, and developed their own social aid programs. In the absence of official political power, and in the face of male-dominated welfare programs, these venues gave women a voice in debates about the direction French society should take. They also gave women a chance to engage in society and help promote the kinds of social change they believed would be good for the nation and other women as well as for their own religious communities.

Women and Social Action

By the end of the nineteenth century, Catholic, Protestant, and Jewish women were all involved in social action aimed at making long-term improvements in the lives of the poor. Many upper-class women, especially Catholic women, held on to the notion that the upper class constituted an intellectual and moral elite. Nonetheless, they made more efforts to understand the causes of poverty and promote workers' rights and collective bargaining. Women leaders recognized that workers faced severe material problems that had nothing to do with morality and everything to do with France's social and economic conditions. At a 1912 Protestant charity meeting, Julie Siegfried encouraged "Christian women" to go to the poor with simplicity, without a "patronizing attitude" but with modesty and kindness. She asked women to study the problems that led to people's moral and economic downfall so that they would be better equipped to lift up those who had fallen into misery and despair.[20] Women's growing understanding of the nature of the French economy and labor system prompted their organizations to move beyond purely moralistic programs.[21] Catholic leader Mme Gautier-Lacaze described women's syndicates as "works of justice."[22] Women leaders hoped their efforts to improve the lives of workers would draw workers away from socialist and communist organizations as well as ameliorate their material and moral conditions. These programs gave women an opportunity to contribute to the economic and social stability of the French nation while at the same time taking religion to the poor.

Catholic Women and Rural Workers

Although Catholic women created social programs throughout France for both urban and rural women and children, their work in rural areas exemplified their goals for the poor, the French nation, and the Catholic Church. Catholic women actively opposed urbanization, which they believed moved people away from the healthy, moral countryside to potentially unhealthy, immoral cities. In the eyes of many Catholics, the process of urbanization led directly to family destruction, unhealthy workers, and further depopulation. It also undermined France's identity as a nation of small farmers. In a 1908 speech given to women members of the Action Sociale de la Femme (ASF), Georges Noblemaire warned that the "invasion of the city" by rural people contributed to depopulation because so many of these uprooted migrants contracted tuberculosis in Paris and died. Disease spread through "factory conditions, unhealthy air, and unhealthy dust," which he contrasted with the "healthy air of the countryside."[23] Similarly, in 1913 the Marquise de Juigné complained to the Ligue Patriotique des Françaises (LPDF) that there were no longer enough people in the provinces to cultivate the land. This meant that large farms had to employ foreign workers from Germany, Belgium, Italy, and Spain. Small farmers, whom she considered "one of the forces of France" and instrumental to its prosperity, disappeared. Meanwhile, cities were flooded with workers who lived in "moral and physical misery" and contributed to social unrest.[24] Catholic women generally accepted the view that country life was healthier or at least potentially healthier than life in cities. Thus, retaining people in areas where they could breathe the fresh, healthy country air would automatically benefit France by reducing disease and mortality rates. As the Marquise de Juigné pointed out, it would also reduce the number of potential revolutionaries in cities, thereby contributing to social peace.[25]

Catholic women understood that a central part of keeping women and girls from migrating was providing them with work and improving their material conditions. Small farms had to remain financially viable. The Countess Keranflec'h-Kernezne, an LPDF leader in rural regeneration programs, noted that rural people's "desire[s] for stability, wellbeing, and a better future" were "strong and simple feelings." These feelings were a "precious treasure for the national soul of which women were the national guardians."[26] As a result, Catholic women developed numerous work assistance programs, many of them focusing on lace and needle trades, to provide employment for rural women. Rural work programs had multiple benefits in the minds of Catholic women. They improved material conditions in rural areas, protected the health and morality of the French population, and preserved or restored "traditional" French industries.

Catholic women realized that small farms often had a difficult time making ends meet. Their primary goal with rural work programs was to provide women with employment and skills to help augment their families' income. Rural women's syndicates such as L'Aiguille à la Campagne supplied women instructors to teach lace-making and offered apprenticeships for its members. This program claimed to furnish women with "remunerative" lace-making skills. In 1903, the branch of this organization in La Franche-Comté made 250,000 francs in sales. It paid women about 2 francs a day.[27] Another program, the Œuvre Sociale de la Dentelle, was created after a fishing crisis hit the coast of Brittany. This program offered work to the wives and daughters of fishermen that they could do at home. Even after fishing conditions improved, the program remained in operation to prevent women and girls from looking for jobs in large cities. One workshop at Concarneau employed 140 girls as well as 150 women who worked from their homes. The women who directed these workshops, some of them nuns, also provided moral and religious training for their students.[28]

Catholic women believed that successfully providing jobs to keep rural women and girls from migrating could also help protect French culture by preserving the French tradition of producing high-quality, creative goods and limiting the introduction of "foreign" and "low quality" products. In 1908, the ASF published an article promoting the Comité de Relèvement des Petites Industries Rurales, which aimed at reviving traditional craftwork in the countryside. The author argued that such programs would keep girls from urban "misery and vice" and benefit France by making available "solid," "artistic," and elegant products that were very different from the "pretentious, perishable rubbish" that people bought at "bon marché." In addition, such programs would prevent the introduction of inferior quality products from abroad that "invade the market in the countryside to paralyze or ruin" the "creative initiative, the free ingenuity of their inhabitants."[29]

A similar article appeared in 1913 in the magazine of the LPDF, expressing particular concerns about German economic competition. An author described "with sadness" the "worrisome invasion of foreign products." She noted that in "all domains" France had become a "tributary to Germany." While many French workers were unemployed, Germany was becoming rich through French expenditures. She promoted a program called Rural Work, which employed about 1,125 workers in rural industries. Its goal was to "present the Parisian public with irreproachable products" that were "always original" and food products that were "absolutely pure [and] paid for with a just salary."[30] If the countryside could be made clean and distribution networks established, then cities would also benefit from the availability of healthy products. These products would enrich rural areas, prevent the invasion of foreign goods, and strengthen the physical constitution of all French people.

Involvement in rural work also provided Catholic women with an opportunity to think about their relationship to the ideas of tradition and modernization. French Catholic women couched their rural aid programs in rhetoric emphasizing the need to preserve France's traditions and heritage. However, they understood that the countryside had to change, and they recognized that rural areas were not without faults. As Eugen Weber has pointed out, by the late nineteenth century, rural France was modernizing. Free and compulsory state schools, roads, railroads, and mass-produced consumer goods were altering traditional ways of life.[31] Rather than allow the process of modernization to be directed entirely by others, Catholic women wished to take control of it or at least influence it in an effort to assure that modernization did not lead to rural or national depopulation, increased class tensions, or further secularization.

Catholic women did not wish to rewind the clock and go back to some mythical moment in the French past when everyone got along. Rather, they advocated for more scientific farm practices, collective action on the part of workers for better prices, better education, improved hygiene, and a greater interest on the part of the nation in the well-being of rural areas. Catholic women hoped to transform the real conditions in France into their ideal image of traditional France: small, prosperous family farms, healthy rural life, Christian peasants, and peaceful class relations. Catholic women were trying to create an updated version of traditional France formed by modern, more progressive Catholics.

Women of Faith and the Urban Poor

In urban areas, Catholic, Protestant, and Jewish women's organiza-tions all developed similar kinds of programs. They created special women's syndicates, free milk programs, and work assistance opportu-nities for poor and unemployed women. Women's syndicates, such as those created by Catholic leader Marie-Louise Rochebillard in Lyon, aimed to improve the health, employability, and morality of women workers. Rochebillard's syndicates organized women in commerce and needle-working trades and offered a number of advantages to women who joined.[32] Women members had access to professional courses and apprenticeship positions. The syndicates recruited instructors to teach lessons once a week in accounting, stenography, sewing, mending, and embroidery. During the first year, 250 students attended courses, but that number quickly rose to between 600 and 700 students a year, taught by about 100 professors.[33] The associated mutual insurance society permitted women to pay 1.25 francs each month in order to receive free medical care, reduced prices on medicine, and unemploy-ment aid in case of illness.[34]

Faith-based women's outreach to improve the health of the urban working class also included children's programs. Women's organiza-tions created vacation colonies, ran orphanages, and developed after-school programs to keep children safe and teach them religious lessons. Many of these projects included some element of healthcare and/or occupational training. Programs to provide milk to babies were espe-cially popular, not only among faith-based women but in French soci-ety as a whole. These programs provided free sterilized milk for young children in an effort to reduce high infant mortality rates among the poor. They often provided free medical care as well. Along with offer-ing milk for babies, programs such as the Catholic-sponsored Œuvre de la Goutte de Lait offered free medical care to nurslings. Every night beginning at 6:00 p.m., mothers who could not nurse their babies received bottles of sterilized milk prepared for the following day. Mothers also received counsel by "devoted women" about how to care for their babies; they learned about vaccinations, and a doctor was available to see ill children for two hours on Wednesdays. By 1913, the program enrolled about seventy children up to two years of age. The results were encouraging from both a physical and religious standpoint. All of the children involved in the program were baptized at the urging of Catholic volunteers. Organizers hoped to turn these children and their families into healthy French people and good Catholics so they could morally and physically strengthen French society.

Catholic women clearly linked free milk and similar programs with the protection of the French nation. Directly underneath an article describing the Goutte de Lait, the LPDF printed an advertisement titled "20 Germans to 1 French." This article encouraged people to have more children in order to prevent a future defeat by the Germans. The notice stated that it would be cowardly to refuse the nation this request. Those who could not or did not want to have children could show their patriotism by protecting the health and well-being of poor children through programs such as the Goutte de Lait.[35] Women workers were potential mothers, the producers of future soldiers for the French nation. As such, they and their babies merited special care not only for their own health but also for the sake of France.

The French Protestant and Jewish communities did not create programs designed primarily for rural populations. The largest Protestant and Jewish populations existed in cities, so those communities focused their attention on urban problems. Unlike Catholic women, who generally resisted interfaith cooperation, many Protestant and Jewish organizations encouraged participation from all women with similar moral and social goals. Protestant and Jewish women demonstrated their desire for interfaith cooperation on social issues through their participation in the Conférence de Versailles. Evidence of this cooperation appears in *La femme*, the magazine that represented the Conférence de Versailles and served as a general forum for discussing social and women's issues. The Conférence de Versailles and *La femme* were created and directed by Protestant women from well-known families, including Julie Siegfried, Mme Frank Puaux, Sarah Monod, and Elisa Sabatier.[36] It had a stated Christian base. However, Gabrielle Alphen-Salvador, who was Jewish, was listed as a "collaboratrice" of the magazine, and a number of other Jewish women contributed articles and spoke at meetings.

Each year the Conférence de Versailles brought together women involved in religious and secular social programs to discuss their work and develop ideas about how to improve social conditions in France. Despite its largely Protestant leadership, few of the programs discussed had a noticeably religious character. At the 1907 conference, women heard reports about the Œuvre de la Rue de Berlin, a Protestant program aimed at providing work assistance to poor women. However, they also heard about the Union des Œuvres d'Assistance, a nonconfessional program that facilitated communication and cooperation between existing social programs. Other women gave talks on topics ranging from summer camps to programs that provided milk to poor infants.[37] The following year, 1908, Mme Léon Lévy, a moderate Jewish feminist, spoke about the École des Bonnes d'Enfants, a nonconfessional program that trained young women to work as childcare providers either in private homes or in kindergartens.[38] At the same conference, Cecile Braunschweig discussed the Fédération des Services de Placement, which encouraged cooperation between placement bureaus that tried to find jobs for unemployed workers.[39] Gabrielle Lipman, also a moderate Jewish feminist, encouraged women to support the Society for the Protection of Animals and demanded laws preventing cruelty to animals.[40]

Protestant and Jewish women developed many of the same kinds of programs as Catholic women. However, their methods for achieving a better future for France differed from Catholics in important ways. Protestant and Jewish women maintained a clear attachment to their faith. However, many of these women were willing to promote Judeo-Christian values rather than a specifically religious agenda. Protestants and Jews did not see themselves as the only true representatives of the nation. Rather, these women propelled France toward becoming a more moral state that offered greater protection and more rights to all women. They also wished to assure France's future as a nation that accorded equal worth to all its citizens regardless of religious background.

Celine Leglaive-Perani suggests that philanthropy can act as a mirror reflecting the donor's motivations and conception of their place in society. Philanthropy can demonstrate loyalty to a religious community, but philanthropy not attached to religious confession also acts as a declaration of belonging to the national community. It demonstrates the giver's loyalty to the nation and their right to be equal citizens.[41] In the case of Jews, Leglaive-Perani argues that funding or creating philanthropic projects allowed Jews to present themselves as "useful and generous citizens toward all French people." Philanthropy became a way to express their gratitude to France. It also provided Jews with access to nonconfessional associations where they could interact with non-Jews, combat anti-Semitism, and show that they were loyal, productive citizens like everyone else.[42] Leglaive-Perani's work focuses on Jews, but similar arguments can be made for the Protestant community. Protestant and Jewish women presented themselves and their communities as devoted citizens working toward the health, stability, and well-being of the nation by improving the lives of other women and children. These women's work with the poor symbolized their communities' openness and democratic spirit while at the same time providing opportunities to reinforce faith and reduce misery in France.

Engagement with nonconfessional programs did not inhibit Protestant and Jewish women from assisting their own communities. Jewish women felt they had a critical responsibility to contribute to Jewish aid programs, owing to the large population of Eastern European Jewish immigrants and refugees and the anti-Semitism they faced. The most important social welfare program in the French Jewish community was the Comité de Bienfaisance Israélite, founded in 1809. By 1906, it assisted about 7,000 people a year. The status of the Comité de Bienfaisance Israélite extended beyond the Jewish community; the organization received a silver medal for high-quality charitable work at the Universal Exposition in 1900.[43] Although women did not participate in the organization's directing board, they operated subsections that aided women and children. Jewish women leaders directed both the Comité de Patronage des Enfants et Familles Assistés, which

oversaw aid to families and children, and the Comité des Dames Vis-
iteuses des Femmes en Couches, which worked with pregnant women
and mothers with newborns. Through these organizations, women
leaders dispensed material and educational aid to children, cared for
poor pregnant women, and provided legal assistance to women who
ran afoul of the law and ended up in jail. These programs not only
aided poor Jews, but also tried to improve the health of Jewish children
and assure their future welfare. The Comité de Patronage furnished
children with medical care, and women directors sent the most delicate children to vacation colonies in the countryside.[44] Women also
placed orphans in homes to ensure that they received basic schooling
as well as some sort of apprenticeship to learn a trade or continue their
education.[45]

The organizations that Jewish women headed not only aided
the poor, but also worked to strengthen the French Jewish community. They improved the health of poor members of the community,
reduced the number of women seeking assistance at secular or state
welfare programs, and minimized infant mortality among Jewish children. Jewish women leaders focused more attention on the material
aid of women and girls than on increasing their faith. However, Jewish
women's participation in religious social programs nonetheless helped
strengthen the Jewish community by providing Jewish support networks that prevented poor Jewish mothers and their children from
becoming detached from the Jewish community.

Conclusion

It is hard to measure how impactful women's programs were on the
lives of the working poor. They undoubtedly offered needed support
to women and children, especially in the absence of a broad state-
run welfare system. However, these programs did not always help
workers. Catholic employers sometimes formed mixed syndicates
that were headed by the employer or female members of the employer's household. Patricia Hilden suggests that these syndicates often
served as mechanisms to control workers rather than as representative

institutions for workers' rights. Workers tended to view them with suspicion.[46] Employers could use religious obligations to "press workers into submission," and women suffered particularly under this policy. Women who transgressed the moral bounds set by the Church could be fired. Unmarried factory women who became pregnant were often fired, and women could lose their jobs for talking to men outside of the factory who they did not plan to marry.[47]

What is interesting about women's social work is not so much the impact it had on workers' lives but what it says about women leaders' desire to protect France physically and engage in the process of national identity construction. Catholic women saw their work as centrally important to France. The Countess Keranflec'h-Kernezne declared that women involved in rural work programs were protecting "patriotism, respect for traditions, the cult of glories of the country, religious faith," and "eternal homes, which feed the vital energy of the race."[48] Despite the conflicts between the Catholic Church and the Third Republic in the early years of the twentieth century, Catholic women were unshakable patriots, if not toward the French government then toward the French nation. In their minds, strengthening France was inextricably linked with assisting poor workers and preventing the rural exodus as well as bringing the nation back to the Catholic faith. Catholic women shied away from suffrage, but they accepted the responsibility to "save" the nation from physical, material, and spiritual decline, partly through their social work.

Defining national identity rested at the heart of Catholic women's rural and urban programs. Women wanted to protect their image of France—a France that was Catholic and had strong rural traditions. Herman Lebovics argues that the early twentieth century saw both the French left and the French right claiming to represent French heritage.[49] Caroline Ford notes that by the early Third Republic, republicans explicitly defined the nation in opposition to the Catholic Church."[50] Catholics, on the other hand, saw themselves as the heart of the French nation and the keepers of French heritage. As one woman wrote in 1902, "the French soul is a Catholic soul."[51] Catholic women wanted to make sure they were involved in the process of defining

French identity and keeping Catholicism as a central part of that identity. As Keranflec'h-Kernezne suggested, the "holy and noble traditions" of the French nation resided in the hearts of French women.[52] Women had a special responsibility as the bearers of culture to engage in the struggle over what constituted French identity. In the absence of political rights, agricultural and worker aid programs gave them a means to shape identity by influencing the poor, engaging in debates about rural education, and protecting the health of working women. These women had considerable faith in their own abilities to understand the problems faced by rural people and to guide France into a more prosperous, "authentically French" future.

Although faith played an important role in the creation of aid associations among Protestant and Jewish women, their social programs exemplify the flexible boundaries between religious and secular social work. Like Catholics, they hoped to see France become a more moral, peaceful, powerful nation. They created programs that would improve the health and well-being of members of their communities as well as the nation as a whole. That said, they were more likely than Catholics to emphasize cooperation to achieve these goals. Protestant and Jewish women did not envision a France dominated by either Protestantism or Judaism. They understood that as minority communities, they could sometimes accomplish more by cooperating with a broad spectrum of people rather than remaining closed in their own denominational organizations. Promoting interdenominational work allowed Protestant and Jewish women to support an image of France that was tolerant and equally protected the rights of all its citizens regardless of faith background, wealth, or gender. Interfaith social work allowed Protestant and Jewish women to present their communities as cooperative and willing to work toward religious and social harmony in France.

Catholic, Protestant, and Jewish women all wanted to improve class relations, ameliorate the plight of the poor, and make France more moral. At the same time, they wished to present a favorable image of their faith communities and ensure that their communities retained a place as part of the moral and religious identity of the nation. Women in all three communities recognized that their methods for social reform had to change. Religion had to be modernized to cope with changing social conditions, and women were at the forefront of this modernization. Women actively expanded their own public action and contributed to the modernization of religious social policy. Marguerite Billat, a writer for a Catholic journal, presented syndicates as an example of this modernization. She warned Catholics not to be the "wrecks of the past that waves of rising generations submerge and reject endlessly." Instead, she encouraged Catholics to draw from the "living sources of true Christianity" the forces that they needed without imposing limits on their actions.[53] Women's increased interaction with France's social problems pushed them to look for new solutions and to find new sources of engagement for themselves. Women in all three communities were no longer content to pray at home or only enter the public sphere in the shadows of philanthropy. Rather, they asserted their right to speak and act publicly for the good of their faith and their nation. In the process, they broadened their own definition of citizenship and membership in their communities. Religious organizations gave them the flexibility to shape France in ways that were important to them while at the same time working to preserve or enhance the position of their religious communities and that of women.

5

A Voyage of Faith

Religious Women and International Work

Around 1889, a young woman from Geneva, Switzerland, left home to accept a post as a domestic worker for a family outside of Warsaw. Sometime after her arrival in Poland, she stopped writing to her family, sending her mother into a state of panic. With few options to find out what had happened to their daughter, the parents turned to the Union Internationale des Amies de la Jeune Fille (International Union of Young Women's Friends, hereafter, Amies), founded in 1877 by Swiss Protestant women in Neuchâtel. The Geneva branch of the association then sent a letter to a member of the Amies in Poland asking for information about the girl. After a long and rather difficult quest, a Polish member discovered that the young domestic worker had become very ill and had been abandoned in a hospital by the family that hired her. Once the Amies located the girl, the organization arranged for her to be repatriated, much to the relief of her worried parents.[1]

By the second half of the nineteenth century, women of faith throughout Europe began developing organizations such as the Amies to assist immigrant and migrant women and girls as they traveled and looked for work.[2] These associations endeavored to protect young travelers from moral downfall and the "white slave trade" while instilling them with religious values and strengthening their religious identity. This chapter explores the actions taken by the French branches of the Amies and the Association Catholique Internationale des Œuvres de Protection de la Jeune Fille (International Catholic Association of Protection Programs for Young Women, hereafter, ACI) to protect migrant and immigrant women and girls, strengthen their faith, and combat the increasingly secular nature of French society under the Third Republic.[3] It also compares Catholic and Protestant efforts to cope with arriving immigrants with the efforts of the French Jewish community, which faced an influx of Jewish refugees from Eastern Europe after 1880. Women leaders in all three religious communities worried about immigrants' moral and spiritual welfare. The internal anxieties within each community, as well as differences in the immigrant and migrant populations that each group assisted, shaped the programs that women developed. Participation in these organizations allowed Catholic, Protestant, and Jewish women to extend their civic and religious responsibilities, provide critical support for immigrant and migrant women and children, and reinforce the importance of religion throughout Europe in the late nineteenth and early twentieth centuries.

The development of associations such as the ACI and the Amies became especially important during the second half of the nineteenth century as young, often unmarried, working-class women came to constitute a more significant part of the new migration system. Women immigrant and migrant workers increasingly found jobs as private teachers, seamstresses, textile workers, and especially domestic servants. These prospects drew young women from the French countryside and from abroad to cities where they hoped to find not only adequate work, but also more exciting experiences than their rural villages could provide.[4] However, social reformers were quick to warn that young women traveling alone could become victims of the "white slave trade" if they were tricked by fake employment ads or met at train stations by traffickers of prostitutes posing as employers looking for domestic workers. Few sources provide statistics documenting the numbers of trafficked women, but Celine Leglaive-Perani has demonstrated that fears about the "white slave trade" were based more on myth than fact. Concerns about white slavery linked it to broader concerns about migration, race mixing, and the new roles of women in social and professional work.[5] Nonetheless, by the late nineteenth century the trade in women had become a cause for international concern. Sensationalized stories filled the press, telling of innocent virgins tricked by depraved men.[6] Protestant social activist Sarah Monod underscored these fears at an 1894 meeting of the Amies where she cautioned that girls arriving alone "in the astonishment of the first moments," were "only too disposed . . . to follow the first person who, under the pretext of helping with their baggage or finding them a car . . . often leads them to supposed placements [for employment or housing] which are places of perdition that they can only leave with difficulty."[7]

Although social reformers may have overestimated the extent to which young women risked being victimized by the "white slave trade," their concerns about the moral and physical safety of immigrant women were by no means unfounded.[8] Historians disagree about the extent of the traffic in women, but the image of young virgins forced into prostitution was a powerful motivator for middle-class Europeans.[9] Likewise, the "white slave trade" was not social reformers' only concern. Young immigrant and migrant women faced real problems finding employment that paid a living wage. Rachel Fuchs and Leslie Page Moch have convincingly argued that without familial networks, young immigrant and migrant women were more at risk for unwed pregnancies and abandonment by their partners, which could quickly lead to both destitution and prostitution.[10]

In addition to the physical and moral dangers that threatened traveling women and children, women of faith feared that poor women and girls who lived far from their families, their communities, and their places of worship risked a loss of spiritual consciousness, religious beliefs, and religious identity. This last issue posed a particular problem since these women were or would become mothers. Catholics, Protestants, and Jews all insisted on the primary role mothers played in transmitting faith to their children. Rabbi Emile Lévy noted in 1906 that Jewish mothers affirmed their "attachment to God" in the home, where they deployed their "benevolent and salutary action for the safety and preservation of Judaism."[11] As a result, the Amies, the ACI, and Jewish aid programs all made instilling religious values and fortifying religious identity central to their overall missions. One male speaker who praised the ACI in 1907 urged Catholic women to protect migrant and immigrant girls' "moral and physical valor" to ensure that France would have a large force of women to defend it in an "era in which abominable doctrines threaten to dry up the life sources of our national prosperity."[12] Although women were excluded from holding clerical and pastoral positions, caring for immigrants allowed them to share their faith and develop their own religious ministry through their social work. These women also ensured that France maintained an international presence in solving pressing social problems.

French Catholic, Protestant, and Jewish women's work to support poor immigrant and migrant women and children was by no means unique. The late nineteenth and early twentieth centuries saw an explosion, in Europe and elsewhere, of secular and religious women's organizations aimed at improving the condition of women and children as well as enhancing women's political power. Anne Firor Scott found that after 1860, American women created a plethora of new reform associations including the Woman's Christian Temperance Union, settlement houses, and educational and political societies. African American women also joined together in a variety of mutual aid and poor relief organizations in the years following the Civil War.[13] Likewise, Australian women engaged in "campaigns for better housing, safer childbirth, [and] reduced infant mortality," among other causes, and Shurlee Swain notes that many women "made careers from what was initially a philanthropic interest."[14] British reformers, such as Josephine Butler, campaigned against state-regulated prostitution. In Germany, Bertha Pappenheim taught members of her organization, Women's Welfare, to use modern techniques of social work to provide more effective care for poor women and children.[15] Seth Koven and Sonya Michel have also noted that middle-class women throughout

Europe and the United States took a greater part in their countries' "maternalist politics" by developing healthcare programs that shaped developing state-sponsored welfare proposals.[16]

The goals of secular and religious organizations concerned with improving the conditions of women or promoting morality often overlapped in significant ways. In fact, people who identified as Christians or Jews often populated secular social organizations. Religious women in France frequently worked in religious and nonreligious programs at the same time. In addition to participating in the Conseil National des Femmes Françaises (CNFF), Protestant women such as Sarah Monod and Julie Siegfried held leadership positions in the Amies. The Conférence de Versailles shared a journal with the Amies, which strengthened ties between those two organizations. Monod also served as one of the French delegates to the 1899 international conference of the National Vigilance Association, which was formed to study and prevent the trade in women.[17] Emilie de Morsier, also an active member of the Amies, participated in the British and Continental Federation for the Abolition of Prostitution along with her husband, Gustave. In addition, she belonged to the French Association for the Abolition of Official Prostitution.[18] Similarly, Clarisse Simon engaged in the Jewish Association for the Protection of Girls and Women, the Toit Familial (Familial Home), a foyer for Jewish girls living away from their families, and the Œuvre Libératrice (Philanthropy of Liberation), a nonconfessional organization aimed at rehabilitating "fallen" women. Similar ideas about morality made it possible for secular and religious social aid organizations to cooperate. In France, the Amies worked in conjunction with the Ligue Française pour le Relèvement de la Moralité Publique (French League for the Recovery of Public Morality), an organization aimed at opposing immoral and pornographic literature.[19] Even Catholic women involved in the ACI, who participated only reluctantly in non-Catholic programs, sometimes cooperated with the Amies or the Association pour la Repression de la Traite des Blanches (Association for the Repression of the White Slave Trade) as they looked for ways to keep traveling girls safe.[20]

As these examples suggest, women of faith did not necessarily see religious societies as the exclusive way to achieve their goals. Rather, religious organizations formed one part of a multilayered strategy that women of faith used to improve the lives of other women and girls. These religious organizations contributed to the growing web of international programs that brought people across Europe and the United States together to promote morality and improve the condition of the poor. The religious aspect of the Amies, the ACI, and Jewish programs was important to women who wished to engage in a mission of proselytization, or in the case of Jews, to protect their communities from anti-Semitism. Women's participation in strictly religious organizations allowed them to strengthen their faith communities by preserving or gaining new members, while at the same time protecting vulnerable women and girls. It also allowed them to enhance French prestige in international aid organizations.

Les Amies de la Jeune Fille

Protestant women in Paris founded a branch of the Amies in 1884. Like earlier branches in Lyon and Marseilles, it offered numerous services for immigrant and migrant girls.[21] These services included free employment placement bureaus, hospitality homes where girls could stay once they arrived in the city, and volunteers to meet girls at train stations to protect them from traffickers.[22] In 1893, Mme R. Coste, the national president of the French Amies, sent a letter to the Paris branch describing the successful workings of the train station mission in Orlèans. Paris, as well as other cities, had similar missions. In the case Mme Coste described, a young girl named Amélie, aged fourteen, from the department of Cher, arrived in Orlèans expecting to be met by another girl from her region who had promised to help her find lodging and work. That girl never arrived and Amélie found herself stranded at the Orlèans train station. Employees at the station took pity on her, gave her food, and allowed her to sleep in the station for the night. The next morning, they called the police, who took Amélie to the home of a member of the Amies, who then located a shelter for her until she could find work.[23]

At their 1894 congress, the Paris Amies presented Amélie's case as an example of the association's success in aiding young migrant girls. Her story provided an ideal, if idealistic, example of the workings of the Amies. For the Paris branch, it also acted as advertisement to drum up support for the association's programs. Although Amélie came to the Amies by way of the police, in most cases individuals in the Amies coordinated a girl's trip so that upon her arrival in Paris, Lyon, Orlèans, or numerous other cities, she would be met at the train station by respectable women who could protect her. A correspondent would write to the Amies indicating the hour a girl would arrive at a train station so an Amie could be there to meet her, take her to a welcome center or place of employment, or accompany her to the connecting train that would take her to her final destination.[24] The same year Amélie received help from women in Orlèans, the Paris branch received a letter of thanks from the Amies at Lausanne, Switzerland, for welcoming girls sent by that committee.[25] This protection worked equally well for French girls who wished to work abroad. The organization's 1900 report noted that requests for "French, Parisian, and if possible Protestant" girls came from Germany, Holland, and England.[26] These kinds of relationships played a central part in the successful functioning of the Amies' programs, since the total membership remained relatively small.[27]

In addition to physically protecting immigrant and migrant girls, the Amies also tried to influence them morally and spiritually.[28] One speaker at the 1899 conference of the Paris Amies declared that "with the aid of God," the Amies would continue "to prevent many [moral] falls [and] guarantee the pure and useful existence of many young women." Preventing moral downfall, as this speaker noted, was particularly important because of the difficulty of "raising a poor fallen creature," whose "depraved habits" had already "become second nature."[29] Some women volunteers also took opportunities to influence young workers with Protestant religious values. A 1906 report describing a welcome center associated with the Amies lauded its acceptance of both Catholic and Protestant girls "with the same good will," although all girls had to attend morning and evening religious services that were undoubtedly Protestant in nature.[30] Directors of the Amies' foyers often held their own prayer meetings designed to "turn the girls' attention" toward God, as one writer explained.[31]

The actions taken by the Amies elicited considerable support from important Protestant men as well as other organizations that had similar goals. A number of very prominent pastors, especially those involved with the Ligue pour le Relèvement de la Moralité Publique, gave their support to the work of the Amies.[32] Pastor Th. Fallow, the secretary of the Ligue pour le Relèvement de la Moralité Publique, opened the 1887 Paris Amies meeting by expressing his solidarity with its members' work.[33] Other prominent men in the Protestant community, including pastors Wagner and Allier, who were also members of the Ligue de la Moralité Publique, offered to assist the Amies in developing ideas to prevent the migration of girls away from their families and wrote supportive articles about the Amies.[34] The Amies provided women with an "apolitical"—yet public—social and religious mission, and their work brought them support from well-respected, important men within the community.

Association Catholique Internationale des Œuvres de Protection de la Jeune Fille

For twenty years after the creation of the Amies, no Catholic counterpart existed that offered international protection to immigrant girls and women.[35] This fact was not lost on European Catholic women who worried about the success of the Amies and the lack of coordination among existing Catholic programs. In 1897, a group of Catholic women headed by Louise de Reynold in Fribourg, Switzerland, founded the Association Catholique Internationale des Œuvres de Protection de la Jeune Fille (International Catholic Association of Protection Programs for Young Women, hereafter ACI).[36] French Catholic women such as the Baronne de Buat, the first head of the French secretariat, and members of the French Catholic hierarchy quickly gave their support to the new project; by 1898 they had established a French branch. It provided many of the same programs as the Amies, including job placement services, contacts for girls traveling to cities where they would be working, and an active campaign against the "white slave trade."[37] Rather than simply creating new projects, the ACI tried to facilitate cooperation among existing Catholic programs aimed at protecting young women.[38] Organizations such as the ACI served an important function for Catholic women, most of whom, as Anne Cova has noted, refused to participate in interdenominational and feminist associations. Creating specifically Catholic programs allowed women to reject contentious political questions such as suffrage and focus on their primary goal of re-Christianizing France.[39]

As with the Amies, the primary objectives of the ACI were the physical, moral, and spiritual protection of young women traveling alone. In the four years from 1906 to 1909, the Maison de Famille (Familial House) in Dijon, an ACI affiliate, sheltered and provided meals for hundreds of girls and helped many find employment. In keeping with the society's religious and moral mission, the home also furnished a chapel and a chaplain for the girls. At least three of the girls left the Maison to establish "good Christian homes," according to one speaker.[40] By 1911, a committee in Nancy, a city in northeastern France, had created a program that verified press announcements offering employment and lodging to young women both in France and abroad to ensure the ads did not lead to brothels.[41] In addition, the train station missions of cities like Grenoble, Nice, Rouen, Lille, Lyon, and Limoges, among many others, arranged to meet hundreds, if not thousands, of girls at train stations each year to protect them from traffickers of prostitutes.[42]

Religion and the defense of the Catholic faith held a particularly prominent place in the ACI, especially in France, where bitter conflicts divided Catholics and the Third Republic. Although the hostility Catholics felt toward the Republic was relatively muted in the ACI as compared to other Catholic women's organizations, concerns about secularization shaped its programs. Women leaders of the ACI resolutely insisted upon reviving the Catholic faith among the girls who received assistance. In a 1910 report, Mlle Barre affirmed that the ACI's "role would be utterly incomplete if it did not apply itself to providing religious principles to the young girls that God conferred to it." She encouraged the association's affiliated programs to create study circles aimed at Christianizing "these young indifferent, fickle girls, in love with their independence, disdainful of all authority, full of prejudices, saturated with unhealthy reading, and led by bad examples." Barre recognized that not all girls would understand religious teachings to the same degree, but she hoped study circles would train an elite group of young women who would spread the word of God among their peers.[43]

Catholic women paid considerable attention to the spiritual dangers faced by girls coming to France from other traditionally Catholic nations, such as Poland. This became especially important in the years leading up to World War I when, as Gérard Noiriel notes, France saw increasing numbers of Poles coming to work in agriculture.[44] At a 1910 meeting of the ACI's French branch, Mlle de Saint-Seine encouraged members to consider the plight of young Polish girls working in the French countryside. She warned that many young Polish women faced a precarious future because they worked on farms far from one another, where they risked having their faith compromised through contact with the de-Christianized French peasantry. Saint-Seine encouraged the organization to look for more volunteers throughout France who would check on the young Polish workers and assure their protection.[45] For French Catholic women, work in the ACI provided an opportunity to promote Catholicism, protect girls, and reinforce the Catholic Church by ensuring that young migrant women maintained an attachment to Catholicism. Although no French Catholic women considered challenging the Catholic hierarchy to demand greater official leadership roles in the church, their work in immigrant aid programs gave them a public voice and a visible religious mission. It also elevated their importance in the eyes of the Catholic hierarchy, which blessed the ACI's work.[46]

Jewish Immigrant Aid Programs

Although Catholics and Protestants worried about the plight of immigrant and migrant girls, the problem of immigration was a much more pressing issue for French Jewish women. After 1880, large numbers of Jewish refugees began arriving in France in response to waves of anti-Semitic violence in Eastern Europe, and many of those refugees needed assistance from the established French community.[47] The situation of French Jews differed significantly from that of Protestants and Catholics both in the scope of the immigrant problem, and because a rise in anti-Semitism beginning in about the middle of the nineteenth century made Jewish communities all over Europe feel besieged.[48]

The French Jewish community worried, with good reason, that the presence of unassimilated Jewish immigrants in France might increase anti-Semitism. As a result, French Jews developed numerous programs designed to help poor Jewish immigrants materially and to integrate them into French society as quickly as possible.[49] Marion Kaplan has suggested that for German Jews, in the face of increasing anti-Semitism, social welfare acted as a form of "minority self help and self-protection," and this was true for French Jews as well.[50] In 1913, Hippolyte Prague, editor for the conservative Jewish newspaper *Archives israélite*, described the connection between Jewish social welfare programs and community security. He declared that the spirit of solidarity inspired by "the most pure and generous devotion" created a bond between upper-class Jews and their less fortunate "brothers" that had allowed Jews to survive "many empires that had conspired" to destroy them.[51]

Jewish women philanthropists generally worked in women's sections of aid organizations headed by men rather than independent women's associations. They nonetheless played a vital part in all Jewish programs that aided immigrants and the poor. Jewish women's efforts to assist immigrants were much more diverse than those of their Christian counterparts. They created the Toit Familial, a foyer for girls working away from their families, and they participated in the Israelite Association for the Protection of Young Girls, an organization founded in Britain that was similar to the Amies and the ACI.[52] Rather than focusing solely on problems faced by immigrant girls looking for work, they developed numerous local faith-based organizations that assisted immigrant women and children more generally. The Jewish community, especially in Paris, included a substantial population of poor Jewish immigrants who had lost everything as they fled Eastern Europe. As a result, French Jewish women developed programs to meet the range of needs experienced by different immigrant groups.[53]

In the context of rising anti-Semitism, Jewish women worried not only about the plight of Jewish immigrants but also about the Jewish community's image in France. Many social programs assisted immigrants while also trying to promote a positive image of the French Jewish community. In 1911, the Comité de Bienfaisance Israélite (Jewish Welfare Board) asked Hélène-Léopold Enos to check on Jewish women in the region of the Seine who ran afoul of the law and ended up in jail. Enos happily reported that fewer Jewish women had been arrested than the year before—only seventeen, down from twenty-four in 1910, and all of them were "foreign," primarily from Russia. Enos was able to obtain the suspension of three sentences and help free five other women.[54] Her specific notation that fewer Jewish women had been arrested in 1911 and all of them had been immigrants highlights French Jewish concerns about the negative effects that crime and immigration might have on the established Jewish community's image in France.

Jewish women who participated in secular, anti–"white slavery" programs also saw their work as a way to shield the Jewish community from anti-Semitic violence. Jews faced particular concerns about "white slavery." Jews had traditionally been presented as merchants, and although there were no statistics linking any one group with human trafficking, blame often fell on Jews.[55] A number of Jewish women, including Clarisse Simon and Gabrielle Alphen-Salvador, served on the administrative board of the Œuvre Libératrice, a secular organization founded by Ghénia Avril de Sainte-Croix. The Œuvre Libératrice created a variety of programs for morally destitute women, some of whom had been trafficked as prostitutes from other coun-tries.[56] Although most of the women who received assistance were not Jews, Jewish members saw the organization's work as important for the image of the French Jewish community. In a 1902 letter asking for financial support from a French Jewish organization, Clarisse Simon noted that many of "the participants in this shameful and ignoble commerce" were Jewish and that "their poor victims also belong for the majority to our religion." She declared that she would be especially pleased as a Jew if other Jews would generously support the Œuvre Libératrice.[57] As her letter suggests, Simon worried not only about the safety of Jewish girls, but also that the reputation of the French Jewish community might be tarnished by the presence of Jewish pros-titutes and traffickers of prostitutes. By supporting programs against the "white slave trade," she, like Enos, hoped to protect the Jewish community by bolstering its reputation as a defender of morality and a protector of women.[58]

A number of other French Jewish welfare programs focused more specifically on the material problems faced by immigrants and refu-gees arriving in Paris. In 1900, a group of Russian and Romanian Jews created the Asile Israélite de Nuit (Jewish Nighttime Shelter, here-after, Asile) in Paris in response to the arrival of large numbers of refugees from those countries. In 1911, the Asile added a crèche for poor immigrant children, which came to be largely directed by Jew-ish women. The crèche admitted any child who did not have a conta-gious disease, gave milk to babies whose mothers could not breastfeed, and tried to care for sick children.[59] In addition to establishing the crèche, educated Jewish women helped immigrant women assimilate by teaching French and hygiene courses for the Université Populaire Juive (Popular Jewish University, hereafter, UPJ), an organization that offered a variety of adult education courses to immigrant Jews.[60]

Directing the crèche and participating in the UPJ allowed wealth-ier women to fortify the Jewish community in a number of ways. The crèche permitted working-class immigrant women to look for employment so they would be less dependent on welfare from the community. It helped assure the health of immigrant families by providing material support.[61] Likewise, programs such as the crèche kept immigrants from seeking support outside the Jewish community, thus limiting the anti-Semitism that might have developed had Jewish immigrants arrived at non-Jewish welfare programs in large numbers. Classes in hygiene taught women and children the standards for personal comportment, cleanliness, and dress demanded by their new national community. With all of these programs, women leaders hoped to make Jewish immigrants invisible in French society as quickly as possible while at the same time reinforcing their Jewish identity.

Jewish women, like Christian women, believed that they had a moral and religious responsibility to aid their immigrant counterparts. However, in contrast to Christian women, Jewish women involved in organizations such as the Asile, the Comité de Bienfaisance Israélite, and the UPJ focused primarily on the material and physical needs of immigrants, rather than on their spiritual needs. Women sometimes organized Jewish holiday celebrations for poor children, provided gifts for Hanukah, and arranged for holiday celebrations at a foyer for girls with the help of a rabbi.[62] However, reports from Jewish organizations rarely suggest that women philanthropists actively encouraged religious devotion among the immigrant women they helped.

This does not mean that Jewish women leaders rejected the importance of faith or religious identity. Their active participation in programs run by the Jewish community for Jewish immigrants, the praise given to their work by male Jewish leaders, especially rabbis, and their efforts to assure that children and young women participated in Jewish holidays reveal a desire to preserve the Jewish community and the Jewish faith. The directors of the Asile underscored the religious significance of women supporters by using religious language to depict their work. In 1911, the secretary-general described these women as being "like the ideal woman described in the Scriptures who held out bread to the poor and supported the indigent."[63] Likewise, the presence of Jewish welfare programs prevented poor and immigrant Jews from drifting toward secular welfare programs or those developed by other religious communities where they might have been subjected to proselytizing efforts. Women's work with Jewish welfare organizations thus helped reinforce the Jewish identity of all participants as well as a sense of community solidarity.[64]

The lack of a more pronounced religious mission among French Jews may be explained by the fact that no proselytizing mission exists within Judaism that might have mobilized Jewish women to spread their faith as it did Christian women. French Christian women happily converted Jews, nonbelievers, or even Christians of different denominations, but the French Jewish community contented itself with strengthening the religious identity of people who were already Jewish. Nancy Green has noted that Jewish immigrants to France were often associated with a greater degree of "religious orthodoxy" than their French counterparts.[65] In any case, Jewish women's "religious mission" tended to focus on material, moral, and educational support rather than on specifically spiritual concerns.

Women, Religion, and Internationalism

The development of faith-based immigrant aid organizations must be understood within the context of broader European concerns about immigration, changing social conditions, and the growing role of philanthropy. Although religious groups paid particular attention to declining attachment to faith, especially in France, both secular and confessional societies worried about the dangers faced by girls traveling far from their families. Other secular international societies began forming around the mid-nineteenth century to tackle problems associated with the "white slave trade," prostitution, and the perceived dangers faced by young, single women traveling and living alone.[66] Josephine Butler headed up efforts against state-regulated prostitution with the creation of the British, Continental and General Federation for the Abolition of State Regulation of Vice in 1875, and she played a critical role in raising awareness about the dimensions of the "white slave trade."[67] In 1899, the National Vigilance Association "hosted the first international congress dedicated to the trade in women" with the goal of bringing governments and philanthropic groups from different countries together to study the trade in women.[68] The International Association for the Repression of the White Slave Trade also provided people of different faiths throughout Europe with a secular opportunity to challenge forced prostitution.[69] The goals and methods of these secular organizations were similar to those of religious organizations. Molly McGregor Watson notes that the Association for the Repression of the Trade in Women and the Protection of Young Girls, which formed in France in 1901, made monitoring train stations for the arrival of young women central to its mission. This organization also helped girls find respectable work and lodging, similar to the assistance provided by the ACI and the Amies. McGregor Watson also emphasizes the importance both secular and religious anti–"white slave trade" organizations placed on protecting and "preserving" young girls.[70]

Despite the opportunities for secular social work, women of faith continued to be drawn to organizations that allowed them to protect girls physically as well as influence them spiritually. Women's faith identity provided a point of commonality that facilitated cooperation among women of different regions and countries. This was especially important for Catholic women who were reluctant to work closely with non-Catholic organizations. Religious organizations allowed women to construct significant protective networks for traveling women and girls within France and abroad. Protestant and Catholic women regularly corresponded with their counterparts in regional or international branches of the Amies or the ACI, as well as other similar organizations, to assist traveling women and girls. In discussing a welcome center in Paris, Mme de Castellane, regional president of the Paris ACI, noted that many young girls arrived after having already been "recommended by our correspondents" either from abroad or the French provinces. The same was true for the Train Station Mission.[71] In 1911, the ACI praised its regional committee in Nancy for verifying advertisements for lodging and work directed at young women and sharing that information with the secretariats of Metz and Strasbourg. The ACI also praised this committee for the correspondence it exchanged with the Amies in Basel, Switzerland, and the Protection Society of Warsaw to locate girls who experienced problems after their arrival in Poland. The organization noted that correspondence between the Paris secretariat and other institutions in England, Luxembourg, and Germany about placements in Paris had prevented girls from accepting positions that were not respectable.[72]

The same pattern occurred with the Protestant Amies. By 1889 the Amies headquarters at Neuchâtel had put together a list of 535 hospitality homes, churches, pastors, aid societies, and Christian unions throughout Europe prepared to contribute to the protection of girls.[73] In addition, the Amies Œuvre des Arrivantes (Arrivals Philanthropy) welcomed numerous girls from abroad each year after arranging their trips by correspondence. The Amies' 1914 report noted that the Paris Amies received 1,520 letters regarding girls who would be arriving in Paris.[74] Some of this correspondence came from individuals asking to be met at train stations, while other letters came from other Amies branches or organizations such as the Travelers Aid Society in London who arranged for girls to be assisted by the Amies once they arrived in France.[75]

Catholic and Protestant women understood the novelty of their international work and took pride in having created organizations that linked women in many different countries. Mme Ed. Humbert, in her brief 1889 history of the Amies, declared that "the work of the Union des Amies de la Jeune Fille, with its international character, is very complex, complex in its organizations, in its means of action, even in its goals." Humbert pointed out that women members had a formidable task coordinating communication and correspondence among different countries.[76] Similarly, in 1908, Mme de Montenach, the vice president of the ACI, noted that her organization had overcome considerable difficulties and "prejudices" to "put in place the great enterprise of social and Christian assistance that we have realized." Declaring that "union creates force," she called the organization a "school of formation and rapprochement." Montenach saw the ACI as a model for other Catholic programs in the battle against secularism and anticlerical politics, arguing that it provided Catholics with the ability to "combine their efforts to position themselves against their adversaries . . ."[77]

The diversity of French Jewish women's programs, many of them local rather than international, may be explained by both the nature of Jewish immigration and the context in which those immigrants arrived. A refugee crisis occurred in the wake of the 1881–82 pogroms in Eastern Europe. Another massive wave of Jewish immigration began again after the failed 1905 revolution in Russia. The native French community, which was not very large, quickly found itself overwhelmed by the new arrivals. Paula Hyman argues that the native French Jewish community feared that the arrival of poor Eastern European immigrants who brought different customs, a different language, and a different way of practicing their faith would undermine the integration that native Jews had been working toward since the Revolution of 1789 gave them rights as citizens.[78] Given the conditions of immigration, French Jewish women had no way and, in some cases, no desire to facilitate these immigrants' voyage to France, and could only help ameliorate their condition once they arrived. French Jewish women leaders, like their Christian counterparts, nonetheless depended on networks created among themselves to facilitate the support they provided to immigrant women and children, regardless of how they arrived.

Religion and Leadership for Women

Associations like the Amies, the ACI, and various Jewish programs deemed the physical and spiritual protection of immigrant and migrant women and children their primary objective. These associations did not adopt "feminist" ambitions such as demanding women's suffrage or other political rights per se. Religious organizations nevertheless provided women with important leadership opportunities both in their religious communities and in Europe's efforts at social reform. Kathleen McCarthy argues that in the United States, women's philanthropic work allowed them to create "parallel power structures" outside of areas dominated by men that gave them a means for enacting change.[79] This was true for European women as well. Work in the Amies, the ACI, and Jewish programs allowed Catholic, Protestant, and Jewish women to speak publicly about religious issues and actively spread their faith. Women achieved a greater degree of visibility in the eyes of the clergy. Prominent men often praised their achievements and recognized the importance of women's work in the preservation of religious communities. A male speaker at the 1907 ACI conference referred to women's work as an "apostolic mission."[80] Women did not use these associations to demand greater leadership rights within their churches or synagogues. However, participation provided them with de facto leadership roles without overtly undermining traditional male religious hierarchies, thus making them acceptable and desirable to all three communities.

In addition to expanding women's public participation in religious life, faith-based immigrant aid associations gave women a greater part in global efforts to deal with social ills, and they facilitated acceptance of women's work in the public sphere. For moderate feminists or women who did not wish to demand political rights, these organizations offered a way to promote women's issues without necessarily being "feminist" in an overtly political sense. Women could engage in what Steven Hause and Anne Kenney have called "social feminism," which focused on social reforms rather than political rights.[81] In this context, women's leadership positions in social reform increased rapidly, as is evidenced by the League of Nations' 1922 decision to invite women to serve on a Permanent Advisory Committee on Traffic in Women and Children.[82] Most members of the Amies, the ACI, and Jewish immigrant aid programs did not have specifically feminist goals. Nonetheless, their work in social reform helped to broaden the space available for women's civic action, promote issues important to women, and engender confidence in women's abilities to tackle social and political problems.

Conclusion

The women who engaged in organizations that assisted immigrants believed that they had a religious mission to aid other, less fortunate women and children. The increased immigration and migration of women and children in the second half of the nineteenth century offered women of faith a new opportunity to expand their work protecting other socially, economically, and spiritually vulnerable people. Women's religious affiliations gave their programs institutional support from the broader religious communities while providing a moral base and divine sanction for their social and religious programs. In addition, the creation of faith-based immigrant aid organizations furnished women philanthropists with an opportunity to strengthen their own religious communities, both nationally and internationally. Women leaders fortified the faith of immigrant women through direct proselytization or by incorporating religious activities into social programs. In most cases, women's outreach efforts to immigrants expanded the scope of their social work and affirmed the importance of faith, religious identity, and women's religious activities in an increasingly secular Europe.

6

Battling for God and Nation

Women, Religion, and the First World War

On November 10, 1914, a group of injured soldiers arrived at a hospital patronized by Mme la Baronne Thérèse de Rothschild in Gouvieux, France. During one of Mme de Rothschild's daily visits to the hospital, a gravely injured young soldier stopped her and pleaded with her to bring him a crucifix, explaining that the nurses at the hospital had been unable to procure one. "Very moved" by the request, Mme de Rothschild quickly found a crucifix, and according to her account, the soldier hardly contained his joy upon receiving it, despite the severity of his wounds. He thanked Mme de Rothschild profusely and promised to pray for her. Some days later, he died.[1] Like her male counterpart, Rabbi Abraham Bloch, who also offered a crucifix to a wounded Catholic soldier, Thérèse de Rothschild saw it as her responsibility to provide physical and spiritual care for all of France's soldiers regardless of their religious affiliation.[2] Through their work, women of faith helped to define the *union sacrée*, the sacred union that theoretically united all faith groups in support of the French war effort. Women's wartime service and their contributions to this sacred union became a means through which the Catholic, Protestant, and Jewish

This chapter is adapted from "Soldiers of Faith behind the Lines: Religious Women and Community Patriotism during the First World War in France," *Women's History Review* 22, no. 1 (February 2013), 31–50. http://www.tandfonline.com /loi/rwhr20.

communities shaped the identity of France as well as their own communities' future within the French nation.

In many ways, World War I and the development of the union sacrée was the culmination of France's efforts to reconstruct a religious identity for the nation. The union sacrée welcomed Catholics, Protestants, and Jews into the pact that committed everyone to the defense of France. It created a rhetoric that officially recognized Catholicism, Protestantism, and Judaism as accepted building blocks of French culture. Even so, the Catholic, Protestant, and Jewish communities did not take inclusion into the union sacrée for granted. Instead, all three communities worked very hard to prove their devotion to the nation. These communities pointed to their women's wartime work as community leaders, nurses, and social workers to prove their loyalty, worthiness, and usefulness to France.

All three religious groups equally declared support for the sacred union binding the nation in defense against the Germans. That said, the definition of the union sacrée within these three communities and their long-term goals for it differed considerably. As symbols of the home front, religious women's wartime service came to play a central role in shaping the union sacrée in ways meant to have sustainable benefits for their faith groups. Protestants and Jews were minorities who had a history of persecution in France and who had been accused of foreignness. They wanted the sacred union to fortify France's identity as a nation that equally accepted all of its members regardless of religious affiliation. Protestants and Jews held up the spiritual and social work of their women as proof of their commitment to France, their worth to the nation, and their right to be equal citizens. Catholics, on the other hand, had seen their position in France undermined by church/state conflicts and secularization over the course of the late nineteenth and early twentieth centuries. As a result, Catholics saw the union sacrée as a reestablishment of the broken bond they believed existed between the Church and the nation. Catholics called on their women to bring the nation back under Catholic leadership and confirm the right and worth of the Catholic Church to be the spiritual leader of France.

The crisis provoked by the First World War made women even more valuable to their religious communities both in terms of the work women accomplished and how that work reflected the communities' national reputation. Each group believed that their value to France and their perceived integration and patriotism would be judged partly by women's actions. The war revealed the extent to which women had become vital symbols of their communities' importance to France, especially during moments of crisis that brought into question citizens' loyalty to the nation.

Women's Wartime Responsibilities

With the commencement of World War I, women of faith, like most women, rapidly assumed responsibilities to assist the war effort on the home front. They engaged in all manner of social and religious support for soldiers, civilians, and their religious communities. Catholic women assisted overworked priests, sent packages to soldiers in the trenches, aided poor families, and tried to bring people back to the Catholic faith. Protestant women took over the direction of parishes in the absence of pastors, sent packages to soldiers, and assisted war orphans. Likewise, Jewish women worked in a variety of social aid programs, assisted immigrant Jewish families who had men fighting for France, and patronized hospitals. Women in all three communities worked as nurses and actively tried to sustain morale among soldiers and civilians alike.

Women's wartime activities were not entirely new. As many historians have pointed out, the years leading up to the war saw women engaging in new forms of philanthropy and social action that required a much greater public presence. At the same time, women all over the world began developing new kinds of social programs aimed at making long-term improvements in the lives of poor women and children. Margaret Darrow argues that a discourse developed in turn-of-the-century France that expanded women's duties to society and the nation. This discourse furthered the notion that women had an important role to play in social welfare, education, and health services, as well as programs to aid the poor.[3]

Once the war began, women organized themselves into numerous aid programs, took new types of jobs, and joined the Red Cross. Françoise Thébaud suggests that serving became "the order of the day for bourgeois women and feminists" alike in France. The feminist journal *La fronde*, headed by Marguerite Durand, was published during the war "not to ask for political rights for women but to help them [women] accomplish their social duties."[4] Within days of the declaration of war, Marguerite de Witt-Schlumberger, head of the Union Française pour le Suffrage des Femmes, and Julie Siegfried, head of the Conseil National des Femmes Françaises, who both had sons in uniform, called on their members to support the war effort.[5]

Although women of faith's wartime service differed little from that of other French women, it took on greater meaning for their communities. Religious women not only represented themselves or their women's organizations. Their work also contributed to the image of their entire community as solidly behind the French war effort. Religious magazines frequently published articles praising women involved in various forms of secular and religious wartime work. The Rabbi J. H. Dreyfuss, for instance, affirmed the pride the Jewish community took in women's assistance for the poor, suffering, sick, elderly, and children. He encouraged people to remember its "heroines of charity," who had husbands, sons, and brothers fighting on French soil.[6] For all three faith communities, women became symbols of religious and national devotion on the home front and representatives of the integration and patriotism of their faith communities.

Women, Religion, and the Union Sacrée

At its most fundamental level, the union sacrée was simply a resolve to defend France against the Germans. It did not eliminate all prewar political and religious divisions, nor did it have one single, unchanging meaning for everyone.[7] Jay Winter suggests that people on the home front enjoyed a privileged status away from the fighting, and the way they displayed that privilege was very important. Civilians came under criticism for failing to appreciate their privileged place and for making light of soldiers' sacrifices.[8] The existence of social divisions in wartime France meant that the sacred union had to be defended and its importance reaffirmed constantly. It could also be shaped and refined to meet the changing needs of the nation or individual groups as the war progressed.

Catholic, Protestant, and Jewish women were all eager to publicly show their worthiness of the sacrifice of soldiers. Marthe de Vélard called on members of the Ligue Patriotique des Françaises (LPDF) to "fraternize in sacrifice and the gift of themselves." Women had to act against discouragement and spread "affectionate" and comforting words "inspired by faith and patriotism."[9] Marguerite de Witt-Schlumberger, who saw five of her sons and her son-in-law leave to fight in the war, made similar statements.[10] De Witt-Schlumberger warned women that for the sake of national defense and out of duty to the nation, they had to "guard themselves against all weakness" and remember that their "interior attitude" reflected on their faces. Rather than discouraging soldiers with worries about home, de Witt-Schlumberger reminded women to impart courage to their husbands, sons, and brothers.[11] Jewish women expressed the same determination to support the French war effort at all cost. Thérèse de Rothschild decried the "cruel, cold, and premeditated acts" committed by the Germans as they entered France.[12] Likewise, Suzanne Bloch, a contributor to the Jewish magazine *Le peuple juif,* declared that French Jewish blood flowed "for the only homeland (patrie) that we know." She affirmed that French Jews had already made the "pilgrimage" of their lives not to Jerusalem but to France.[13]

In the context of concerns about shirkers and profiteers, people in wartime Europe developed what Jean-Louis Robert calls a "moral language" with the sacrifice of soldiers at its heart. "Sins" within this moral discourse included egotism, incompetence, cynicism, and frivolousness, a charge often leveled against women.[14] A 1917 book of cartoons "featured a woman angered by an offensive because it meant that she would only be able to go to the theater twice a week."[15] Religious communities in France worked very hard to situate themselves within this moral discourse. They insisted that none of their members were among those who failed to contribute to the war effort or caused divisions within French society. Publicly supporting soldiers and the defense of France allowed religious women to position themselves and their communities as unwavering patriots who would do whatever it took to protect the nation.[16]

Definition of the Union Sacrée

Although widely adhered to throughout the war, the union sacrée carried different meanings for different groups. It united the nation in the battle against the Germans, but its underlying goals were uniquely framed by different faith and political communities. For Catholics, the sacred union could reaffirm France's identity as a Catholic nation. On the eve of World War I, Catholics faced a France in which their value to the French nation had been severely challenged by the anticlerical Third Republic and by declining religiosity among French citizens. Despite the unifying message of the union sacrée, prewar anticlericalism did not disappear once the war began. Catholics faced an "infamous rumor," a series of accusations blaming them for the war and questioning their patriotism. Some rumors suggested that priests or religious orders wanted a war so that they could take revenge for the anticlerical politics of the Republic. Others claimed that Pope Benedict XV was the friend of Germany and that priests shirked during combat.[17] Catholics, who saw themselves as the heart and soul of the French nation, sharply resented this challenge to their patriotism.

Although Catholics generally accepted the idea of a sacred union that could unite divergent groups in French society for the defense of France, many continued to see Catholicism as the "backbone of French patriotism." Some never saw Protestants, Jews, or any non-Catholics as equal members of the nation.[18] In December 1916, one priest warned members of the LPDF that although they might have heard that Protestants were "good and charitable," Protestantism was a religion "without absolute morals." He described it as "one of the errors of the age."[19] Odile Sarti notes that Catholic women, such as those involved in the LPDF, "could not divorce their nationalism from a deep attachment to Catholicism . . . to defend the faith also meant to defend the nation. If Catholicism was in danger, the nation was in peril."[20] Rather than pointing to women's wartime service simply to prove their patriotism, Catholics depended on it to reestablish their position as spiritual leaders of the nation. They hoped the war, as well as women's apostolic work, would show France the error of its secular ways and demonstrate the necessity of a strong Catholic faith.

Catholics' desire to make the sacred union a Catholic union was an unacceptable goal for the Protestant and Jewish communities. Both Protestants and Jews interpreted the union sacrée and their service to the nation as ways to reinforce equality and equal acceptance of all faith communities in France. Like their Catholic counterparts, Protestants' and Jews' pasts shaped their reaction to the war. At various moments throughout their history, both communities had been denied rights as citizens and had suffered discrimination, persecution, and outright violence. France's legacy of persecution against minority religious communities profoundly marked their psychology. In 1886, staunch anti-Semite Edouard Drumont published *La France juive*, "the first best-seller on anti-Semitism in France." His magazine, *La libre parole*, soon followed and accused Jews of trying to destroy Catholicism and control the French financial system for their own personal gain, among other things. At about the same time, anti-Jewish attacks increased in the Catholic daily newspaper *La croix*.[21] The French Jewish community had worked very hard throughout the nineteenth century to show their patriotism and "Frenchness" in hopes of reducing anti-Semitism. However, the frequent anti-Semitic articles published in the Catholic and nationalist presses, as well as the Dreyfus Affair, revealed the fragility of Jews' position in France. By 1900, Protestants felt more secure in their position within the French nation. However, the anti-Semitism experienced by Jews exacerbated both communities' concerns about their security. Many Protestants worried that, after the Jews, they might be the next victims.[22] Likewise, anti-Protestant literature often presented Protestants as foreigners who were not truly French. With the commencement of the war, Protestants tried hard to prove that they had no connection with German Protestants and were, in fact, devoted French citizens.[23]

World War I offered both communities another opportunity to prove their patriotism. Protestants' and Jews' uneasiness about their acceptance into France contributed to their staunch devotion to the union sacrée. For them, it was a union that recognized different groups as equal contributors to the life and survival of the nation. Throughout the war, Protestant pastors avowed the determination of the Protestant community to see France achieve victory.[24] One Protestant speaker declared in 1916, "We Protestants have adhered to the *Union sacrée* with a unanimous spirit . . . We have rightly estimated that in tragic hours, when the nation is in danger, we don't have to ask ourselves if we are Protestant, or Catholic, or Israelite, or Free Thinkers; we are and we can only be Frenchmen who, hand in hand, rush to the aid of our common mother who has been odiously attacked."[25] Jews also used religious language to describe the conflict and present their wartime service as a civic duty blessed by God. At a meeting in June 1915, the grand rabbi of Paris, M. J.-H. Dreyfus, declared "when called by the *Patrie*," Jews responded "like Abraham to God saying, 'We're here'; we are ready, ready to share with all our compatriots the duty, the peril, and the honor of defending our common mother, our adored France."[26] Despite the power of the union sacrée, the Protestant and Jewish communities continually looked for opportunities to demonstrate their devotion and solidarity with France. In this context, women's wartime service took on special importance. Women's social work and spiritual leadership on the home front exemplified the patriotism and "Frenchness" of their entire faith groups.

Women and Devotion to France

The Catholic community saw patriotism as the responsibility of all French Catholics, but it depended on women in particular to maintain high morale and patriotism both on the home front and among soldiers. Early in the war, one priest had admonished women to keep their sadness quiet when they lost their men on the field of honor. All Catholics "had to renounce their own lives and the lives of those they loved for the salvation of the Nation."[27] Catholic women demonstrated their devotion to both the nation and the Church by engaging in apostolic work as well as by reacting against defeatism, demanding support for the war and accepting suffering and sacrifice in the service of the nation.

Within days of the declaration of war, Marthe de Vélard, president of the LPDF, announced that she had placed her organization at the service of the Red Cross. In August 1914, she proclaimed to LPDF women, "the hour has come for us to show ourselves valiant enough to remain at our posts so that our members may prove themselves willing to go wherever the menaced nation calls." She reminded women that their "devotion" had to be carried to all "fields of action."[28] The following month, the LPDF declared that "like men, they [women] had heard the call of the nation and valiantly [and] joyously, had mobilized in the service of their beloved France."[29] Vélard strongly cautioned women that "the work that true LPDF members had to tirelessly accomplish" was to "make war against those who complained and who spread suspicion, fear, [and] discouragement." She warned that LPDF members would be "guilty" if they "let slip the least word of discouragement" or if they permitted "a sentiment of defeatism" to "creep into their souls . . ."[30] Catholic women understood the importance of publicizing their wartime work both to prove their patriotism and to motivate other women to join wartime programs. The LPDF section at Cambrai continued its wartime efforts to help the poor despite German occupation. In response, one writer declared that "such examples of vitality and courage" had to be published because they could excite "zeal and devotion" in other LPDF members throughout France.[31]

As with their Catholic counterparts, Protestant and Jewish women's service lay at the heart of their communities' efforts to demonstrate patriotism and solidarity with the nation. In April 1915, nine months after the commencement of World War I, Pastor M. Russier declared before an assembly of fellow Protestants, "Our sisters are mobilized to surround the injured with care as they arrive in ambulances . . . Thus, we have confirmed before our compatriots that Protestantism has its place in our nation where we know how to shoulder the responsibilities that come to us."[32] In this declaration, Russier clearly linked Protestants' integration into France with women's contributions to the war. In December 1914, an anonymous writer for *L'univers israélite* made a special effort to recognize women for "combining feminine goodness with Jewish piety," and offering "their care in all ambulances, their work in all social programs, [and] their adherence to all committees." This writer concluded that "everywhere there is a need, there is a Jewish hand held out . . ."[33] Likewise, the Grand Rabbi Meiss of Marseille praised women for reinforcing the confidence of those around them that France would achieve a just victory. He referred to women as "true combatants behind the front."[34]

Like all French women, Protestant women suffered heavy losses during the war. They lost husbands, sons, and brothers, and they mourned with the rest of the nation. Despite the losses, Protestant newspapers presented an image of their women as solidly behind the war effort regardless of its cost. In August 1914, the Protestant newspaper *Le huguenot* published a letter written by a Protestant woman, who described the pain and worry she felt at having her husband at the front but also the strength she found in her faith. When her husband received mobilization orders he gave up hope, declaring, "It's finished, I'm leaving, but I won't ever come back." She asked God to help her stay calm and encourage him to fulfill his duty to the nation. She prayed that God would help her say "Father, not my will but yours!" if her husband "had to be one of those who would remain lying on the field of battle."[35] *Le christianisme au XX siècle* published a similar letter written by a woman who had lost all three of her sons to the war and whose brother had been gravely injured. Despite this personal tragedy, she affirmed that she proudly gave her sons to save France.[36]

These women's letters exemplify Protestants' belief that women could boost the morale of the nation and sustain the war effort. These were perfect examples of Protestant women, who, with God's help, accepted enormous sacrifices for the good of France. Their example instructed other women about their responsibilities, the kind of attitude they should have, and how they should draw on their faith to enhance their own courage as well as that of their husbands. Their letters presented an image of strong women who met the challenges they faced and sacrificed their own happiness for the good of the nation. This kind of message remained consistent in the Protestant press throughout the war. On March 7, 1917, Mlle Morin, a leader in the Unions Chrétiennes de Jeunes Filles (UCJF), signed a declaration in the name of the UCJF. This declaration reaffirmed French Protestant women's "acceptance of all sacrifices" needed to win the war and promised to fortify courage among those around them.[37]

When Jewish women, and especially Jewish immigrant women, spoke about their wartime service, they used it as a sign of their integration and devotion to France as well as that of their fellow Jews. In 1918, Sophie Fridmon, a nurse at a Red Cross–affiliated hospital, received a commendation from the Ministry of Health for the care she had given to injured soldiers. In expressing her gratitude to the government, Fridmon declared that she felt particularly honored as a "foreign nurse" to receive the commendation. She avowed that she would never forget what France had done for immigrant Jews who had been persecuted and driven from their homes in other countries. She praised soldiers fighting for freedom and peace, and affirmed that nurses as their "devoted and faithful sisters" shared their suffering. Fridmon proclaimed that Jews in France saw all of their wartime service as a duty they owed to the nation. She promised that Jewish women's "husbands and sons will go to help you chase the enemy out of France, and we will sing with you at the final Victory!"[38]

Paula Hyman argues that World War I "enabled both native and immigrant Jews to demonstrate their patriotism and to benefit from a broad *union sacrée* . . . that characterized French society during these years."[39] Fridmon's case is peculiar in that her immigrant status allowed her to represent not only the French Jewish community but also the immigrant Jewish community. Her emphasis on Jewish devotion to France echoed the writings of other French Jewish women. All of these women understood and embraced their role as representatives of the Jewish community's solidarity with France. As minority religious communities, Protestants and Jews could not present themselves as the natural, God-appointed leaders of France like Catholics. Rather, they felt compelled to prove themselves worthy of their French citizenship. The Protestant and Jewish communities emphasized the commitment of soldiers and pastors on the battlefield to assert their right to be considered equal members of the nation. They also pointed to women's service on the home front as nurses, parish leaders, and social aid workers. The combination of men and women's work affirmed the community's willingness to devote itself fully to France by contributing to its physical defense as well as to its moral and spiritual direction.

All this said, published letters and articles written by women claiming to be proud to sacrifice their men or happy to sustain the war should be viewed with a degree of skepticism. Françoise Thébaud suggests that it was not easy for women to send sons, husbands, or boyfriends off to war. Not everyone did so with the intense patriotism suggested in the above-mentioned letters. Many women cried, some fainted, and by 1917, hundreds of thousands of working women were on strike against low salaries and the duration of the war.[40] Kathleen Kennedy found that in the years leading up to the United States' entry into World War I, American women involved in the war preparedness movement also expressed willingness to give their sons for the nation.[41] Kennedy argues that the presence of this message in women's organizations' propaganda indicates that the values of "patriotic motherhood" were not universally supported.[42] The same could be said for France. The Protestant press seized upon these examples not because they represented the sentiments of all women but to educate or remind women about their wartime responsibilities.

Women and Wartime Spiritual Leadership

Catholic women worked hard to prove their devotion to the nation, but their war effort was also about bringing people back to the faith.

Most Catholic women's programs included a strong element of spiritual outreach. The war offered significant opportunities for Catholic women to take leadership in spiritual matters. With so many men mobilized, including priests, women were largely left with the responsibility to carry on with religious services and community spiritual support. Marie Frossard, secretary of the LPDF, encouraged members to assist the few priests who remained on the home front in caring for believers and bringing people back to the Church. She commanded women to arm themselves "with the necessary energy" to be ready "for the incomparable redemptive work" in which they engaged.[43] As the majority religious group in a nation that had been historically Catholic, Catholics saw themselves as the natural, God-ordained spiritual leaders of France. Catholics had a sense of ownership of the nation and a feeling that only they could be its true representatives. As an anonymous Catholic woman noted in 1902, the "French soul is a Catholic soul."[44]

In the absence of many priests and Catholic men in general on the home front, Catholic women made themselves symbols of Catholics' devotion to the nation as they worked feverishly to bring people back to the faith. Since the Republic considered Catholic women's organizations to be anti-republican, police reporters kept close tabs on what these women did. Throughout the war, the LPDF held numerous meetings, conferences, pilgrimages, and church services attended by police reporters. With normal religious life disrupted by the war, Catholic women's organizations offered an alternative avenue for spirituality not necessarily available in churches. In May 1915 one officer reported about a meeting of 450 LPDF members led by Mlle Paloteau, who told members in attendance to devote themselves to charity and prayer and to unite in "suffering and action." She reminded women to be patient while they waited for the victory and peace that would "with the grace of God" make "France stronger than ever."[45]

During the war, LPDF meetings often drew hundreds of people, which allowed them to spread their religious message and mobilize women for the war effort. Although the LPDF drew most of its support from the middle and upper classes, members also looked for creative ways to reach a broader audience with their message. In April 1915, the LPDF held a meeting attended by 600 people, many of them working class, who were encouraged to join the LPDF. The police reporter who attended the meeting noted that most of the crowd had come because the LPDF was showing a film about the war.[46] Although most attendees may have come to see the movie, they undoubtedly had to listen to the religious and political messages of the LPDF first.

Many Protestant women worked in nonconfessional wartime associations such as nursing programs, but other women devoted their time to assuring the spiritual stability of their religious communities in the absence of pastors. During the war, French Protestants lost thirty-six pastors, fifty-two theology students, and 166 pastors' sons, some of whom probably would have become pastors themselves.[47] Many more served in the trenches. As a result, numerous pastors' wives and other women had to take over the direction of parishes for the duration of the war. The Protestant community took considerable pride in their work. In October 1916, Marguerite de Witt-Schlumberger placed an announcement in several Protestant newspapers asking women to describe their activities since the beginning of the conflict, especially areas in which they had replaced mobilized men.[48] She published nineteen responses describing women's efforts to continue the operation of their churches and parish life in general. Most of the responses came from women, but several men also wrote to praise the work of their wives or other women for the central role they played in safeguarding religious life in the absence of pastors and other male religious leaders.

The men who wrote to de Witt-Schlumberger expressed considerable admiration for the work that women accomplished. One pastor explained that he had not wanted to "oblige" his wife to "speak of her work in our church," so he wrote for her. In his absence, she had "made pastoral visits," provided religious services for the sick and elderly, organized meetings for girls, and worked in numerous aid programs for soldiers and civilians in invaded regions. By cooperating with the wife of another pastor of the same region, she had also improved relations with a church that had previously been a rival. Her husband affirmed that her influence "seemed blessed to him." Other pastors praised the work of women they knew who composed "meditations" for the faithful, directed Sunday and Thursday schools, and engaged in all manner of wartime aid programs. All of these men expressed admiration for the work accomplished by women for the good of Protestant communities and the French nation.[49]

Women who provided spiritual leadership for their parishes aided both the Protestant community and France by maintaining morale, assuring continuity in people's spiritual lives, and providing material aid to the most needy. Maintaining communities' normal spiritual activities helped people deal with the harshness imposed by the conflict and the grief of the losses they suffered. Likewise, holding religious services in the absence of pastors helped prevent detachment from the Protestant faith, which might have occurred had people been unable to attend services for the duration of the war. Thus, women's spiritual leadership helped reinforce people's religious identity and their willingness to continue supporting the war.

Jewish women did not see notable expansion in their opportunities for spiritual outreach or spiritual leadership. Again, this is partly because Jews do not proselytize so there was no need for them to engage in outreach outside the community. There is no evidence that Jewish women took the place of rabbis. Male Jewish leaders and Jewish women themselves preferred to focus on women's work in nursing and social services. Although Jewish women often worked in programs that aided people regardless of faith, they also engaged in some community-specific programs. Jewish women understood the necessity of creating social aid programs for Jews, but they made special efforts to reject any accusation of separatism. In 1915, a group of Jews founded the Œuvre des Orphelins Israélites de la Guerre, which primarily organized women to help care for children who had lost one or both parents during the war. Although this organization specifically aided Jewish children, its first bulletin published in January 1916 affirmed that each religious group's "heartfelt effort to glorify its dead and offer special protection to the children that they had left behind them" did not prevent the "unity of the Nation."[50] Jewish women carefully justified the decision to create such programs while at the same time affirming their commitment to France. Jewish women saw national unity as central to all of their programs, and they understood the important role they played in symbolizing the patriotism of their community. As Paula Hyman notes, Jewish wartime service "illustrated the way in which religion reinforced love of country." Wartime service also allowed Jewish leaders to suggest that it was, in fact, anti-Semites who were unpatriotic by "attacking an entire category of fellow citizens in wartime."[51]

Women and Nursing

Women in all three communities volunteered as nurses and engaged in numerous programs to aid soldiers and civilians who were injured during the conflict. Their social and nursing work made them an important part of the physical presence of their communities on both the home and war fronts. In the Catholic community, nuns and laywomen alike joined nursing services such as the Red Cross. Many received commendations from the army for their bravery and dedication. Sister Jeanne-Juliette Perdon was commended in 1915 for calmly evacuating her hospital, despite great danger to her own life, after a bomb destroyed the hospital.[52] Nuns, in particular, brought with them a long nursing tradition, which made them especially valuable to the military. As Véronique Leroux-Hugon notes, the list of nuns who died "under the banner of the Red Cross" was extensive.[53] Members of the LPDF who decided to join the Red Cross sometimes worked closely with nuns. One nurse affirmed that the Augustine Sisters working with the eager members of the LPDF had supplied several nurses to the war effort.[54] Women involved in the LPDF also organized workshops where working-class women received a wage for making clothing and linens for soldiers and priests serving in the trenches. They created information bureaus that provided families who were unable to visit soldiers in hospitals with information about their husbands and sons who had been wounded, and they developed diverse programs to aid war orphans.

Even hostile republican police reporters assigned to keep tabs on LPDF activities had to acknowledge women's dedication to wartime service. One officer noted that since the beginning of the war, the LPDF had been "very active in the organization of war programs." He indicated that many members had become nurses at the war front and on the home front and some of them had been given commendations by the army. In addition, women had distributed 100,000 francs in salaries to poor women involved in its work assistance programs.[55] LPDF leaders were careful to encourage other members to make their Catholic identity known as they engaged in their nursing work. One LPDF speaker assured her audience that soldiers would feel "at home and comforted" by the "attentions of LPDF nurses" who made their Catholic identity known by wearing the daisy, the symbol of the LPDF.[56]

Protestant women actively engaged in wartime service as well. They worked as nurses, aided orphans, and sent care packages to soldiers.[57] Protestant journals frequently praised women who had received honors for their dedication to helping soldiers.[58] Some of these nurses died from their exposure to contagious diseases in military hospitals. In October 1917, *Le christianisme au XXe siècle* published a short article recognizing Eva Dürrleman, the sister of pastors André and Freddy Dürrleman and the head nurse for a team with the Union des Femmes de France. Eva received honors from the military health service for having shown "strong moral valor" and for devotion to her work.[59] That same year, both *Le christianisme au XXe siècle* and *Le huguenot* reported on the commendation accorded to Cécile Vallette, a nurse with the Armée d'Orient who had received the *Croix de Guerre avec Palme*. She died in service after being pricked accidentally by an infected needle while caring for a Russian soldier. Vallette had an uncle and a brother who were pastors.[60]

Like the Catholic and Protestant communities, the French Jewish press took great pains to publicize the honors individual women received, especially those who worked as nurses. Women's work in nonconfessional nursing organizations such as the Red Cross confirmed Jews' willingness to serve the entire nation and contribute to the union sacrée. In 1916, *Archives israélites* praised Blanche Lévy, a nurse who had received the *Croix de Guerre*. Lévy was commended for being "indifferent to danger, showing composure in the midst of two bombardments, watching over the security of the injured, remaining at the hospital during a bombardment, and placing herself at the disposition of the chief doctor."[61] Two months later, *Archives israélites* noted that both Mme Saint-Paul and Mlle Gimpel (first names not given) had received medals from the Ministry of War for their work as nurses.[62]

Many such notices recognizing the service of women nurses appeared over the course of the war. Hippolyte Prague, editor of *Archives israélites*, asserted that Jewish nurses expressed the "passion to do good" inherent in the "Jewish heart," and had developed a "sacred ministry" though their wartime work. He recognized the many nurses who, in caring for wounded soldiers, had themselves fallen on the "field of battle" in military hospitals, succumbing to illnesses contracted during their service. He proclaimed that these young Jewish women who belonged to the "best families" had "sacrificed themselves" in an effort to serve France and humanity. Prague's statements not only emphasized the dedication of Jewish women and thereby the Jewish community to France, but also valorized women's work in general. Using the language of religious devotion, Prague raised women's service as nurses to the level of soldiers. He emphasized that as Jews and as women they brought assistance to France and pride to the Jewish community.[63]

All three communities carefully chronicled their women's wartime service. Even women who did not work in specifically faith-based programs were recognized by their communities for their religious identities and their nonreligious social work. The goal was to instill pride in the community and reveal the community's solidarity with the nation. Praising women's service in both confessional and nonconfessional wartime programs allowed faith-based groups to bring the admirable work of their members to the attention of the public. Moreover, Françoise Thébaud has noted that not all women became nurses for patriotic reasons. Some hoped to find husbands and others liked the status attached to wearing a uniform. Those who joined the nursing corps to be fashionable quickly abandoned the "thankless work."[64]

The Catholic, Protestant, and Jewish press wished to demonstrate that their women joined nursing corps for the right reasons and remained until death if necessary. This helped place all three communities solidly within the wartime "moral discourse" by underscoring women's seriousness and their worthiness of the sacrifice of soldiers.

Conclusion

The union sacrée was most successful in uniting all French citizens in defense against the Germans. It also created a rhetoric that incorporated Catholicism, Protestantism, and Judaism as foundational aspects of the French nation and French identity. It brought to an end the years of religious unrest and church/state battles that had characterized the prewar years. The success Catholics, Protestants, and Jews had in using the union sacrée to shape France in the postwar era is less easily defined. Very few sources exist to indicate changes in people's attitudes toward each faith group. However, police reports suggest that Catholic women's wartime activities may have helped improve the relationship between Catholics and the French state. Reporters who monitored the activities of Catholic women's organizations commented on women's patriotism and their dedication to wartime work. In 1917 the Préfet of Paris wrote to the minister of the interior describing the attitudes of French Catholic women in response to a proposed international pacifist women's meeting in Switzerland. Although the reporter described French Catholic women as "reactionary," he also wrote that the ASF, LFF, and LPDF "have all declared themselves in favor of the struggle until a final victory and that they are absolutely opposed to any pacifist idea." All three groups rejected any invitation to the proposed peace conference.[65] In the aftermath of World War I, the relationship between French Catholics and the Third Republic improved markedly. Women were not the only cause of this improvement, but their wartime work provided an alternative focus to prewar anticlericalism.[66] This, of course, was not the massive return to the Church that Catholics had hoped for, but it does suggest women's potential importance in shaping the reputation of French Catholicism.

The situation for Protestants and Jews was mixed. Anti-Protestantism largely disappeared in the aftermath of World War I as Protestants became more accepted as French citizens by the rest of the nation. In that respect, the union sacrée does seem to have accomplished Protestants' goals. Women's wartime work undoubtedly played a part in this growing acceptance. This was not the case for Jews. Anti-Semitism continued to plague French society. Patrick Cabanel suggests that the influx of Jewish immigrants from Central and Eastern Europe into France in the interwar years exacerbated anti-Jewish feelings.[67] The continued presence of anti-Semitism validated the belief among Jews that they needed to remind others of the sacrifices men and women in their communities made for the nation.

The results of the war for women were also mixed, although historians generally agree that it produced no great leap forward for women's rights. The war did create many new, competing images of women. Women appeared as patriots who sent their men off to war while they managed homes and businesses alone. As wartime workers, women kept factories running in the absence of men. However, these images were countered by those depicting women as frivolous, coddled, and immoral beings who refused to recognize or appreciate the sacrifice of soldiers. As Mary Louise Roberts notes, soldiers gendered the division between home front and war front. The "male" battlefield was in opposition to the "female" home front. All women were expected to prove their devotion to the nation, and women of faith had to demonstrate their importance to multiple communities. For some soldiers returning on leave, "the relative comforts that women enjoyed at home seemed to throw into relief the hardships, sacrifices, and humiliations of trench life."[68] The wartime work religious women took on gave them an opportunity to prove their worth as women as well as citizens and members of their faith communities. As Marguerite de Witt-Schlumberger's study of pastors' wives indicates, women still committed to motherhood, but they also became heads of households, pastors, parish ministers, and community leaders.[69] The publicity religious communities gave to women's wartime work helped contribute to a positive portrayal of women of faith as public religious leaders, brave nurses, effective social aid workers, and determined patriots. Motherhood continued to be central to most women's identities during and after the war, especially Catholic women, but the war also opened up some new avenues for women's religious leadership.

In Marian Kaplan's study of German Jewish women in the nineteenth century, she notes that historians have moved away from discussing the separate spheres of men and women and toward thinking about how those spheres have connected.[70] The boundaries between public and private, the world of men and the world of women, have never been concrete. They have overlapped, shifted, and blurred at different points in time. World War I helped to blur the religious spheres of men and women further. The crisis produced by the First World War revealed the place women were coming to occupy as an important part of the public face and voice of their communities. Each community wanted to make sure that women's identities as members of their religious communities were not lost beneath their identities as women or French citizens. Religious communities believed they could prove their patriotism and integration by pointing to the sacrifices their women made for the nation.

Conclusion

The early twentieth century was a period of intense social and religious conflict in France. The French battled among themselves to determine the appropriate place for religion and women, and they fought the Germans to protect their status and national sovereignty. The religious conflicts France experienced in the late nineteenth and early twentieth centuries shattered France's religious identity as an unquestionably Catholic nation. The fissures created by church/state conflicts created an opportunity for Catholics, Protestants, and Jews to refashion a new religious identity favorable to their communities. The atmosphere of religious uncertainty encouraged each community to rethink the religious and social positions of women. It gave women unprecedented access to religious leadership positions. For each of these three groups, gendered religious traditions came to represent the values upon which they wished to build the nation as well as their own reputation within France. Women's faith-based work helped each community carve out a space for itself as France reconstructed its religious identity in the midst of church/state crises and trends toward secularization.

France is again in the midst of an identity crisis as it tries to integrate increasing numbers of non-European immigrants and people of recent immigrant descent into the nation. Debates about Muslim women's clothing and equality (or lack thereof) for women in Muslim communities have once again made women important symbols for their faith group. For many Europeans, Muslim women's decision to wear hijabs, burqas, or burkinis represents a perceived inability or refusal on the part of Muslim communities to integrate into European culture or to accept European values. France banned headscarves in public schools in 2004 and banned the wearing of burqas in most public places in 2010.[1] In December 2009, then-President Nicolas Sarkozy began holding town hall meetings across France about French national identity. He pitched these meetings as a way to "help clarify and reaffirm the nation's values in an age of mass immigration." Critics claimed the meetings were little more than a "ploy to win over right-wing voters." Hundreds of debates occurred across France posing questions about what it means to be French. At one such meeting in Nanterre, "the local mayor led a group of about 45 people in discussing French history, culture, and the importance of symbols like the flag."[2]

Tensions about Muslim women's attire have intensified in the wake of numerous terrorists attacks in the last few years. The summer of 2016 saw France embroiled in a heated debate about burkinis (full-body swimsuits often worn by conservative Muslim women) on French beaches. About thirty French municipalities made failed attempts to ban burkinis from their town's beaches. In August, the small city of Villeneuve-Loubet banned from swimming "anyone failing to wear correct attire respecting good morals and the principle of laïcité"—in sum, women wearing burkinis.[3] This ban, and others like it, were overturned by one of France's highest courts, but not before provoking both support and outrage around the world. The political right and a more authoritarian populism have profited from fears about immigration, Islam, and identity loss in France. Marine Le Pen, leader of France's far-right National Front Party, moved to the second round of voting in the presidential election in May 2017.

Women and religion are again at the heart of debates about French identity. In the late nineteenth and early twentieth centuries, the state believed that providing women with secular education was essential to preserving the Republic. Women, as teachers of morality in the home, held the key to turning sons and husbands into good republican voters, but only if they could be extracted from the power of the Catholic clergy. Similarly, religious communities saw women as defenders of the faith and transmitters of religious beliefs across generation. For both anticlericals and people of faith, women were critically important to France's future and the transformation of its culture. The rhetoric in the current debate about Muslim women is very similar.

The inflexible approach that France has taken to school head-scarves and burqas must be understood in the context of France's religious history in general. It is true that racism, xenophobia, and a fear of Islamic radicalism have played a part in encouraging contemporary France to view Islam as incompatible with French values. But when the French claim they are protecting secularism by preventing women from wearing certain clothing, they mean it. The French are genuinely skeptical about religion that needs to be practiced outside of the home or the place of worship. French Jews in the early twentieth century understood this. Part of Jews' efforts to integrate into France and prove their loyalty included minimizing public signs of their faith. France fought hard to separate the state from the Catholic Church. The French are reluctant to see new groups bring religion back into the public sphere through dress, special food accommodations in schools, or times throughout the day to pray.

The 2003 decision on the part of the French state to target Muslim girls wearing hijabs in an effort to protect laïcité was not a new policy. The French state made similar efforts to secularize Catholic women and girls in the 1880s. There is a long history in France of seeing women as both politically important and politically unreliable because of their stronger attachment to religion. France has traditionally accorded women the responsibility of teaching religion, morals, and the values of citizenship in the home. Women have been presented as the bearers of French culture; they educate children first. Republicans in the 1880s who created France's state-run, secular school system saw girls' education as central to breaking the power of priests over women and making them good republican mothers. Joan Scott argues that the headscarf debate in France shifted older concerns about women and religion onto Islam. Muslim girls had to be protected from the "supposed pressure from their fathers, brothers, and imams to wear headscarves" like Catholic girls in the past had to be protected from the antirepublican influence of priests.[4] Part of the reasoning behind forcing girls to remove their headscarves in schools is to train them in secular republican values that they can take home. The state takes them out from under the power of their "backward" religious families and puts them under the power of the "enlightened" Republic.

There are significant differences between France's current religious problems and their early-twentieth-century ones. The international radicalization of Islam and the specter of terrorism create a unique and more hostile environment for France's current religious conflicts. France's large Muslim community is relatively new. Much of it is poor and marginalized. Its members, especially young men, struggle to find a place for themselves in the French economy and French culture. Whether France's efforts to secularize its Muslim population by banning certain items of clothing are effective remains to be seen. So far, it does not seem to be working.

Despite the differences, there are certain elements of France's early twentieth century battles that might provide guidance for its current ones. Religious upheaval and its link with women's rights had two positive effects. First, they encouraged France's Catholic, Protestant, and Jewish communities to rethink traditional teachings about women and create more equal positions for women within religious institutions. Second, they helped to mobilize hundreds of thousands of women for religious and social work. Through their faith-based organizations, women engaged with the important social and religious questions of the day. They thought critically about their position within their communities and gradually challenged some religious teachings. Women pushed the limits of acceptable public action taught by religious leaders. Faith communities were forced to pay more attention to women's concerns. The confidence women gained through their religious work, even if it started out very conservative, helped accustom them to having a more equal place with men in society.

French Muslim women need an environment that encourages their participation in religious and national debates. Even if women choose conservative doctrines initially, speaking in public and engaging in public political and social action tend to have a liberalizing impact on entire communities. Encouraging women's religious action might also lead women to look for less conservative branches of Islam that are amenable to a more equal position for women. France has shown itself capable of building a religious foundation that incorporates a multiplicity of belief systems. It asks that religious communities show proof of their commitment to French values such as liberty, equality, and laïcité in return. The international climate of violence, fear, and political fearmongering creates special challenges for French Muslims and the rest of the nation. National religious identity is never static. It is fluid, malleable, and subject to change. Accepting Islam as a positive aspect of French religious identity will require compromises on the part of the Muslim community and the rest of France. Encouraging Muslim women to play a more prominent role in both national and community discussions could be a good first step in that direction.

Notes

Bibliography

Index

Notes

Introduction

1. Leila Ahmed argues that the interpretative nature of faith allows it to adapt to changing social conditions. Catholicism, Protestantism, and Judaism have all transformed in significant ways over the centuries of their existence. They live not only within sacred texts but also within the interpretations of those texts and the actions of people who practice them. See Leila Ahmed, *A Border Passage: From Cairo to America—A Woman's Journey* (New York: Farrar, Straus and Giroux, 1999).

2. Joan Wallach Scott, *The Politics of the Veil* (Princeton, NJ: Princeton Univ. Press, 2007), 15.

3. Comtesse de Keranflec'h-Kernezne, *Madame Chenu, 1861–1939* (Paris: Action Sociale de la Femme et le Livre Français, 1940), 10. For more information, see Sylvie Fayet-Scribe, *Associations féminines et catholicisme XIXe–XXe siècle* (Paris: Éditions Ouvrières, 1990), 93–97.

4. Steven Hause and Anne Kenney, "The Development of the Catholic Women's Suffrage Movement in France, 1896–1922," *Catholic Historical Review* 67, no. 1 (January 1981): 15–16.

5. Bruno Dumons, *Les dames de la Ligue des Femmes Françaises (1901–1914)* (Paris: Les Éditions du Cerf, 2006), 27.

6. Mme de Vélard, "Séance du vendredi matin," *Congrès de la Ligue Patriotique des Françaises à Lourdes, 6–10 Octobre 1910*, 76. Archives Action Catholique Générale Féminine Box H 172.

7. For a history of the LPDF, see Odile Sarti, *The Ligue Patriotique des Françaises, 1902–1933: A Feminine Response to the Secularization of French Society* (New York: Garland Publishing, 1992).

8. Patrick Cabanel, *Les protestants et la république de 1870 à nos jours* (Paris: Éditions Complexe, 2000), 19; Paula Hyman, *From Dreyfus to Vichy: The Remaking of French Jewry, 1906–1939* (New York: Columbia Univ. Press, 1979), 28.

9. André Encrevé, *Les protestantes en France de 1800 à nos jours* (Paris: Éditions Stock, 1985), 29. Encrevé also provides numbers of Protestants living in different

areas of France as well as numbers participating in France's various denominations. See chapter 1 of his book.

10. Nadia Malinovich, *French and Jewish: Culture and the Politics of Identity in Early Twentieth-Century France* (Liverpool: Liverpool Univ. Press, 2011), 3.

11. Paula Hyman, *The Emancipation of Jews of Alsace: Acculturation and Tradition in the Nineteenth Century* (New Haven, CT: Yale Univ. Press, 1984), 60–61.

12. "Notre histoire: Une fondatrice de l'action catholique feminine," Action Catholique des Femmes, accessed March 12, 2018, https://actioncatholiquedes femmes.org/notre-association/notre-histoire/.

13. Magali Della Sudda, "Les femmes catholiques à l'épreuve de la laïcité: La Ligue Patriotique des Françaises ou la première mobilization feminine de masse (1902–1914)," in *Politiques de la laïcité au XXe siècle*, ed. Patrick Weil (Paris: Presses Universitaires de France, 2007), 131–39.

14. Geneviève Poujol, *Un féminisme sous tutelle: Les protestantes françaises— 1810–1960* (Paris: Les Éditions de Paris, 2003), 237–38.

15. Poujol, *Un féminisme sous tutelle*, 265–66.

16. Céline Leglaive-Perani, "Les juifs français dans la lutte contre la traite des blanches (1880–1930)," *Archives juives* 44, no. 2 (2011): 63–65.

17. Della Sudda, "Les femmes catholiques à l'épreuve de la laïcité," 131–39.

18. Poujol, *Un féminisme sous tutelle*, 257.

19. Despite the fact that religion had become somewhat "feminized" over the course of the nineteenth century, James McMillan reminds us that many men continued to practice in their respective faiths and just because they did not practice the faith to the same extent as women does not necessarily mean they were hostile to religion. Many also stood out as leaders in movements such as the social Catholic and social Christianity movements as well as in organizations such as the Jewish Welfare Board and the Alliance Israélite Universelle. See James McMillan, "Religion and Gender in Modern France: Some Reflections," in *Religion, Society and Politics in France since 1789*, eds. Frank Tallett and Nicholas Atkin (London: Hambledon Press, 1991), 55–61.

20. Jean-Marie Mayeur and Madeleine Rebérioux, *The Third Republic from Its Origins to the Great War, 1871–1914*, trans. J. R. Foster (Cambridge: Cambridge Univ. Press, 1984), 101–6.

21. Ernst Renan, *Souvenirs d'enfance et de jeunesse*, in *Histoire religieuse de la France contemporaine, 1880–1930*, eds. Gerard Cholvy and Yves-Marie Hilaire (Toulouse: Éditions Privat, 1985), 171.

22. Charles Sowerwine, *France since 1870: Culture, Politics and Society* (New York: Palgrave, 2001), 44. He cites Ralph Gibson for some of his statistics.

23. Hugh McLeod, *Secularisation in Western Europe, 1848–1914* (London: Palgrave Macmillan, 2000), 126. Although more women than men attended mass and

received communion, the numbers of women regularly performing these duties was not always high either. McLeod found that in 1898 only 15 percent of women in the diocese of Chartres received communion during Easter.

24. Gerard Cholvy and Yves-Marie Hilaire, *Histoire religieuse de la France contemporaine, 1880–1930* (Toulouse: Éditions Privat, 1986), 173. Cholvy and Hilaire provide a very detailed description of religious trends in departments throughout France.

25. For a detailed discussion of the division that occurred among liberal and conservative Protestants in the late nineteenth century, see André Encrevé, *L'expérience et la foi: Pensée et vie religieuse des Huguenots au XIXe siècle* (Geneva: Labor et Fides, 2001), ch. 3.

26. Some French Jews hoped that the arrival of more religious Eastern European immigrants after 1880 might raise the level of religiosity of the entire community. See Nancy Green, "The Contradictions of Acculturation: Immigrant Oratories and Yiddish Union Sections in Paris before World War I," in *The Jews in Modern France*, eds. Frances Malino and Bernard Wasserstein (Hanover, London: Univ. Press of New England, 1985), 57.

27. McLeod, *Secularisation in Western Europe*, 142.

28. David Landes, "Two Cheers for Emancipation," in *The Jews in Modern France*, eds. Frances Malino and Bernard Wasserstein (Hanover, London: Univ. Press of New England, 1985), 291; Hyman, *From Dreyfus to Vichy*, 40–42. Hyman argues that the Jewish community faced particular problems because the community claimed religion as "the sole legitimate basis of Jewish identity." It had a difficult time countering the appeal of free thought to many nonobservant Jews. Jewish institutions, even philanthropic ones, had a difficult time attracting people who were either "indifferent to Judaism" or who saw Judaism as a liability to integration into French society. Hyman argues that "the situation of mass indifference which confronted the religious leadership of French Jewry stimulated vain attempts at creative religious reform within the framework of traditional Jewish law. Proposals were considered with a view to lowering the number of persons legally required for a *minyan* (the quorum for public prayer) and to counting women as eligible for at least part of that quorum. Equally reflective of the religious status of French Jewry was the 1911 decision of the Association of French Rabbis to admit uncircumcised male children to courses of religious instruction (while denying them authorization for the celebration of the *bar-mitzvah*)."

29. Bronwyn Winter, *Hijab & the Republic: Uncovering the French Headscarf Debate* (Syracuse, NY: Syracuse Univ. Press, 2009), 55.

30. Winter, *Hijab & the Republic*, 70.

31. Sowerwine, *France since 1870*, 41.

32. Cholvy and Hilaire, *Histoire religieuse*, 22. For an extended discussion of the development of laïcité in France, see Jean Baubérot, *Histoire de la laïcité en France*

(Paris: Presses Universitaires de France, 2000); Paul Airiau, *Cent ans de laïcité françaises, 1905–2005* (Paris: Presses de la Renaissance, 2005).

33. Sowerwine, *France since 1870*, 43–44.

34. Jules Ferry, speech at the Salle Molière, Apr. 10, 1870, cited in Winter, *Hijab & the Republic*, 30.

35. Jules Ferry, quoted in Mayeur and Rebérioux, *The Third Republic*, 89.

36. Ibid.

37. James McMillan, *Housewife or Harlot: The Place of Women in French Society, 1870–1940* (New York: St. Martin's Press, 1981), 50.

38. Maurice Larkin, *L'église et l'état en France: 1905: La crise de la séparation* (Toulouse: Éditions Privat, 2004), 25–26.

39. Carol Harrison, *Romantic Catholics: France's Postrevolutionary Generation in Search of a Modern Faith* (Ithaca, NY: Cornell Univ. Press, 2014), 3.

40. Stephen Schloesser, *Jazz Age Catholicism: Mystic Modernism in Postwar Paris, 1919–1933* (Toronto: Univ. of Toronto Press, 2005), 5.

41. Harrison, *Romantic Catholics*, 296.

42. Thomas Kselman, *Death and the Afterlife in Modern France* (Princeton, NJ: Princeton Univ. Press, 1993).

43. Thomas Kselman, "The Dechristianisation of Death in Modern France," in *The Decline of Christendom in Western Europe*, eds. Hugh McLeod and Werner Ustorf (Cambridge: Cambridge Univ. Press, 2003), 145.

44. Lynn Sharp, *Secular Spirituality: Reincarnation and Spiritism in Nineteenth-Century France* (Lanham, MD: Lexington Books, 2006), ch. 5.

45. Sarah Curtis, *Civilizing Habits: Women Missionaries and the Revival of French Empire* (Oxford: Oxford Univ. Press, 2010), 6.

46. Curtis, *Civilizing Habits*, 2.

47. Ralph Gibson, *A Social History of French Catholicism, 1789–1914* (London, New York: Routledge, 1989).

48. Rebecca Rogers, "Retrograde or Modern? Unveiling the Teaching Nun in Nineteenth-Century France," *Social History* 23, no. 2 (May 1998): 146–48. In 1878, 135,000 women were part of a religious order, and teaching orders in particular became popular after the 1850 Falloux Law, which allowed "religious women to open schools without a teaching diploma."

49. Ruth Harris, *Lourdes: Body and Spirit in the Secular Age* (New York: Viking, 1999), 12.

50. Christopher Clark, "The New Catholicism and the European Culture Wars," in *Culture Wars: Secular-Catholic Conflict in Nineteenth-Century Europe*, eds. Christopher Clark and Wolfram Kaiser (Cambridge: Cambridge Univ. Press, 2003), 11. Jacqueline LaLouette tackles questions about whether the 1905 separation law made France secular. Some have argued that secularization happened before the

1905 law, since the French state had equally recognized Catholicism, Protestant-ism, and Judaism since the French Revolution. LaLouette notes that even after the separation, a relationship continued to remain between church and state. It did not eliminate contact between the government and religious institutions; it simply regulated that contact in different ways. See Jacqueline LaLouette, *La séparation des églises et de l'état: Genèse et dévelopment d'une idée (1789–1905)* (Paris: Éditions du Seuil, 2005), 11–16.

51. Claude Langlois, *Le catholicisme au feminin: Les congregations françaises à supérieure générale au XIXe siècle* (Paris: Les Éditions du Cerf, 1984), 14.

52. Ralph Gibson, "Le catholicisme et les femmes en France au XIXe siècle," *Revue d'histoire de l'église de France* 78, no. 202 (1993), 63–67.

53. Caroline Ford, *Divided Houses: Religion and Gender in Modern France* (Ithaca, NY: Cornell Univ. Press, 2005), 6.

54. Harris, *Lourdes*, 18.

55. Patrick Pasture, "Beyond the Feminization Thesis: Gendering the History of Christianity in the Nineteenth and Twentieth Centuries," in *Beyond the Feminization Thesis: Gender and Christianity in Modern Europe*, eds. Patrick Pasture et al. (Leuven: Leuven Univ. Press, 2012), 9–10, 31.

56. Bernhard Schneider, "The Catholic Poor Relief Discourse and the Feminization of the Caritas in Early Nineteenth-Century Germany," in *Beyond the Feminization Thesis: Gender and Christianity in Modern Europe*, eds. Patrick Pasture et al. (Leuven: Leuven Univ. Press, 2012), 35–55.

57. Michael O'Sullivan, "A Feminized Church?: German Catholic Women, Piety, and Domesticity, 1918–1938," in *Beyond the Feminization Thesis: Gender and Christianity in Modern Europe*, eds. Patrick Pasture et al. (Leuven: Leuven Univ. Press, 2012), 191–211.

58. Ford, *Divided Houses*, 6.

59. See Pasture et al., *Beyond the Feminization Thesis: Gender and Christianity in Modern Europe* (Leuven: Leuven Univ. Press, 2012).

60. Ben-Ammi, "La question du 'minyan,'" *L'univers israélite* 63, no. 47 (August 7, 1908): 645–49.

61. Anthony Steinhoff, "A Feminized Church? The Campaign for Women's Suffrage in Alsace-Lorraine's Protestant Churches, 1907–1914," *Central European History* 38, no. 2 (June 2005): 220–21.

62. Matthieu Bréjon de Lavergnée, *Histoire des filles de la charité (XVIIe–XVIIIe siècle)* (Paris: Fayard, 2011), 23. By the early nineteenth century, the Société de Saint-Vincent-de-Paul began drawing devout Catholics into the modern age by employing more transparent modes of action and operating with less secrecy. See Matthieu Brejon de Lavergnée, *La Société de Saint-Vincent-de-Paul au XIXe siècle: Un fleuron du catholicisme sociale* (Paris: Cerf, 2008), 602.

63. Claude Langlois, "Le catholicisme au féminin," *Archives de sciences sociales des religiones* 57, no. 1 (January–March 1984): 37–49.

64. Rogers, "Retrograde or Modern?" 147.

65. Curtis, *Civilizing Habits*, 3.

66. Langlois, "Le catholicisme au féminin," 29–53. For a further discussion about the feminization of the Catholic Church in the nineteenth century and reasons for this feminization, see Gibson, "Le catholicisme et les femmes," 63–93.

67. Hazel Mills, "Negotiating the Divide: Women, Philanthropy and the 'Public Sphere' in Nineteenth-Century France," in *Religion, Society and Politics in France since 1789*, eds. Frank Tallett and Nicholas Atkin (London: Hambledon Press, 1991), 48–52.

68. Sarah Curtis, "Charitable Ladies: Gender, Class and Religion in Mid-Nineteenth Century Paris," *Past & Present* 177, no. 1 (November 2002): 122–25, 156.

69. Marie-Emmanuelle Chessel, *Consommateurs engagés à la Belle Époque: La ligue sociale d'acheteurs* (Paris: Presses de Sciences Po, 2012), 291–92.

70. Anne Cova, *Au service de l'église, de la patrie et de la famille: Femmes catholiques et maternité sous la IIIe république* (Paris: L'Harmattan, 2000), 207–8.

71. Magali Della Sudda, "La politique malgre elles: Mobilisations féminines catholiques en France et en Italie (1900–1914)," *Revue française de science politique* 60, no. 1 (2010): 57.

72. Dumons, *Les dames de la Ligue des Femmes Françaises*, 26–28.

73. Dumons reinforces the notion that secularization and religious revival often go hand in hand. His work makes clear that Catholic women's mass mobilization, and their use of "modern tools" of political participation, was directly linked to the secular political policies of the French Third Republic. See Bruno Dumons, "Resistances des ligues féminines catholiques a l'idee laique," in *Le pouvoir du genre: Laïcités et religions, 1905–2005*, ed. Florence Rochefort (Toulouse: Presses Universitaires du Mirail, 2008), 96–97. Odile Sarti, in her study of the Ligue Patriotique des Françaises, argues that the LPDF "taught Catholic women that their religion was not solely a private matter of prayer and sacrament," and taught them to lead and manage others. Steven Hause has described the development of a suffrage movement among Catholic women in the years leading up to World War I. See Sarti, *The Ligue Patriotique des Françaises*, ix; Hause, "The Development of the Catholic Women's Suffrage Movement," 11–30.

74. Florence Rochefort, "Contrecarrer ou interroger les religions," in *Le siècle des féminismes*, eds. Elaine Gubin et al. (Paris: Éditions de l'Atelier, 2004), 348.

75. Florence Rochefort, "Féminisme et protestantisme au XIXe siècle, première rencontres, 1830–1900," *Bulletin de la Société de l'Histoire du Protestantisme* 146 (January–March 2000): 69–87.

76. Yolande Cohen, "Protestant and Jewish Philanthropies in France: The Conseil National des Femmes Françaises, (1901–1939)," *French Politics, Culture and Society* 36, no. 3 (2018): 74–76.

77. Florence Rochefort, "Ambivalences laïques et critiques féministes," in *Le pouvoir du genre: Laïcités et religions, 1905–2005*, ed. Florence Rochefort (Toulouse: Presses Universitaires du Mirail, 2007), 3.

78. Rita Felski, *The Gender of Modernity* (Cambridge, MA: Harvard Univ. Press, 1995), 11. See also Christopher Clark's discussion of modernity in the context of nineteenth-century culture wars between Catholics and liberals: Clark, "The New Catholicism," 11–47.

79. Astradur Eysteinsson, *The Concept of Modernism* (Ithaca, NY: Cornell Univ. Press, 1990), cited in Schloesser, *Jazz Age Catholicism*, 11.

80. Clark, "The New Catholicism," 12–13, 45.

81. Jay Berkovitz, "Ritual and Emancipation: A Reassessment of Cultural Modernization in France," *Historical Reflections* 32, no. 1 (Winter 2006): 11.

82. Langlois, *Le catholicisme au féminin*, 642.

83. Della Sudda, "Les femmes catholiques," 135–38.

84. Chessel, *Consommateurs engagés à la Belle Époque*, 297.

85. Schloesser, *Jazz Age Catholicism*, 4.

86. Other writers have linked modernity with "modern science and technology, a longing for freedom, the emergence of the masses on the historical stage . . . and globalization." K. Jaspers, cited by Yves Lambert, "New Christianity, Indifference and Diffused Spirituality," in *The Decline of Christendom in Western Europe, 1750–2000*, eds. Hugh McLeod and Werner Ustorf (Cambridge: Cambridge Univ. Press, 2003), 64.

87. Julie Kalman, *Orientalizing the Jew: Religion, Culture and Imperialism in Nineteenth Century France* (Bloomington: Indiana Univ. Press, 2017), 2–6.

1. Religious Identity and the Challenge of Feminism

1. Jane Misme, "Émancipatrices: Mlle Sarah Monod," *Le figaro* (July 7, 1899): 2.

2. By the woman question, I mean the place of women in society broadly. That includes suffrage, education, employment opportunities, women's rights as wives and mothers, and their social engagement.

3. Sarti, *The Ligue Patriotique des Françaises*, 32.

4. Mme de Vélard, "Séance du vendredi matin," Congrès de la Ligue Patriotique des Françaises à Lourdes, 6–10 Octobre 1910, 76. Archives Action Catholique Générale Féminine Box H 172. By 1911, the UFSF had only 2,600 members. See Steven Hause and Anne Kenney, *Women's Suffrage and Social Politics in the French Third Republic* (Princeton, NJ: Princeton Univ. Press, 1984), 138.

5. Patrick Cabanel, *Juifs et protestants en France, les affinités électives XVIe–XXIe siècle* (Paris: Fayard, 2004), 112.

6. Emile Lévy, *La femme juive: Deux sermons* (Imprimerie E. Seitz, 1906), 10–14.

7. Hause and Kenney, *Women's Suffrage and Social Politics*, 9–10.

8. For detailed explanations, see Hause and Kenney, *Women's Suffrage and Social Politics*; Karen Offen, *European Feminisms, 1700–1950* (Stanford, CA: Stanford Univ. Press, 2000); Laurence Klejman and Florence Rochefort, *L'égalité en marche: Le féminisme sous la Troisième République* (Paris: Press de la Fondation Nationale des Sciences Politiques, 1989).

9. Evelyne Diebolt, "Women and Philanthropy in France: From the Sixteenth to the Twentieth Centuries," in *Women, Philanthropy, and Civil Society*, ed. Kathleen D. McCarthy (Bloomington: Indiana Univ. Press, 2001), 44–45.

10. Karen Offen, "Defining Feminism: A Comparative Historical Approach," *Signs: Journal of Women in Contemporary Culture and Society* 14, no. 1 (1988): 134–36, 147.

11. Klejman and Rochefort, *L'égalité en marche*, 24–27. James McMillan also notes that for many French feminists, reforming the Napoleonic Code took precedence over demanding the right to vote. See James McMillan, *France and Women, 1789–1914* (London, New York: Routledge, 2000), 192–95.

12. Archives privées de Mariel Brunhes-Delamarre, lettre d'Adèle Moreau du 9 octobre 1900 à Henriette Brunhes. Cited in Cova, *Au service de l'église*, 65–67.

13. Steven Hause provides membership numbers for the most prominent moderate, militant, and Catholic women's rights organizations. See Hause and Kenney, *Women's Suffrage and Social Politics*, Table 5.

14. Christine Bard, *Les filles de Marianne: Histoire des féminismes 1914–1940* (Paris: Fayard, 1995), 10–11.

15. Cohen, "Protestant and Jewish Philanthropies in France," 79–80.

16. Bard, *Les filles de Marianne*, 28–33. Bard provides a good overview of most of the feminist organizations that formed in the years leading up to the war.

17. McMillan, *Housewife or Harlot*, 26–27.

18. McMillan, 46–58.

19. Mary Louise Roberts, *Disruptive Acts: The New Woman in Fin-de-Siècle France* (Chicago: Univ. of Chicago Press, 2005), 2–8.

20. Lynn Abrams, *The Making of Modern Woman* (London: Pearson Education, 2002), 3.

21. Mayeur and Rebérioux, *The Third Republic*, 101–6. Social Catholicism was first introduced after the Franco-Prussian War with the work of Albert de Mun, who wanted to bring Catholicism to workers while at the same time improving their material conditions. Social Catholicism developed in the 1880s and 1890s, encouraged by the Rerum Novarum and later by the work of Frédéric Le Play, who

encouraged the study of social problems and called on "authorities" to develop solutions to those problems. Christian democracy, which was headed largely by priests, rejected the notion of a hierarchical society, recognized people's desire to have a voice, and aimed to find solutions to social problems. It also rallied to the Republic. Mayeur and Rebérioux discuss both movements in chapter 6. The policies of Leo XIII and the development of Christian democracy and Social Catholicism in the 1890s helped bring some people back to the faith, but Catholics nonetheless saw irreligion as a serious and growing problem in the years leading up to the war.

22. "Audience pontificale accordée à l'Union des Femmes Catholique d'Italie, à la Ligue des Femmes Françaises, et à la Ligue Patriotique des Françaises," *Echo de la Ligue Patriotique des Françaises* 7, no. 78 (May 15, 1909): 2–3.

23. Archives privées de Mariel Brunhes-Delamarre, lettre d'Adèle Moreau du 9 octobre 1900 à Henriette Brunhes. Cited in Cova, *Au service de l'église*, 65–67.

24. Emile Ollivier, "Le féminisme," *Bulletin de l'Action Sociale de la Femme* 1, no. 10 (January 10, 1903): 215–25.

25. M. M., "Discussion sur le vote des femmes au cercle catholique de dames," *Bulletin du Devoir des Femmes Françaises* 8 (August 1906): 288–89.

26. Della Sudda, "Les femmes catholiques," 137.

27. Anatole Le Roy-Beaulieu, "Conférence: De la liberté de l'enseignement pour les mères de famille," *Bulletin de l'Action Sociale de la Femme* 2, no. 3 (April 10, 1903): 331–45.

28. Hause and Kenney, "The Development of the Catholic Women's Suffrage Movement," 25–30.

29. Rochefort, "Féminisme et protestantisme," 69–72.

30. Hélène du Pasquier, "De vraies françaises!," *Journal de la Jeune Fille* (July 1914): 167–73. She is referring to the decision by most Protestant churches to grant women the right to vote in church elections by 1906.

31. Wilfred Monod, "Masculin et féminin," Discours prononcé au musée social, à l'assemblée annuelle de la ligue d'électeurs pour le suffrage des femmes, le 11 février, sous la présidence de M. Ferdinand Buisson (Epinal: Imprimerie Nouvelle, s.d.), 1–8. He mentions the sinking of the Titanic in 1912 and he cites a number of texts dated 1902–6, so it is likely that he gave this speech around 1912 or 1913.

32. Lévy, *La femme juive*, 10–14.

33. R. M., "La justice et le féminisme," *L'univers israélite* 64, no. 48 (August 13, 1909): 677–82.

34. "Audience pontificale accordée à l'Union des Femmes Catholique d'Italie, à la Ligue des Femmes Françaises, et à la Ligue Patriotique des Françaises," *Echo de la Ligue Patriotique des Françaises* 7, no. 78 (May 15, 1909): 2–3.

35. J. B. Piolet, "Renseignements pratiques: L'Action Sociale de la Femme," *Bulletin de l'Action Sociale de la Femme* 1, no. 7 (October 10, 1902): 159.

36. Philip Nord, *The Republican Moment: Struggles for Democracy in Nineteenth-Century France* (Cambridge, MA: Harvard Univ. Press, 1995).

37. Jean-Marie Mayeur and Madeleine Rebérioux have noted that by the time of the 1902 parliamentary elections, the nature and maybe the existence of the Republic seemed to be at stake against this new right-wing nationalist movement that was antirepublican and antiparliamentarian. Mayeur and Rebérioux, *The Third Republic*, 220. See also Peter Davies, *The Extreme Right in France, 1789 to the Present: From de Maistre to Le Pen* (London: Routledge, 2002), 55–56.

38. The efforts of the Third Republic to secularize the state and to separate politics from religion offered Protestants and Jews an opportunity to secure their place in the nation as equal citizens. For Protestants and Jews, laïcité meant the "conquest of . . . public space for those who were not part of the 'natural' religion of France." See Cabanel, *Juifs et protestants en France*, 112.

39. Wilfred Monod, "Masculin et féminin," 1–8.

40. Louis Lafon, "Le vote des femmes," *Evangile et liberté: La vie nouvelle et le protestant unis* 29, no. 22 (May 30, 1914): 193–94.

41. Gabrielle Lipman, "Le féminisme et le judaïsme," *L'univers israélite* 64, no. 2 (September 25, 1908): 52–54.

42. Emile Cahen, "À l'étranger comme en France," *Archives israélites* 77, no. 17 (April 27, 1916): 66.

43. Pierre Birnbaum, *Jewish Destinies: Citizenship, State, and Community in Modern France*, trans. Arthur Goldhammer (New York: Hill and Wang, 2000), 3–4.

44. Hause and Kenney, "The Development of the Catholic Women's Suffrage Movement," 15.

45. Cholvy and Hilaire, *Histoire religieuse*, 156.

46. For more information about Catholic women's international work, see Emily Machen, "French Women and the Global Fight for Faith: Catholic International Religious Outreach in Turn-of-the-Century France," *Catholic Historical Review* 100, no. 2 (Spring 2014): 292–318.

47. Keranflec'h-Kernezne, *Madame Chenu, 1861–1939*, 25.

48. Mme Gautier-Lacaze, "Rapport sur le Secrétariat International de l'Action Sociale de la Femme," *Bulletin de l'Action Sociale de la Femme* 9, no. 6 (June 1910): 256.

49. Monod, "Masculin et féminin," 1–8. Monod discusses Buisson's feminist positions at this conference.

50. French Protestants confronted violence at many points in their history in France. They wished to carve out a space for their faith as part of the foundation of the Republic. Even in the nineteenth century, when Protestants gradually received greater acceptance in society, the Restoration, the Second Empire, and the Moral Order showed an "evident sympathy for Catholicism" and increased the obstacles for Protestants to freely practice their faith and evangelize. Protestants' "historic

experience . . . led [them] to rally massively to the secular, republican" Third Republic. Their suspicion toward any alliance between politics and Catholicism contributed to their "passionate choice in favor of anticlericalism and secularism." The same was true for Jews. See Cabanel, *Les protestants et la république*, 30.

51. Paula Hyman, "Gender and the Shaping of Modern Jewish Identities," *Jewish Social Studies* 8, nos. 2–3 (Winter/Spring 2002): 155.

52. Gabrielle Lipman, "Le féminisme et le judaïsme," *L'univers israélite* 64, no. 2 (September 25, 1908): 52–54.

53. Malinovich, *French and Jewish*, 3.

54. Michel Winock, *Nationalism, Anti-Semitism, and Fascism in France* (Stanford, CA: Stanford Univ. Press, 1998), 85–93.

55. For a history of Jews in Modern France, see Birnbaum, *Jewish Destinies*; Vicky Caron, *Between France and Germany: The Jews of Alsace-Lorraine, 1871–1918* (Stanford, CA: Stanford Univ. Press, 1988); Michael Graetz, *The Jews in Nineteenth-Century France: From the French Revolution to the Alliance Israelite Universelle* (Stanford, CA: Stanford Univ. Press, 1996); Hyman, *From Dreyfus to Vichy*; Paula Hyman, *The Jews of Modern France* (Berkeley: Univ. of California Press, 1998); Frances Malino and Bernard Wasserstein, eds, *The Jews in Modern France* (Hanover: Univ. Press of New England, 1985); Bèatrice Philippe, *Les juifs à Paris à la Belle Epoque* (Paris: Albin Michel, 1992). For information on Catholics and anti-Semitism, see Pierre Pierrard, *Juifs et catholiques français: de Drumont à Jules Isaac (1886–1945)* (Paris: Fayard, 1970).

56. Hyman, "Gender and the Shaping of Modern Jewish Identities," 155.

57. L. Suffète, "Le féminisme à l'institut," *L'univers israélite* 66, no. 16 (December 30, 1910): 485–90.

58. Rochefort, "Féminisme et protestantisme," 71.

59. M. M. Déchelette, "Renseignements pratiques l'Action Sociale de la Femme—But de l'œuvre," *Bulletin de l'Action Sociale de la Femme* 1, no. 1 (April 10, 1902): 18.

60. Elsia Sabatier, *Madame Jules Siegfried, 1848–1922* (Privas: Imprimerie Loubarie et Fils, s.d. [1924?]), 33–41.

2. The Development of Women's "Ministries" in France

1. Lévy, *La femme juive*, 3–4.

2. Caroline Ford has studied the "feminization" of Catholicism in nineteenth-century France. Her work tries to define what the "feminization" of religion actually means. She argues that it was "a reflection of a perceived rejection of Catholicism by men, which threw women's religiosity into sharp relief." See Ford, *Divided Houses*, 6.

3. McLeod, *Secularisation in Western Europe*, 62.

4. Paulin, Évêque de Marseille, "Évêché de Marseille," *Echo de la Ligue Patriotique des Françaises* 2, no. 14 (February 1904): 297–98.

5. Mlle de Noaillat, "Rapport sur l'apostolat des dizainières," *Congrès de la Ligue Patriotique des Françaises* (1909), 216–23. A *dizainières* was a woman in charge of ten others who worked as an apostle and used various means to strengthen the Ligue and evangelize (Sarti, 171, cited *Echo*, June 1921, 5–6).

6. Un Anduzien, "L'église d'Anduze aujourd'hui," *Le Huguenot: Journal mensuel des églises réformées des cévennes et du sud-est* 17, no. 7 (June 21, 1902): 64. Despite men's indifference to the practice of their faith, the author suggests that men were ready, as their ancestors had been, to defend their temple and their religion if it were attacked. Despite its drop in numbers, Anduze possessed a number of charitable establishments such as the Asile Bon-Secours, a home for the elderly, an orphanage for young girls, and a crèche for small children. The church also had chapters of the Unions Chrétiennes de Jeunes Gens et de Jeunes Filles. Likewise, individual charity continued to be strong despite the drop in the population, meaning the church was able to fund all of its programs and create new ones. Since the church was composed primarily of women, women most assuredly played a large role in these works. The author concludes that while the number of faithful and lively Christians was small, "a little leaven could leaven the whole cake."

7. Ben-Ammi, "La question du 'minyan,'" *L'univers israélite* 63, no. 47 (August 7, 1908): 645–49.

8. Pierre Pierrard argues that although Catholics were reactionary in many of their political and social positions, socialists and Freemasons who expressed hostility to the Church and drew many members did challenge the position of the Church in France. See Pierre Pierrard, *Un siècle de l'église de France, 1900–2000* (Paris: Desclée de Brouwer, 2000). Other historians, such as André Encrevé, have argued that Catholics' determination to blame a Judeo-Mason plot for secularization resulted from laziness and a refusal to "reflect on its own errors." See Encrevé, *Les protestants en France*, 203.

9. *Le devoir des femmes françaises par l'une d'elles* (Paris: M. J. Caplain, 1902), 6, 27–31.

10. Letter from Mme de Cuverville to Mme de Laubier, Paris, le 21 décembre 1902. Archives Action Catholique Générale Féminine, Box H 565—Folder: 1902—Sub-folder: Documents relatifs aux Conseils et Comités de la Ligue des Femmes Françaises, Comité de Paris, Period allant d'octobre 1901–juin 1902.

11. Noaillat, "Rapport sur l'apostolat des dizainières," 216–17. Archives Nationales de France F7 13215.

12. "Retraites fermées," *Echo de la Ligue Patriotique des Françaises* 7, no. 75 (February 15, 1909): 4–5. In 1905, Rennes hosted two retreats with sixty-two participants from nineteen communes, and in 1908, Saint-Servain held a retreat with 114 participants from twenty-three communes. "Retraite des dames catéchistes," *Bulletin des œuvres catholiques de femmes dans le diocèses de Viviers; Œuvre d'adoration en union*

avec Montmartre; Œuvre des catéchismes: Œuvre catholique de la protection de la jeune fille 2, no. 14 (November 1908): 33–34. In 1909, the Ligue organized eight such retreats that, according to a report by the Vicomtesse de Vélard, met with considerable success. One workers' retreat managed to draw 250–300 participants. See "Rapport de la Vtesse de Vélard," *Congrès de la Ligue Patriotique des Françaises* (1909), 24–30. Archives Nationales de France F7 13215.

13. "Nouvelles de la Ligue," *Echo de la Ligue Patriotique des Françaises* 6, no. 69 (August 15, 1908): 8–11.

14. "La Ligue Patriotique des Françaises à Lourdes," *La croix* (July 18, 1916): 2.

15. Harris, *Lourdes*, 17.

16. This is a quote from an uncited source, not the words of Babut himself.

17. Charles Babut, preface to Marie Merle Bianquis, *La vocation de la femme d'après la bible: Etudes bibliques dédiées aux Unions Chrétiennes de Jeunes Filles* (Paris: Librairie Fischbacher, 1903), 5–9.

18. M. Anne, évangéliste laïque à Sous-le-Bois, "La vocation d'évangéliste est-elle aussi une vocation de femmes: Une réponse par des faits," *Journal de l'Évangélisation* 17, no. 2 (February 15, 1909): 36–40.

19. Lévy, *La femme juive*, 6–8, 16. For a further example, see Louis Lévy, "Sermons de M. J.-H. Dreyfuss," *L'univers israélite* 64, no. 10 (November 20, 1908): 306.

20. Gabrielle Bauer, "La mission de la femme juive," *Foi et réveil: Revue trimestrielle de la doctrine et de la vie juives* 1 (May 1913): 67–71.

21. "Rapport de la Vtesse de Vélard," *Congrès de la Ligue Patriotique des Françaises* (1909), 24–30. Archives Nationales de France F7 13215.

22. Le Parisien, "Dames catéchistes," *Echo de la Ligue Patriotique des Françaises* 7, no. 78 (May 15, 1909): 8.

23. Mlle de Noaillat, "Rapport sur l'apostolat des dizainières," *Congrès de la Ligue Patriotique des Françaises* (1909), 216–23. Archives Nationales de France F7 13215.

24. Police Report—Paris, December 28, 1904. Archives de la Préfecture de Police, Paris Box BA 902—Folder: BA 902.

25. *Rome et la Ligue Patriotique des Françaises, 1908* (Paris: Ligue Patriotique des Françaises, 1908), 22–24.

26. See Langlois, *Le catholicisme au féminin*. Nineteenth-century women's leadership could take a variety of forms. Suzanne Desan found that during the French Revolution, "women created power and identity and carved out a sphere of cultural influence as the dominant leaders of goal-oriented religious riots." See Suzanne Desan, *Reclaiming the Sacred: Lay Religion and Popular Politics in Revolutionary France* (Ithaca, NY: Cornell Univ. Press, 1990), 167.

27. "Menus propos: L'évangile de la femme," *L'église libre* 39, no. 31 (August 2, 1907): 242.

28. E. Borel-Brun, "Christ et la femme," *Journal de la jeune fille* (October 1905): 256–57.

29. Marthe Rohr, "Reine du foyer," *Journal de la jeune fille* (June 1914): 137–43.

30. Charles Babut, preface to Bianquis, *La vocation de la femme d'après la bible*, 5–9.

31. "Conférences Pastorales générales," *Le christianisme au XX siècle: Journal de l'église réformée de France* 33, no. 17 (April 21, 1904): 130.

32. R. T., "Le féminisme et le judaïsme," *L'univers israelite* 56, no. 48 (August 16, 1901): 677–80.

33. Mathieu Wolff, "Encore à l'occasion de Hanoucca," *L'univers israélite* 61, no. 15 (December 29, 1905): 471–73.

34. "Association des rabbins français," *L'univers israélite* 63, no. 45 (July 24, 1908): 587–89.

35. Ben-Ammi, "La question du 'minyan,'" *L'univers israélite* 63, no. 47 (August 7, 1908): 645–49.

36. "Rapport de Monsieur Lehmann, 1er Partie," Archives de la Consistoire Israélite de Paris—Dossier 1A 9-12—Dossier Anciennement coté 1A4—Chemise 9: Organisation—F: Réforme du Minyan Rapport Lehmann, 1908–1909—Folder: Rapport de Monsieur Lehmann 1 et 2 Partie, 2–12.

37. Following this decision, circumstantial evidence suggests that some rabbis allowed women to participate in or lowered the number of people needed for the minyan. In 1914, H. Prague commented that synagogues in the provinces could not unite even seven faithful members and prayers had to be said with a congregation that barely reached half a dozen, even counting women. Evidently, some rabbis continued to have difficulty gathering a quorum even if they were willing to include women. See H. Prague, "L'assemblée consistoriale: Notes et impressions," *Archives israélites* 75, no. 23 (June 4, 1914): 181–82.

38. "Nouvelles diverses," *Archives israélites* 29 (July 21, 1921): 115.

39. "Nouvelles diverses," *Archives israélites* 37 (September 15, 1921): 148; "Nouvelles diverses," *Archives israélites* 2 (January 12, 1928): 8.

40. O. Douen, *Histoire de la société biblique protestante de Paris* (Paris: Agence de la Société Biblique Protestant, 1868), 323–29. Archives Nationale de la France (F19 19170); E. Sagnol, "Chronique des églises: Marseille," *Echo de la vérité: Organe des église évangéliques, dites baptistes* 23, no. 13 (July 2, 1901): 181. A semipublic ministry for women was not entirely new to the Protestant community. Protestant women had a long tradition of engaging in activities that required them to teach the Bible, and Protestantism's emphasis on each individual's responsibility to read the Bible made women theologically educated enough to engage in the work of proselytization. Protestant women had always been given a more important, if limited, role in receiving religious education and in taking part in evangelization than their

Catholic counterparts. In the 1830s, Protestant women from leading Protestant families such as Mme Frédéric Monod, Mme Jules Mallet, and Mme la duchesse de Broglie formed a women's section for the Société Biblique Protestant de Paris. The Société Biblique Auxiliaire des Dames de Paris sent women to visit the homes of Protestant families to encourage religious zeal. The women distributed Bibles and asked for donations for religious causes. By 1863, the women involved in this organization had distributed 5,577 Bibles, and in 1854, the Comité des Dames added an evangelist who spent her time visiting families and probably reading the Bible to illiterate women and children or teaching them about the Protestant faith, although her exact responsibilities are not entirely clear from available sources. By 1862, the society had also added a "Biblewoman" or "lectrice de la Bible" who made 600 visits in eight months. The position of "lectrice de la Bible" continued into the twentieth century. In 1901, the journal *Echo de la vérité* asked its readers to remember Mlle Bruguneau, who was a "lectrice de la Bible" in the Church of Marseille, because her mother had recently died. See also J. Dalencourt, *Mission évangélique aux femmes de la classe ouvrière: Œuvre de Mme Dalencourt* (Paris, 1881), 3–5. The Mission Évangélique aux Femmes de la Classe Ouvrière, founded in 1870 right after the Franco-Prussian War, encouraged women to become evangelists and to study the Bible. The organization held regular meetings where women, especially poor women, could come and discuss Bible readings that had been handed out in advance. A woman describing the project in 1881 declared that she took great pleasure in seeing the interest of women who came, especially those who previously had little experience with the Bible.

41. Mlle de Noaillat, "Rapport sur l'apostolat des dizainières," *Congrès de la Ligue Patriotique des Françaises* (1909), 216–23. Archives Nationales de France F7 13215.

42. P. LeJeune, "L'apostolat: La conquête d'une âme," *Association des mères chrétiennes: Charleville: Revue Mensuelle* 4, no. 44 (April 1909): 254–55.

43. René Doumic, "Echo des conférences: L'état contre la famille," *Bulletin de l'Action Sociale de la Femme* 1, no. 2 (May 10, 1902): 23–26; Anatole Leroy-Beaulieu, "Conférence de la liberté de l'enseignement pour les mères de famille," *Bulletin de l'Action Sociale de la Femme* 2, no. 3 (April 10, 1903): 331–46; "Chronique de l'Action Sociale de la Femme," *Bulletin de l'Action Sociale de la Femme* 4, no. 4 (April 20, 1905): 565–71.

44. "Ligue Patriotique des Françaises: Conférence," Cabinet du Préfet de la Dordogne, 4 Décembre 1909. Le Préfet du département de la Dordogne à Monsieur le Présidente du Conseil, Ministre de l'Intérieur. Archives Nationales de France F7 13217—Folder: Orgeat—Subfolder: Dordogne.

45. "Ligue des femmes françaises," *La croix* (December 22, 1911): 4.

46. "Propagande par la presse, les chants, les images," *Echo de la Ligue Patriotique des Françaises* 2, no. 121 (September 1904): 450–52.

47. Mme de Boury, "Rapport sur la presse," *Echo de la Ligue Patriotique des Françaises* 6, no. 68 (July 15, 1908): 2–5.

48. Encrevé, *Les protestants en France*, 75–78, 92–93.

49. *Le foyer de l'ouvrière: Exercice 1899–1900* (Châteauroux: Imprimerie Typographique et Lithographique L. Badel, 1900), 3–8; "Statuts," *Le foyer de l'ouvrière: Exercice 1900–1901* (Châteauroux: Imprimerie Typographique et Lithographique L. Badel, 1901), 3–4.

50. Pauline Allier, "Le Foyer de l'étudiante," *Le Christianisme au XX siècle* 39, no. 46 (November 18, 1910): 379.

51. Monica Miniati, *"Les 'Émancipées': Les femmes juives italiennes aux XIXe et XXe siècles (1848–1924)* (Paris: Honoré Champion, 2004), 265–68. Miniati has noted that for Italian Jewish women, emancipation after 1848 "made the family the only center of gravity for the Jewish life, the only actor in the process of educating new generations of young Jews and where women played a central role. In this new environment, women had to assume a double responsibility and take on a double mission, that of Jewish mother and Italian mother which balanced the delicate equilibrium between the religious and national patrimonies. Maternal influence quickly became linked to the vitality of the Jewish future and the community developed a number of initiatives designed to provide women with the tools and references they needed to accomplish their difficult mission of mediation."

52. Maurice Samuels, *The Right to Difference: French Universalism and the Jews* (Chicago: Univ. of Chicago Press, 2016), 187.

53. Birnbaum, *Jewish Destinies*, 60.

54. Emile Ollivier, "Conférence: La femme dans les luttes religieuses," *Bulletin de l'Action Sociale de la Femme* 2, no. 10 (December 10, 1903): 615–22.

3. Political Engagement, Community Voting Rights, and Women's Pastorate

1. R. M., "Après le scrutin," *L'univers israélite* 63, no. 10 (22 Novembre 1907): 293–98.

2. "Appel de la Ligue des Femmes Françaises," *Echo de Paris* (19 Mars 1906): 2.

3. "Comment les femmes peuvent-elle voter?," *Bulletin de l'Action Sociale de la Femme* 5, no. 3 (March 20, 1906): 82.

4. For a good discussion about the law on associations, see C. S. Phillips, *The Church in France 1848–1907* (London: Society for Promoting Christian Knowledge, 1936), 259–75.

5. "8ème Conseil," s.d. Archives de l'Action Catholique Générale Féminine, Box 565—Folder 1901–1902—Subfolder: Documents relatif aux conseils et Comités de la Ligue des Femmes Françaises, Comité de Paris. For more information about the

development of the far right in France and its relationship with the Catholic Church, see Oscar Arnal, *Ambivalent Alliance: The Catholic Church and the Action Française, 1899–1939* (Pittsburgh: Univ. of Pittsburgh Press, 1985); Davies, *The Extreme Right in France*, ch. 3.

6. John McManners and Jean Marie Mayeur and Madeleine Rebérioux provide a good discussion of the 1902 elections. See John McManners, *Church and State in France, 1870–1914* (New York, London: Harper & Row, 1972), 129; Mayeur and Rebérioux, *The Third Republic*, 220–22.

7. "Protestation," *Bulletin du devoir des femmes françaises* 2 (February 1905): 41.

8. Marie Maugeret, "Signatures de femmes," *Bulletin du devoir des femmes françaises* 7 (July 1905): 251. It is impossible to verify this number of signatures. The LPDF claimed that it had collected 189,818 signatures. It is likely that the Congrès Jeanne d'Arc and the LPDF worked together in gathering names. See "On Proteste," *Echo de la Ligue Patriotique des Françaises* 3, no. 29 (May 1905): 602.

9. For more information about Catholics' decision not to create *association cultuelles* see Phillips, *The Church in France*, 275–89.

10. For a very good discussion of the politics of Pius X, see Arnal, *Ambivalent Alliance*, ch. 4. Pius X forced some bishops who had wanted to compromise with the French government to resign from their positions.

11. Steven Hause and Anne Kenney argue that World War I "stimulated Catholic suffragism." I agree that the war did alter conditions in France to make suffrage more acceptable for Catholic women. However, women's political work in the prewar years prepared them for more direct political action once the Vatican agreed in 1919. See Hause and Kenney, "The Development of the Catholic Women's Suffrage Movement," 11–30.

12. La Baronne Reille, "Pas de politique," *Echo de la Ligue Patriotique des Françaises* 1, no. 1 (January 1903): 8–9.

13. Police Report, "D'un correspondent: Les ligues féminines réactionnaires préparent les élections," Paris, le 16 Février 1910. Archives Nationales de France, F7 13215—Folder: Historiques, Comités central, Comités locaux—Subfolder: Elections 1905–1914.

14. Police Report, "La Ligue Patriotique des Françaises," Paris, May 27, 1913. Archives Nationales de France F7 13215—Folder: Historiques, Comités central, Comités locaux—Subfolder: Elections 1905–1914. For more on the Action Libérale Populaire, see Arnal, *Ambivalent Alliance*, 37–40.

15. Police Report, "D'un correspondant," Paris, November 6, 1913. Archives Nationales de France, F7 13215—Folder: Historiques, Comités central, Comités locaux—Subfolder: Elections 1905–1914.

16. Communication de M. Piou au Comité de la Ligue, Paris, May 24, 1902. Archives Action Catholique Générale Féminine, Box—Folder: 1901–1902—Subfolder:

Documents relatif aux Conseil et Comités de la LFF, Comité de Paris, Période allant d'octobre 1901–juin 1902—Second subfolder: 6ᵉ Réunion de Comité.

17. "Chronique locale: Les femmes et la politique," *Le bulletin catholique semaine religieuse du Diocèse de Montauban* 28, no. 30 (July 25, 1903): 482–83. Archives Nationales de France, F 19 5631.

18. Marie-Madeleine, "Croquis synodal à propos de l'éligibilité des femmes," *Le Huguenot: Journal mensuel des églises réformées des cévennes et du sud-est* 2, no. 13 (July 1, 1911): 102–3.

19. E. Barnaud, "Le vote des femmes dans l'église," *L'éclaireur: Journal populaire évangélique* 11, no. 7 (April 1, 1900): 51–53.

20. Barnaud, 51–53.

21. "Troisième séance, mercredi 7 juin," *Actes et décisions du synode général officieuse des églises réformées de France tenu à Bordeaux du 6 au 14 juin 1899* (Alençon: Imprimerie Veuve Félix Guy et Cie., 1899), 26. Société de l'Histoire du Protestantisme Français, Box 2414.

22. "Rapport de M. Mailhet sur l'électorat des femmes dans l'église," Église réformée de France—Synode Particulier des Alpes et du Jura XXe Circonscription—Compte Rendu de la Vingtième Session Tenue à Mens (Isère) les 12, 13, et 14 Mai 1900 (La Roche: Imprimerie Typographique J.-A. Fetz, 1900), 9.

23. S. G.-V., "A propos du droit des femmes dans l'église," *Le protestant libéral* 19, no. 50 (December 10, 1904): 406. He criticized a conference of liberal churches for denying women equal rights with men in liberal churches and for providing no good reasons for doing so. Some people objected because of the dependence of churches on the state, which posed questions about the legality of making such a change without approval from the government. However, the author noted that some members had questioned the mental capacity of women, suggesting that "mental fatigue" prevented them from dealing with "grave and arduous problems." The author argued that this was "excessive and displaced," noting that very few men or pastors were really tired and crushed by the "weight of ecclesiastical questions."

24. The Synode de Bolbec voted 13–11 against allowing women's suffrage, with six abstentions. Neuilly-sur-Seine voted in favor of allowing widows and single women over the age of thirty to vote in church elections. It justified its decision by noting that women should have a say in the nomination of pastors and by acknowledging the injustice in denying women heads of households the right to vote. The Synode de Saint-Laurent-du-Cros also agreed in theory to allow women to vote, although it did not accord them the right immediately. At its meeting, one member noted the "danger" in "revealing to young women some delicate information relative to pastoral candidates," and he warned about the "inevitable conflicts" that would occur between feminine assemblies and the presbytery councils. In an effort to prepare its parishes for an eventual women's vote, the Synode de

Saint-Laurent-du-Cros gave women a consultative and deliberative voice from the age of 21. "Le Synode de Bolbec"; "Le Synode de Neuilly-sur-Seine"; Alfred Jaulmes, "Synode de Saint-Laurent-du-Cros," *Le christianisme au XX siècle* 30, no. 27 (July 5, 1901): 214–18.

25. Commission exécutive du Synode du Poitou, *Le Synode: Son passé—son present* (Cahors: Imprimerie Typographique A. Coueslant, 1900), 1–6.

26. Encrevé, *L'expérience et la foi*, 18–19.

27. "Troisième séance: L'électorat paroissial des femmes," Église réformée de France—Synode Particulier de la Basse-Ardèche (XVIIe Circonscription)—Compte-Rendu de la Vingt-et-Unième Session tenue à LaGorce les 27 et 28 Novembre 1901 (Privas: Imprimerie Nouvelle, 1902), 6–7. Archives de la Société de l'Histoire du Protestantisme Français—Synodes Régionaux, 2e–9e circonscriptions (3)—Folder: Synodes Régionaux 17e circonscription (P. 2418).

28. "Le Synode de Générac," *Le christianisme au XX siècle* 30, no. 24 (May 24, 1901): 169.

29. G. M., "Etudes synodales: L'électorat féminine," *Le christianisme au XIX siècle* 29, no. 29 (July 26, 1900): 229–30.

30. "Deuxième séance," Église réformée de France—Synode Régional Officieux des Églises Réformées Évangéliques de la IVe Circonscription (Ouest)—XXIIIe Session tenue dans le Temple de Brest les 12 et 13 Juin 1901—Compte-Rendu Analytique des Séances (Nantes: Imprimerie du Commerce, 1902), 4–5.

31. "Nouvelles et Faits Divers: France," *Le témoignage: Journal de l'église de la confession d'Augsbourg* 43, no. 32 (August 9, 1907): 259.

32. "Synode de Gémozac—XXXIXe session, 13 Avril 1915," *Union régionale des Charentes, vie circonscription: Compte rendu de la dixième assemblée générale tenue à Gémozac le 13 avril 1915* (Saintes: Imprimerie A. Gay, 1915), 4–7. Archives de la Société de l'Histoire du Protestantisme Français—P. 2418—Synodes régionaux, 4e–9e circonscriptions (2)—Folder: Synodes Régionaux 6e Circonscription.

33. Marguerite de Witt-Schlumberger, *Le rôle des femmes de pasteurs en France pendant la guerre* (Paris: Librairie Fischbacher, s.d. probably 1916 or 1917), 7. De Witt-Schlumberger, a very active member in moderate feminist/suffragist work, had clear feminist aims with this pamphlet. In 1918 she published an article arguing explicitly that women be ordained. See Marguerite de Witt-Schlumberger, "Tribune libre: Ministères féminins," *Le christianisme au XXe siècle* 47, no. 34 (August 22, 1918). The Protestant press and synod reports frequently note that many women were filling the positions of mobilized pastors.

34. Une femme de pasteur mobilisé, "Les femmes peuvent-elles prêcher?" *Le christianisme au XX siècle* 45, no. 34 (October 26, 1916): 339–40.

35. "Synode Particulière de Montbéliard: III—De l'institution éventuelle d'un pastorat féminine," *Recueil officiel des actes du synode général et des synodes particuliers*

de l'eglise evangélique luthérienne de France: Nouvelle série: Tom V (1916–1918) (Cahors: Imprimerie Typographique Coueslant, 1916), 17–19.

36. M. le professeur H. Bois, "Rapport sur les activités féminines," *Actes et décisions du synode national des églises réformées évangéliques de France tenu à Paris (Batignolles) les 20–21 juin 1916,* Publié par les soins de la Commission permanente, 108. Archives de la Société de l'Histoire du Protestantisme Français—P. 2417—Synodes—Églises Réformées Évangéliques 1914–27.

37. Jean-Paul Willaime found that the Reformed church of France admitted women to the pastorate without restrictions in 1965, and most other French denominations followed suit. Even the Independent Reformed Evangelical Church, one of France's most conservative denominations, finally admitted women to the pastorate in 1994. By 1995, women made up about 15 percent of the pastoral corps in France. See Jean-Paul Willaime, "Les mutations des cadres de la vie ecclésial dans les églises protestantes," in *Histoire du christianisme, v. 13: Crises et renouveau (de 1958 à nos jours),* eds. Roger Aubert et al. (Paris: Desclée, 2000), 250.

38. Jean Baubérot et Jean-Paul Willaime, *Le protestantisme* (Solar, 1987), 152–53. See also Willaime, "Les mutations des cadres," 246–54; Anne-Marie Heitz-Muller, "L'ouverture du ministère pastoral aux femmes dans les églises protestantes d'Alsace et de Lorraine," *Revue d'histoire et de philosophie religieuses* 83, no. 3 (2003): 301–23.

39. "Église réformées de France: Union nationale des églises réformée évangéliques: École supérieur d'enseignement religieux," *Le christianisme au XX siècle* 50, no. 27 (July 7, 1921): 384. These courses were offered by the École Supérieur d'Enseignement Religieux with support from the École de Service Chrétien.

40. Martin Haag, "Statut des femmes dans les organisations religieuses: L'exemple de l'accès au pouvoir clérical," *Archives de sciences sociales des religions* 95 (July–September 1996): 48–51.

41. The following sources discuss the creation of diaconesse-évangélistes in both the Reformed and Lutheran communities: Poujol, *Un féminisme sous tutelle,* 100–101; "Activité féminine dans l'église," *Recueil officiel des actes du synode général et des synodes particuliers de l'église évangélique luthérienne de France: Tom VI (1919–1921)* (Imprimerie Typographique Coueslant, 1919), 34–40. Archives de la Société de l'Histoire du Protestantisme Français—P. 2413—Synodes Églises Évangéliques Luthérienne de France; "Église réformée de France: Union nationale des églises réformée évangéliques: École supérieur d'enseignement religieux," *Le christianisme au XX siècle* 50, no. 27 (July 7, 1921): 384; Heitz-Muller, "L'ouverture du ministère pastoral," 301–23. Heitz-Muller found that four women attended theology school at the Facultés de Strasbourg in 1920 and fourteen attended in 1933. In 1928, the Church of the Confession of Augsburg of Alsace-Lorraine adopted a rule allowing women who completed studies in theology to receive the title of pastor's aide and act as a second or third pastor. The first woman ordained as a pastor in France was Berthe Bertsch,

who was ordained by the Reformed Church of Alsace and Lorraine in 1930, but who began her ministry in 1927. See also Willaime, "Les mutations des cadres," 249. Not until 1949 did the Reformed Church of France ordain a woman, and this was still a rare case. See Poujol, *Un féminisme sous tutelle*, 256.

42. Nord, *The Republican Moment*, 64–65.

43. Lisa Moses Leff, *Sacred Bonds of Solidarity: The Rise of Jewish Internationalism in Nineteenth-Century France* (Stanford, CA: Stanford Univ. Press, 2006), 4.

44. Nord, *The Republican Moment*, 79. Nord provides the following citation: I. Cahen, "La crise israélite," *Archives israélites* (May 15, 1870): 297–98.

45. McManners, *Church and State in France*, 147–48.

46. Phyllis Cohen Albert, *The Modernization of French Jewry: Consistory and Community in the Nineteenth Century* (Hanover, MA: Brandeis Univ. Press, 1977), 123.

47. Mathieu Wolff, "Pour être électeur," *L'univers israélite* 60, no. 37 (June 2, 1905): 336–38.

48. H. Prague, "Le féminisme dans la communauté," *Archives israélites* 67, no. 34 (August 23, 1906): 265–67.

49. I counted the statutes that exist in the Archives Nationales de France. Archives Nationales de France F19 11158.

50. Prague, "Le féminisme dans la communauté," 265–67.

51. R. M., "Après le scrutin," *L'univers israélite* 63, no. 10 (November 22, 1907): 293–98.

52. Philip Nord includes these quotations in *The Republican Moment*, p. 79. He cites the following sources: I. Cahen, "Les intérêts moraux et le communisme," *Archives israélites* (April 15–June 15, 1871): 78; "Le panthéisme et la démocratie," *Archives israélites* (October 15, 1872): 624; "Les élections législatives et les israélites," *Archives israélites*, (May 1, 1869): 259–61; Astruc, as cited in Cahen, "Le livre récent de M. le Grand-Rabbin Astruc," *Archives israélites* (March 1, 1870): 145.

4. Faith for Social Progress

1. Comtesse de Keranflec'h-Kernezne, "Les cercles de fermières en France et en Belgique," *ACI: Compte rendu du IXe Congrès National Français* (Dijon, 1913), 183–89.

2. Herman Lebovics, *True France: The Wars over Cultural Identity, 1900–1945* (Ithaca, NY: Cornell Univ. Press, 1992), 24–27. Catholic women's organizations also mirrored ideas held by other conservative groups such as the Fédération Régionaliste Française, arguing for educational reforms that would "emphasize practical and moral training" and maintain "the vitality of such moral guides as the family, country life, and religious practice" as well as address problems such as depopulation of the countryside.

3. Judith Stone, *The Search for Social Peace: Reform Legislation in France, 1890–1914* (Albany: State Univ. of New York Press, 1985), xiii.

4. Stone, *The Search for Social Peace*, x–xi.

5. For more information on various national reform efforts, see Sonya Rose, "Protective Labor Legislation in Nineteenth-Century Britain: Gender, Class and the Liberal State," and Kathleen Canning, "Social Policy, Body Politics: Recasting the Social Question in Germany, 1875–1900," in *Gender and Class in Modern Europe*, eds. Laura Frader and Sonya Rose (Ithaca, NY: Cornell Univ. Press, 1996), 193–237.

6. Rachel Fuchs, "France in a Comparative Perspective," in *Gender and the Politics of Social Reform in France, 1870–1914*, eds. Elinor Accampo, Rachel Fuchs, and Mary Lynn Stewart (Baltimore, MD: Johns Hopkins Univ. Press, 1995), 163–64.

7. Fuchs, "France in a Comparative Perspective," 166.

8. Fuchs, 158.

9. Alisa Klaus, "Women's Organizations and the Infant Health Movement in France and the United States, 1890–1920," in *Lady Bountiful Revisited: Women, Philanthropy and Power*, ed. Kathleen McCarthy (New Brunswick, NJ: Rutgers Univ. Press, 1990), 158–59.

10. Mary Lynn Stewart, "Setting the Standards: Labor and Family Reformers," in *Gender and the Politics of Social Reform in France, 1870–1914*, eds. Elinor Accampo, Rachel Fuchs, and Mary Lynn Stewart (Baltimore, MD: Johns Hopkins Univ. Press, 1995), 108. Social Catholicism developed in France in the mid-nineteenth century under the leadership of men such as Frédéric Ozanam, who founded the Société de Saint Vincent de Paul. Ozanam initiated the process of moving Catholics away from charity and toward social action, which produced long-term improvements in the lives of the poor. However, the social Catholic movement remained small until the Commune of 1871 revealed the stark class divisions that existed in France. This realization motivated Catholics to take action to improve the material and spiritual condition of the poor. The social Catholic movement grew under the leadership of men such as Albert de Mun and René de la Tour du Pin. In 1891, the movement received critical support from the Vatican when Pope Leo XIII issued the *Rerum Novarum* calling on Catholics to go to the people and take a more active social role. See A. R. Vidler, *A Century of Social Catholicism, 1820–1920* (London: SPCK, 1964), 77–78.

11. Stone, *The Search for Social Peace*, xv.

12. Klaus, "Women's Organizations and the Infant Health Movement," 158–59.

13. Seth Koven found that the British government frequently left social welfare up to local communities where women tended to have the most influence since they could be elected and appointed to various official positions. Koven argues that "women's voluntary associations contributed to the success and stability of the Victorian and Edwardian state—and they were equally important as sites for the expression

and growth of women's civic and political consciousness. Educated middle-class women used voluntary associations to carve out for themselves political identities and a variety of new professions such as health and district visiting and social work." This allowed them to "exercise power outside the home." Seth Koven, "Borderlands: Women, Voluntary Action, and Child Welfare in Britain 1840–1914," in *Mothers of a New World: Maternalist Politics and the Origins of Welfare States*, eds. Seth Koven and Sonya Michel (New York, London: Routledge, 1993), 123–24.

14. Klaus, "Women's Organizations and the Infant Health Movement," 158.

15. Klaus, 166–67.

16. Protestants also played an important part in women's access to the position of inspectress in primary schools and other government aid programs. Linda Clark suggests that the government's decision about the "appointment of primary school inspectresses" derived largely from the work of Ferdinand Buisson, the liberal Protestant director of primary instruction from 1879 to 1896. Another Protestant, Henri Monod, was instrumental in expanding women's roles as inspectors beyond education to other government-run programs for women and children. Likewise, Pauline Kergomard, also a Protestant, became "inspectresse general of nursery schools" in 1879. As noted above, she was eventually elected to serve on the Ministry of Public Instruction's chief advisory committee and was an active proponent of women inspectresses. See Linda L. Clark, "Bringing Feminine Qualities into the Public Sphere: The Third Republic's Appointment of Women Inspectors," in *Gender and the Politics of Social Reform in France, 1870–1914*, eds. Elinor Accampo, Rachel Fuchs, and Mary Lynn Stewart (Baltimore, MD: Johns Hopkins Univ. Press, 1995): 133–40.

17. Pauline Kergomard, "Les femmes dans l'enseignement primaire," *Revue pédagogique*, 14 (May 1889): 417–27, cited in Clark, "Bringing Feminine Qualities into the Public Sphere."

18. Clark, "Bringing Feminine Qualities into the Public Sphere," 134, 150–51.

19. Fuchs, "France in a Comparative Perspective," 183.

20. Albert Valez, "2e Congrès des diaconats et des associations protestante de bienfaisance," *Le christianisme au XX siècle* 41, no. 25 (June 21, 1912): 206.

21. McManners, *Church and State in France*, 81–83. Beginning in the 1870s, Count Albert de Mun and René de la Tour du Pin became interested in the misery of the working classes and their alienation from the Church. To deal with these problems, de Mun founded the Œuvre des Cercles Catholiques d'Ouvriers (Catholic Workers' Circles), a paternalistic association run by the upper class that tried to make the lives of workers better by providing them with entertainment and cultural activities such as concerts and billiards. De Mun was criticized for his paternalistic methods, but he opened the way for social Catholics to work toward a better understanding of the harsh conditions created by industrialization.

22. "Chronique de l'Action Sociale de la Femme," *Bulletin de l'Action Sociale de la Femme* 5, no. 3 (March 20, 1906): 101–2.

23. Georges Noblemaire, "Emigrés et déracinés," *Bulletin de l'Action Sociale de la Femme* 7, no. 5 (May 20, 1908): 219.

24. La Marquise de Juigné, "Nécessité de retenir les femmes dans leur pays: Moyens à employer par la Ligue dans ce but," *Congrès de la Ligue Patriotique des Françaises* (Paris: 1913), 170.

25. La Marquise de Juigné, "Nécessité de retenir les femmes dans leur pays," 170.

26. Keranflec'h-Kernezne, "Les cercles de fermières," 192.

27. Henry Reverdy, "La pratique de l'action sociale à la campagne," *Bulletin de l'Action Sociale de la Femme* 3, no. 7 (July 20, 1904): 268.

28. "Œuvre sociale de la dentelle," *Supplément à l'Echo de la Ligue Patriotique des Françaises* 11, no. 128 (July 15, 1913): 76.

29. "Industries rurales," *Bulletin de l'Action Sociale de la Femme* 7, no. 9 (November 20, 1908): 453–54.

30. "Chronique internationale—Le travail rural," *Fédération internationale des Ligues Catholiques Féminines—Supplément à l'Echo de la Ligue Patriotique des Françaises* 122 (January 15, 1913): 49.

31. Eugen Weber, *Peasants into Frenchmen: The Modernization of Rural France, 1870–1914* (Stanford, CA: Stanford Univ. Press, 1976), part II.

32. Marie-Louise Rochebillard, *Syndicats d'ouvrières lyonnaises* (Paris, Lille: Imprimerie de l'Action Populaire, c. 1904?), 11–14.

33. Rochebillard, *Syndicats d'ouvrières lyonnaises*, 14–16.

34. Among the syndicates most strongly supported by the Catholic community were those created by Marie-Louise Rochebillard in Lyon. Unlike other Catholic women's syndicates, these were not mixed but they did involve upper-class Catholic women. Rochebillard began by creating two very small syndicates in Lyon, one for women in commerce and the other for needle workers. Each syndicate had about twenty members to start with, but by about 1904, the Syndicat des Dames Employées de Commerce had 225 members, the Syndicate de l'Aiguille had about 275, and the silk workers syndicate, which was created a few years after the other two, had about sixty members. See Rochebillard, *Syndicats d'ouvrières lyonnaises*, 19–25.

35. M. L., "Œuvre de la Goutte de Lait du VI arrondissement sous le patronage de la Ligue Patriotique des Françaises," and "20 allemands contre 1 français," *Petit Echo de la Ligue Patriotique des Françaises* 11, no. 160 (June 1913): 3.

36. In 1899, Sarah Monod, Gabrielle Mallet, E. Fisch, Isabelle Bogelot, and Julie Siegfried, all of whom actively participated in projects within the Protestant community, served on the conference's directing board.

37. See the journal *La femme* 30, nos. 6–7 (June–July 1908). The entire edition was dedicated to talks given at the Conférence de Versailles.

38. Mme Léon Lévy, "Rapport sur 'L'École des Bonnes d'Enfants' de la rue de Alésia," *La femme* 3, nos. 6–7 (June–July 1908): 101–2.

39. Mme Léon Braunschweig, "L'organisation d'une association ou fédération des services de placement," *La femme* 3, no. 8 (August 1908): 113–14.

40. Gabrielle Lipman, "Pour les bêtes," *La femme* 9, no. 30 (September 1908): 136–38.

41. Celine Leglaive-Perani, "De la charité à la philanthropie: Introduction," *Archives juives* 1, no. 44 (2011): 3, 14.

42. Celine Leglaive-Perani, "Donner au féminin: Juives philanthripes in France (1830–1930)," *Archives juives* 2, no. 48 (2015): 11–15.

43. Celine Leglaive-Perani, "Le judaïsme parisien et la Comité de Bienfaisance Israélite (1830–1930)," *Archives juives* 1, no. 44 (2011): 37–38.

44. "Rapport du Conseil d'Administration," *Comité de Bienfaisance Israélite de Paris: Assemblée générale du 18 Mars 1901: Rapport présenté par le Conseil d'Administration* (Paris: Simon Franck, 1901), 14.

45. "Rapport présenté par le Conseil d'Administration," *Comité de Bienfaisance Israélite de Paris: Assemblée générale du 27 Mai 1903: Rapport présenté par le Conseil d'Administration: Exercice 1902–1903* (1903), 12–13.

46. Patricia Hilden, *Working Women and Socialist Politics in France, 1880–1914: A Regional Study* (Oxford: Clarendon Press, 1986), 112–14.

47. Hilden, *Working Women and Socialists Politics*, 115–22. A number of obstacles also hindered women's involvement in syndicates and prevented mass participation of women in syndicates, either Catholic or otherwise. Marriage and childbirth often interrupted women's participation in the workplace. Many women worked for a few years before they married and returned to the workplace once their children were older, but their intermittent involvement in the workplace at different stages of their lives prevented them from developing clear professional identities. See Michelle Perrot, "Les femmes et le syndicalisme au temps de la naissance de la CGT," *Cahiers d'histoire de l'Institut de Recherches Marxistes* 61 (1995): 47–53.

48. Keranflec'h-Kernezne, "Les cercles de fermières," 192.

49. Lebovics, *True France*, xiii.

50. Caroline Ford, *Creating the Nation in Provincial France: Religion and Political Identity in Brittany* (Princeton, NJ: Princeton Univ. Press, 1993), 25.

51. *Le devoir des femmes françaises par l'une d'elles* (Paris: M. J. Caplain, 1902), 29.

52. Keranflec'h-Kernezne, "Les cercles de fermières," 193.

53. Marguerite Billat, "La nouvelle année 1910–1911," *Courrier des syndicats* 2, no. 20 (December 12, 1910): 2–3. Archives de l'Archevêché de Paris Box 3K1, 1d—Syndicats CFTC—Folder: Syndicats féminins de l'Impasse Gomboust.

5. A Voyage of Faith

1. Mme Ed. Humbert, *L'Union Internationale des Amies de la Jeune Fille: Son origine, sa nature, son extension* (Neuchâtel: Imprimerie Attinger Frères, 1889), 9–10.

2. Immigrant women and children came to France from many different countries to look for work and protection against anti-Semitism. Migrant girls generally traveled from the French provinces to cities or larger towns looking for employment.

3. This paper focuses almost exclusively on the Paris branch of the Union Internationale des Amies de la Jeune Fille because I have not been able to find the annual reports of any other branches. The reports from other French branches may exist in archives in Lyon or Marseilles, but the Société de l'Histoire du Protestantism Français in Paris only has the Paris reports. The Bibliotheque Marguerite Durand, also in Paris, has copies of some volumes of *La femme*, the journal that represented the Amies, but information in that journal about other French branches is very incomplete. I therefore have chosen to focus on the Paris branch.

4. Leslie Page Moch, *Moving Europeans: Migration in Western Europe since 1600*, *2nd edition* (Bloomington: Indiana Univ. Press, 2003), 104–21. For more information on immigration to France at the turn of the century, see Gérard Noiriel, *The French Melting Pot: Immigration, Citizenship, and National Identity*, trans. Geoffroy de Laforcade (Minneapolis: Univ. of Minnesota Press, 1996); Yves Lequin, *Histoire des étrangers et de l'immigration en France* (Paris: Larousse, 2006). Both of these works provide important information about the number of immigrants arriving in France, where they came from, and what kinds of jobs they took. Noiriel found that the number of foreign-born women in France has always been considerably less than the number of foreign-born men. In 1891, there were 113 immigrant men for every immigrant woman. Nonetheless, the area of domestic work provided numerous positions for immigrant women. In 1901, one third of immigrant women in France worked in "domestic service." Eugen Weber also provides information about factors that encouraged peasants, including women, to leave the farm and go to cities in the late nineteenth century. See Weber, *Peasants into Frenchmen*, chapter 16.

5. Leglaive-Perani, "Les juifs français," 60.

6. Molly McGregor Watson, "The Trade in Women: 'White Slavery' and the French Nation, 1899–1939," (PhD diss., Stanford University, 1999).

7. "Allocution de Mlle Sarah Monod," *Union Internationale des Amies de la Jeune Fille, Section Parisienne* (Paris: Imprimerie Typographique Harry E Eybord, 1894), 8.

8. Edward Bristow notes that the enslavement of young girls did not occur as often as Victorian social aid workers believed, but he also found that Jewish volunteers working against the white slave trade did encounter traffickers at train stations. See Edward Bristow, *Prostitution and Prejudice: The Jewish Fight against White Slavery 1870–1939* (New York: Schocken Books, 1983), 25. In addition to faith-based

organizations, nonconfessional organizations such as the Association for the Repression of the White Slave Trade also brought people throughout Europe together to combat forced prostitution. See Jane Jordan, *Josephine Butler* (London: John Murray, 2001), chapter 11.

9. Bristow, *Prostitution and Prejudice*, 28–29. Bristow has noted that as prostitution became increasingly profitable over the course of the nineteenth century, the number of procurers also increased, and recruiters of prostitutes waited at prison gates, train stations, and shipping ports for unsuspecting or desperate young women. However, Alain Corbin argues that very few girls were actually kidnapped and forced to work as prostitutes, as many anti–white slavery advocates feared. See Alain Corbin, *Women for Hire: Prostitution and Sexuality in France after 1850*, trans. Alan Sheridan (Cambridge, MA: Harvard Univ. Press, 1990), 285.

10. Rachel G. Fuchs and Leslie Page Moch, "Pregnant, Single, and Far from Home: Migrant Women in Nineteenth-Century Paris," *The American Historical Review* 95, no. 4 (1990): 1007–31.

11. "Échos de la chaire: Le rôle de la femme juive dans la Société moderne," *Archives israélites*, 31 (August 2, 1906): 244.

12. "Discours de M. Louis Rivière, président du Congrès: Résumé des travaux du Congrès, État actuel de l'œuvre," *Association Catholique Internationale pour la Protection de la Jeune Fille: Discours de la journée de clôture du 4me congrès national tenu à Bordeaux les 7 et 8 Octobre 1907* (Fribourg, 1908), 12.

13. Anne Firor Scott, "Women's Voluntary Associations: From Charity to Reform," in *Lady Bountiful Revisited: Women, Philanthropy, and Power*, ed. Kathleen McCarthy (New Brunswick, NJ: Rutgers Univ. Press, 1990), 41–49.

14. Shurlee Swain, "Woman and Philanthropy in Colonial and Post-Colonial Australia," in *Women, Philanthropy, and Civil Society*, ed. Kathleen McCarthy (Bloomington: Indiana Univ. Press, 2001), 159.

15. Marion A. Kaplan, *The Making of the Jewish Middle Class: Women, Family, and Identity in Imperial Germany* (Oxford: Oxford Univ. Press, 1991), 208–11.

16. Seth Koven and Sonya Michel, "Womanly Duties: Maternalist Politics and the Origins of Welfare States in France, Germany, Great Britain, and the United States 1880–1920," in *Gender and History in Western Europe*, eds. Robert Shoemaker and Mary Vincent (London: Arnold, 1998), 319–46. See also Evelyne Diebolt, "Femmes protestantes face aux politiques de santé publique 1900–1939," *Bulletin de la Société de l'Histoire du Protestantisme Françaises* 146, no. 1 (2000): 91–132. Women also came to play a greater part in the French civil administration as inspectors of women's prisons and girls' schools. See Clark, "Bringing Feminine Qualities into the Public Sphere," 128–56.

17. Watson, "The Trade in Women," 14–15.

18. Corbin, *Women for Hire*, 215–31.

19. This league was largely, but not exclusively, Protestant. It worked in conjunction with the British and Continental Federation for the Abolition of Prostitution. See Annie Stora-Lamarre, *L'enfer de la IIIe République: Censeurs et pornographes (1881–1914)* (Paris: Editions Imago, 1990), 89.

20. "Discours de M. Louis Rivière, president du congrès," *ACI: Congrès National Français* (Fribourg, 1908), 6.

21. It's not clear who founded the Paris Amies. The initial reports do not provide a list of members or a board of directors. However, the 1896–97 report suggests that women from very prominent families such as Julie Siegfried and Mme A. Fisch had become associated with the Paris Amies.

22. "Rapport général du comité exécutif de Paris lu le 1er Mai 1888 à la Conférence Internationale de l'Union des Amies de la Jeune Fille," *Amies: Section parisienne* (Paris, 1888), 3–7.

23. "Rapport général," *Amies: Section parisienne* (Paris, 1894), 12–15.

24. Marie Chrétien, "Œuvre des arrivantes," *Amies: Section parisienne* (Paris, 1900), 16. See also Corbin, *Women for Hire*, 285. Although Corbin's research indicates that some young women migrated with the express goal of working as prostitutes, this does not seem to be the case for most girls aided by the ACI or the Amies. The willingness of a girl or her family to contact religious organizations for assistance does not suggest that the girl planned to work as a prostitute. Members of the ACI noted that some girls contacted the organization for assistance upon their arrival in Paris after seeing posters advertising the organization's services. See La Marquise de Castellane, "Rapport sur la Maison d'Accueil de Paris," *ACI: Congrès National Français* (Dijon, 1913), 21–23.

25. "Rapport général," *Amies: Section parisienne* (Paris, 1894), 12–15.

26. E. Meyer, "Rapport du bureau de placement," *Amies: Section parisienne* (Fontenay-aux-Roses, 1901), 22.

27. By 1889 the Amies had 3,500 members in twenty-two different countries and 919 different locations. These women were scattered throughout Europe, as well as in limited locations in Asia, Africa, and Turkey. None of the reports include the number of women members in Paris or France.

28. Maire Chrétien, "Œuvre des Arrivantes," *Amies: Section parisienne* (Fontenay-aux-Roses, 1901), 29–34. Although most of the girls the Amies assisted came from Protestant backgrounds, this society helped girls regardless of their faith. Of the 375 girls aided by the organization in 1900, 298 were Protestant, seventy-six were Catholic, and one was Jewish.

29. "Rapport général sur l'année 1899," *Amies: Section parisienne* (Paris, 1900), 6–10.

30. B-E Wellington, "Rapport sur le home français et international," *Amies: Section parisienne* (Paris, 1907), 31.

31. L. Rourin, "Rapport présenté à l'assemblée générale annuelle des Amies de la Jeune Fille," *La femme* 31, no. 3 (March 1909): 39.

32. This predominantly Protestant organization aimed to eliminate immoral and pornographic material from French society. It encouraged the French government to pass laws repressing pornography and immoral reading material. See Stora-Lamarre, *L'enfer de la IIIe République*, 88–95.

33. Introduction, *Amies: Section parisienne* (Paris, 1887), 2. Th. Fallot is almost certainly Tommy Fallot, a very prominent pastor in the Reformed Church who was instrumental in the development of social Christianity in France. See Cabanel, *Les protestants et la république*, 94–95.

34. "Allocution de Mlle Sarah Monod," *Amies: Section parisienne* (Paris, 1894), 8–9.

35. For more information on the Swiss and international aspects of the ACI's work, see Catherine Galley, "Les formes d'un engagement féminine: L'Association catholique internationale des Œuvres de Protection de la jeune fille," (Mémoire de licence, Faculté des Lettres de l'Université de Fribourg [Suisse], 1996).

36. Letter: Louise de Reynold et le Baronne de Montenach à Votre Emminence, s.d. Archives de l'Archevêché de Paris, Box 3K1, 3B1, Jeunes Filles (Œuvres)—Folder: Protection de la Jeune Fille.

37. The kinds of programs that the Amies and the ACI offered remained fairly consistent during the time considered in this paper, although they did expand over time.

38. "Association Catholique Internationale des Œuvres pour la Protection de la Jeune Fille" (pamphlet), s.d. (after 1907). Archives de l'Archevêché de Paris, Box 3K1, 3b1, Jeune Filles (Œuvres)—Folder: Protection de la Jeune Fille. It linked organizations not only in Europe but also in the US, Brazil, Argentina, Algeria, Tunisia, and Egypt.

39. Cova, *Au service de l'église*, 65.

40. "Rapport sur la maison de famille—le secrétariat—Les correspondantes de la région de Dijon par Mlle d'Arbaumont," *ACI: Congrès National Français* (Dijon, 1910), 43–47.

41. "Rapport national français: Nancy," *ACI: Congrès National Français* (Dijon, 1912), 67–68.

42. "Rapport national français par Mlle de Saint-Seine," *ACI: Congrès National Français* (Dijon, 1910), 55–57.

43. "Rapport sur les cercles d'études et les retraites des midinettes par Mlle Barre," *ACI: Congrès National Français* (Dijon, 1910), 67–72.

44. Noiriel, *The French Melting Pot*, 102. Yves Lequin also notes the increasing number of Italians coming to France toward the end of the nineteenth century. See Lequin, *Histoire des étrangers*, 285.

45. Mlle de Saint-Seine, "Rapport sur l'émigration polonaise," *ACI: Congrès National Français* (Dijon, 1910), 159–65.

46. In 1907 the ACI received a telegram from the Cardinal Merry del Val that included a blessing from the Pope for the society's work. See "Séance de clôture," *ACI: Congrès National Français* (Fribourg, 1908), 2.

47. Paula Hyman estimates that France attracted about 30,000 Jewish immigrants between 1881 and 1914. She also notes that "while estimates as to the number of Jewish immigrants to France vary, all agree that the rate of immigration increased in the years 1905 to 1914, and then rose even higher following World War I. . . . Many of the foreign Jews were merely in transit. The most plausible estimates place the number of immigrants who settled in Paris at approximately 25,000, of whom 85% were from Central and Eastern Europe, the rest from the Balkans and the Levant." See Hyman, *From Dreyfus to Vichy*, 64–65. She cites Michel Roblin, *Les juifs de paris* (Paris: Éditions A. et J. Picard, 1952), 73.

48. The anti-Semitic press also often accused Jews of facilitating the "white slave" trade. Jews were accused of trafficking girls themselves and of financing trafficking operations, as well as profiting from such operations. The Jewish community in France wished to undermine such charges through organizations designed to protect girls from traffickers. See Corbin, *Women for Hire*, 292.

49. Hyman, *From Dreyfus to Vichy*, 63, chapter 5. For more information on Jewish philanthropy, see Nancy Green, "To Give and to Receive," in *The Uses of Charity: The Poor on Relief in the Nineteenth-Century Metropolis*, ed. Peter Mandle (Philadelphia: Univ. of Pennsylvania Press, 1990), 198–99.

50. Kaplan, *The Making of the Jewish Middle Class*, 192.

51. H. Prague, "Solidarité!" *Archives israélites*, LXXIV, no. 18 (May 1, 1913): 137–38.

52. The French branch of this association was founded in November 1910, but very little information exists about it. The only document that I have been able to locate is the proceedings from its first general assembly held in January 1912. This organization headed entirely by women was supported by important men in the community, and had goals very similar to those of the Amies and the ACI. In 1912, it seems to have only existed in Paris, although the women involved wished to create branches in other French cities. It had aided a handful of young women, some of them looking for work and others trafficked as prostitutes. It worked with the Œuvre Libératrice to help young women who had been trafficked as prostitutes. See *Association pour la Protection de la Jeune Fille (Section israélite): Assemblée générale du 28 janvier 1912* (Paris, 1912).

53. Edward Bristow notes that Jews across Europe in the nineteenth and twentieth centuries played a central role in "anti–white slave trade" societies. It is likely that French Jews, including women, participated in such organizations. However, French

Jewish sources, including journals of the period, rarely mention "white slavery" and provide almost no information about French Jewish involvement in "anti–white slavery" work. Bristow argues that the lack of information about "white slavery" in French Jewish journals resulted from Jewish defensiveness in the aftermath of the Dreyfus Affair. See Bristow, *Prostitution and Prejudice*, 216.

54. Hélène-Léopold Enos, "Rapport de Mme Enos déléguée au patronage des prisons," *Comité de Bienfaisance Israélite de Paris: Assemblée générale du 5 juin 1912: Exercice 1911* (1911), 18–19.

55. Celine Leglaive-Perani, "Les juifs français dans la lutte contre la traite des blanches (1880–1930)," *Archives Juives* 2, no. 44 (2011): 61.

56. "Liste de Souscription," *L'Œuvre libératrice: Assemblée générale du 15 mars 1903*, 27–30. Archives de l'Alliance Israélite Universelle, France 1H1—Folder: Œuvre Libératrice 1902–1907. The Œuvre Libératrice aided "fallen women," as well as those who had been forced into prostitution, in finding ways to leave their lives as prostitutes and regain their dignity. It rescued some women and girls from the police department and received others from "anti–white slavery" organizations such as the Œuvre Contre la Traite des Blanches.

57. Letter from Mme C. Eugène Simon and Emilie S. Phiefe (spelling unclear), members of the Œuvre Libératrice, to the President of the AIU, 20 September 1902. Archives de l'Alliance Israèlite Universelle, France 1H1.

58. See also Karen Offen, "Madame Ghénia Avril de Sainte-Croix," 239–55.

59. Dr. Eudlitz, "Rapport moral du conseil d'administration," *L'Asile de Nuit Israélite de Paris* (Imp. Polyglotte N.-L. Dangiz, 1912), 24–28.

60. M. J. Luncz, secrétaire, "Rapport sur l'activité de l'UPJ du 1er novembre 1902 au 31 octobre 1903 présenté à l'assemblée générale du 5 décembre 1903," *Université Populaire Juive: Compte-Rendu annuel et statuts* (Paris: Imprimerie N.L. Danzig, 1904), 5–16.

61. "Allocution de M. Novochelski," *L'Asile de Nuite Israélite de Paris* (Imp. Polyglotte, N.-L. Danzig, 1911), 13, 17–18.

62. "Allocution de Madame Eugène Manuel," *Le Toit Familial: Compte rendu de la séance générale annuelle du 8 juin 1904* (Paris, 1904), 15–21.

63. Dr. Eudlitz, "Rapport moral du conseil d'administration," *L'Asile de Nuit Israélite de Paris: Rapport de l'exercice 1912* (Imp. Polyglotte N.-L. Dangiz, 1912), 29. Jewish feminist scholar Rachel Biale has noted that according to the Jewish legal code, the *Shulhan Arukh*, practicing *tzedakah* (charity or justice) was a requirement for a "worthy daughter of Israel." See Rachel Biale, *Women and Jewish Law: The Essential Texts, Their History, and Their Relevance for Today* (New York: Schocken Books, 1984), 38.

64. This does not mean that Jews within the French Jewish community always got along well; many examples exist, suggesting tensions between upper- and working-class Jews as well as between immigrants and the established Jewish community.

French Jews nonetheless did feel a responsibility to take care of arriving immigrants, even if that meant helping them on to the United States rather than having them remain in France. See Green, "To Give and to Receive," 197–226.

65. Green, "The Contradictions of Acculturation," 59.

66. Leila J. Rupp's work is one of the few studies that examines how women contributed to internationalism. Her project makes a significant contribution to the study of women's international activities but, as she notes, much work still needs to be done before a complete picture of women's contribution to internationalism can be developed. See Leila J. Rupp, *Worlds of Women: The Making of an International Women's Movement* (Princeton, NJ: Princeton Univ. Press, 1997).

67. See Anne Summers, "Work in Progress: Which Women? What Europe? Josephine Butler and the International Abolitionist Federation," *History Workshop Journal* 62 (2006): 216; Jordan, *Josephine Butler*, chapter 11.

68. Watson, "The Trade in Women," 14.

69. See proceedings from the Conférence Internationale pour la Répression de la Traite des Blanches: Bruxelles, 21, 22, 23, et 24 octobre 1912 (Brussels, 1912), 12–20. French women such as Mme Paul de Schlumberger (Protestant), Mme Avril de Sainte-Croix, and Mme Eugène Simon (Jewish), among others, participated in this conference.

70. Watson, "The Trade in Women," 62–65.

71. La Marquise de Castellane, "Rapport sur la maison d'accueil de Paris," *ACI: Congrès National Français* (Dijon, 1913), 21–23.

72. Mlle de Saint-Seine, "Rapport national français: Nancy," *ACI: Congrès National Français* (Dijon, 1912), 67–68, 79–80.

73. Humbert, *L'Union International des Amies de la Jeune Fille*, 1–24.

74. "Œuvre des arrivantes," *Amies: Section parisienne* (Fontenay-aux-Roses, 1914), 29–31. Many of the reports published by the Amies comment on the correspondence within France and abroad to organize girls' trips.

75. F. Dupin de Saint-André, "Quelques expériences d'une membre de l'Union des Amies de la Jeune Fille," *La femme* 31, no. 1 (January 1909): 3–5.

76. Humbert, *L'Union Internationale des Amies de la Jeune Fille*, 5–39.

77. "Discours de Mme de Montenach, vice-president internationale," *ACI: Congrès National Français* (Fribourg, 1908), 15–25. By 1907, the ACI consisted of about 2,000 programs worldwide. The ACI held an international conference every three years that brought women from all over Europe and other parts of the world together to discuss their common goals.

78. Hyman, *From Dreyfus to Vichy*, 63–65.

79. Kathleen McCarthy, "Parallel Power Structures: Women and the Voluntary Sphere," in *Lady Bountiful Revisited: Women, Philanthropy, and Power*, ed. Kathleen McCarthy (New Brunswick, NJ: Rutgers Univ. Press, 1990), 23.

80. "Discours de M. Louis Rivière, président du Congrès: Résumé des travaux du Congrès, État actuel de l'œuvre," *ACI: Congrès National Français* (Fribourg, 1908), 12.

81. Hause and Kenney, *Women's Suffrage and Social Politics*, 23–25. See also Bard, *Les filles de Marianne*. Bard provides a very thorough description of French feminism's development in the first half of the twentieth century, including the moderate feminist and reformist groups such as the Conseil National des Femmes Françaises, headed by prominent Protestant and Jewish women.

82. See Karen Offen, "Intrepid Crusader: Ghénia Avril de Sainte-Croix Takes on the Prostitution Issue," *Proceedings of the Western Society for French History* 33 (2005): 362. Offen found that the International Council of Women nominated Mme Avril de Sainte-Croix to serve on the League's committee. She was appointed in 1922. Although Sainte-Croix was not clearly associated with any religious group, the participation of women in the League's council attests to the status women had achieved in the milieu of social reform through their work in a variety of different anti–white slavery organizations. Mme Montenach served as the ACI representative on this committee in 1922. See "League of Nations Summary of Annual Reports 1922–1945," *Advisory Committee on Traffic in Women and Children: Minutes*, 1922 (microfilm: C. 445. MZ65. 1922 Category IV, 1922–1923 Assembly, Council, Circular Letters reel 2 of 13.)

6. Battling for God and Nation

1. Baronne Thérèse James de Rothschild, *Souvenirs de la Grande Guerre, 1914–1918* (Protat Frères à Mâcon, 1927), 48–50.

2. "Union des associations cultuelles de France et d'Algérie: Rapport moral 1915," *Union des associations cultuelles israelites de France: Comptes rendus 1908–1928*. Archives de la Consistoire Israélite de Paris, no code.

3. Margaret Darrow, *French Women and the First World War: War Stories of the Home Front* (Oxford, New York: Berg, 2000), 21–22.

4. Françoise Thébaud, *La femme au temps de la guerre de 14* (Paris: Editions Stock, 1986), 27.

5. Hause and Kenney, *Women's Suffrage and Social Politics*, 191–92.

6. J. H. Dreyfuss, *Sermons de guerre: Troisième série des sermons et allocutions* (Paris: Librairie Durlacher, 1921), 91–102.

7. Jean-Jacques Becker, *The Great War and the French People* (Oxford, Providence: Berg, 1993), 4.

8. Jay Winter, "Paris, London, Berlin 1914–1919: Capital Cities at War," in *Capital Cities at War: Paris, London, Berlin 1914–1919*, eds. Jay Winter and Jean-Louis Robert (Cambridge: Cambridge Univ. Press, 1997), 14–19.

9. Vicomtesse de Vélard, "Haut les cœurs!," *Echo de la Ligue Patriotique des Françaises* 12, no. 140 (August 15, 1914): 1. For another example, see "Service à l'église N.D. des Victoires pour les soldats mort au champ d'honneur" (police report), November 27, 1914. Archives de la Préfecture de la Police, Paris (BA 902)—Folder: BA 902.

10. Thébaud, *La femme au temps de la guerre de 14*, 24.

11. Marguerite de Witt-Schlumberger, "Appel aux femmes françaises," *Le huguenot* 30, no. 17–18 (September 1/15, 1915), 79. This article also appears in the *Journal des débats* (July 12, 1915) and in *Évangile et liberté: La vie nouvelle et le protestant unis*, 30 (29) (July 17, 1915): 216–17.

12. Rothschild, *Souvenirs de la Grande Guerre*, 1–12.

13. Suzanne Bloch, "Tribune Libre: Lettre d'une Française Juive à la Rédaction," *Le peuple juif: Ancien écho sioniste* 10, no. 6 (July 1, 1916): 8–9.

14. Jean-Louis Robert, "The Image of the Profiteer," in *Capital Cities at War: Paris, London, Berlin 1914–1919*, eds. Jay Winter and Jean-Louis Robert (Cambridge: Cambridge Univ. Press, 1997), 104–5, 131.

15. Mary Louise Roberts, *Civilization without Sexes: Reconstructing Gender in Postwar France, 1917–1927* (Chicago: Univ. of Chicago Press, 1994), 24–25.

16. See Thébaud, *La femme au temps de la guerre de 14*, 32, 134–35.

17. Jean-Marie Mayeur, "Le catholicisme français et la Première Guerre Mondiale," *Francia* 2 (1974): 386.

18. André Latreille, cited by A. Becker in Becker, *The Great War and the French People*, 179. The first days of mobilization saw numerous examples of unity among Catholics, Protestants, Jews, and the state. Jean-Marie Mayeur notes that the religious divisions of the prewar years appeared to be overcome as the "diverse 'spiritual families' came together for national defense." Many priests served either as military chaplains or as soldiers, and priests left on the home front cooperated with Protestants and local authorities in wartime programs. The "massive return to the altars" that occurred in the first months of the war also seemed to prove to Catholics that France had remained Christian. See Mayeur, "Le catholicisme français," 380–85.

19. "Paris le 15 décembre 1916" (police report). Archives National de France F7 13216—Folder: Ligue Patriotique des Françaises (1910–1927).

20. Sarti, *The Ligue Patriotique des Françaises*, 45.

21. Winock, *Nationalism, Anti-Semitism, and Fascism in France*, 85–93.

22. Patrick Cabanel suggests that it would be hard to overestimate the power of the memory of the Saint Bartholomew's Day massacre in 1572, the persecution that followed the revocation of the Edict of Nantes in 1685, the war of the Camisards between 1702 and 1704, or the violence of the White Terror in 1815. Even the governments of the Restoration, the Second Empire, and the Moral Order had shown an "evident sympathy for Catholicism and had multiplied the red tape against

Protestants and their liberty of evangelization of religious practice." See Cabanel, *Les protestants et la république*, 24–30.

23. See Steven Hause, "Anti-Protestant Rhetoric in the Early Third Republic," *French Historical Studies* 16, no. 1 (1989): 187–88.

24. See Laurent Gambarotte, *Foi et patrie: La prédication du protestantisme français pendant la Première Guerre Mondiale* (Geneva: Labor et Fides, 1996), 74–86.

25. *La minorité protestante et l'union sacrée* (January 23, 1916), 31, cited in Laurent Gambarotte, *Foi et patrie*, 78. He attributes this to J. Lafon but does not include his name in the citation.

26. "Discours de M. J.-H. Dreyfus, grand-rabbin de Paris," *L'univers israélite* 71, no. 11 (June 4, 1915): 264–67.

27. Police Report, November 27, 1914. Archives de la Préfecture de Police, Paris BA 902.

28. Vicomtesse de Vélard, "Haut les cœurs!," *Echo de la Ligue Patriotique des Françaises* 12, no. 140 (August 15, 1914): 1. For another example, see "Service à l'église N.D. des victoires pour les soldats mort au champ d'honneur" (police report), November 27, 1914. Archives de la Préfecture de Police, Paris (BA 902)—Folder: BA 902.

29. "Les ligueuses et la guerre," *Petit Echo de la Ligue Patriotique des Françaises* 12, no. 175 (September 1914): 1.

30. Vicomtesse de Vélard, "Lettre aux adhérentes," *Petit Echo de la Ligue Patriotique des Françaises* 12, no. 176 (October 1914): 1–2.

31. "La Ligue à Cambrai," *Petit Echo de la Ligue Patriotique des Françaises* 14, no. 193 (March 1916): 4.

32. H. F., "Assemblées annuelles," *Le christianisme au XX siècle* 44, no. 16 (April 22, 1915): 124.

33. Judaeus, "Le judaïsme français et la guerre: Patrie, religion, charité," *L'univers israélite* 70, no. 11 (December 4, 1914): 27–29.

34. "Echo de la chaire," *Archives israélites* 77, no. 41 (October 12, 1916): 162.

35. "La lettre d'une chrétienne—X . . . 9 Août 1914," *Le huguenot* 29, no. 16–17 (August 15 and September 1, 1914): 133.

36. "Une chrétienne et une française," *Haute les cœurs: Feuille bimensuelle pour les femmes* 31 (July 1, 1916): 1.

37. "Nouvelles des unions: Communication du comité national," *Journal de la jeune fille* (March–April 1917): 68–69. The UCJF was the French equivalent of the Young Women's Christian Association.

38. "Nobles paroles d'un cœur français," *L'univers israélite* 73, no. 26 (March 6 1918), 637–39. It's not clear where Sophie Fridmon came from. However, Philippe Boulanger found that 30,000 foreigners volunteered for wartime service in France at the beginning of the war. See Philippe Boulanger, "Géographie historique de la

conscription et des conscrits en France de 1914 à 1922" (PhD diss., Université de Paris-IV, 1998, 2 vols.). Cited in Stéphane Audoin-Rouzeau and Annette Becker, *14–18: Understanding the Great War*, trans. Catherine Temerson (New York: Hill and Wang, 2000), 100.

39. Hyman, *The Jews of Modern France*, 133.

40. Thébaud, *La femme au temps de la guerre de 14*, 23–25, 260–61.

41. Kathleen Kennedy, *Disloyal Mothers and Scurrilous Citizens: Women and Subversion during World War I*, (Bloomington: Indiana Univ. Press, 1999), chapter 1.

42. Kennedy, *Disloyal Mothers*, 1.

43. "Rapport de Mlle Frossard—La mission de la Ligueuse: Être plus que jamais l'auxiliaire du Clergé et préparer la France de demain," *Echo de la Ligue Patriotique des Françaises* 15, no. 174 (November 15, 1917): 4–7.

44. *Le devoir des femmes françaises par l'une d'elles* (Paris: M. J. Caplain, 1902), 29.

45. Police Report: Préfecture de Police, Paris, le 7 Mai 1915. Archives de la Préfecture de Police, Paris BA 902.

46. Police Report: Préfecture de la Police, 19 Avril 1915. Archives Nationale de France F7 13216—Folder: Department Centrale.

47. Statistics drawn from Gambarotto, *Foi et patrie*, 358–59.

48. In the pamphlet that de Witt-Schlumberger produced, she indicated that she had placed an ad in several Protestant journals. She did not name the journals. See de Witt-Schlumberger, *Le rôle des femmes de pasteurs*, 1.

49. De Witt-Schlumberger, *Le Rôle des femmes de pasteurs*, 9–15. De Witt-Schlumberger included nine examples in the tract, but she does not say how many she received.

50. Œuvre des orphelins israélites de la guerre, supplément au premier bulletin (Paris: Siège Social, November 1916), 3–10. Women made up almost the totality of the active members, and supervised children enrolled in the program. Likewise, women in the regional committee of Algiers held the positions of president, vice president, and treasurer, and the directing committee in Constantine only included women.

51. Hyman, *The Jews of Modern France*, 134.

52. This story is cited in Yvonne Knibiehler, Véronique LeRoux-Hugon, Odile DuPont-Hess, and Yoland Tastayre, *Cornettes et blouses blanches: Les infirmières dans la société française (1880–1980)* (Paris: Hachette, 1984), 101. They cite Abbé Coubé, *Le patriotisme de la femme française* (Paris: Lethielleux, 1916) further down on the page, although it is not clear whether the story comes from this book. The origin of the nurse's commendation is also unclear.

53. Knibiehler, Leroux-Hugon, DuPont-Hess, and Tastayre, *Cornettes et blouses blanches*, 101.

54. "La Ligue à Cambrai," *Echo de la Ligue Patriotique des Françaises* 14, no. 155 (15 Février 1916): 2.

55. Police Report: Paris, 10 Mars 1916. Archives Nationales de France F7 13216.

56. Police Report: Préfecture de la Police, Paris, 31 Mai 1915. Archives de la Préfecture de Police, Paris (BA 902)—Folder: BA 902.

57. For examples of programs to aid soldiers, see Mme A. Philip de Barjeau, "Les orphelins de la guerre," *Journal de la jeune fille* (September–October 1916): 197–98; "Appels et communications pour 'leur' noël," *Le christianisme au XX siècle* 45, no. 45 (November 9, 1916): 357.

58. For more information on French nurses during World War I, see Thébaud, *La femme au temps de la guerre de 14*, part 1, ch. 3; Margaret Darrow, "French Volunteer Nursing and the Myth of War Experience in World War I," *American Historical Review* (February 1996): 80–106.

59. "Nouvelles et faits divers," *Le christianisme au XXe siècle* 46, no. 42 (October 18, 1917): 334.

60. "Nouvelles et faits divers: Distinctions," *Le christianisme au XXe siècle* 46, no. 41 (October 11, 1917): 352. "Armée d'Orient," *Le huguenot* 32, no. 17 et 18 (September 1 and 15, 1917): 69–70.

61. "Échos israélites de la guerre," *Archives israélites* 78, no. 44 (November 1, 1917): 175.

62. "Échos israélite de la guerre," *Archives israélites* 49 (December 6, 1917): 194.

63. H. Prague, "Nos infirmières," *Archives israélites* 79, no. 27 (July 4, 1918): 105–6.

64. Thébaud, *La femme au temps de la guerre de 14*, 87.

65. Police Report: Préfet de Police à Monsieur le Ministre de l'Intérieur, Paris, September 1, 1917. Archives Nationales de France F7 13215—Folder: "Fédération internationale des ligues catholiques (1910–1918)."

66. For more information about the improved relationship between Catholics and the State, see Cholvy and Hilaire, *Histoire religieuses*, 271–82.

67. Cabanel, *Juifs et protestants en France*, 214–15.

68. Roberts, *Civilization without Sexes*, 21–24.

69. De Witt-Schlumberger, *Le rôle des femmes de pasteurs*, 3–15.

70. Kaplan, *The Making of the Jewish Middle Class*, 19–20.

Conclusion

1. For more on this, see Wallach Scott, *The Politics of the Veil*, 1–20.

2. Eleanor Beardsley, "Meetings Debate the Question of French Identity," *All Things Considered—National Public Radio*, December 9, 2009, http://www.npr.org/templates/story/story.php?storyId=121963766.

3. Valentin Graff, "À Villeneuve-Loubet, ville symbole de la polémique de l'été, le burkini reste invisible," *France 24*, August 29, 2016. http://www.france24.com/fr /20160828-villeneuve-loubet-ville-symbole-polemique-burkini-reste-invisible-ete.

4. Wallach Scott, *The Politics of the Veil*, 107.

Bibliography

Abrams, Lynn. *The Making of Modern Woman*. London: Pearson Education, 2002.

Accampo, Elinor, Rachel Fuchs, and Mary Lynn Stewart, eds. *Gender and the Politics of Social Reform in France, 1870–1914*. Baltimore, MD: Johns Hopkins Univ. Press, 1995.

Ahmed, Leila. *A Border Passage: From Cairo to America—A Woman's Journey*. New York: Farrar, Straus and Giroux, 1999.

Airiau, Paul. *Cent ans de laïcité françaises, 1905–2005*. Paris: Presses de la Renaissance, 2005.

Albert, Phyllis Cohen. *The Modernization of French Jewry: Consistory and Community in the Nineteenth Century*. Hanover, MA: Brandeis Univ. Press, 1977.

Arnal, Oscar. *Ambivalent Alliance: The Catholic Church and the Action Française, 1899–1939*. Pittsburgh: Univ. of Pittsburgh Press, 1985.

Aubert, Roger, and Claude Soetens., eds. *Histoire du christianisme, v. 13: Crises et renouveau (de 1958 à nos jours)*. Paris: Desclée, 2000.

Audoin-Rouzeau, Stéphane, and Annette Becker. *14–18: Understanding the Great War*. Translated by Catherine Temerson. New York: Hill and Wang, 2000.

Bard, Christine. *Les filles de Marianne: Histoire des féminismes 1914–1940*. Paris: Fayard, 1995.

Baubérot, Jean. *Histoire de la laïcité en France*. Paris: Presses Universitaires de France, 2000.

Baubérot, Jean et Jean-Paul Willaime. *Le protestantisme*. Solar, 1987.

Becker, Jean-Jacques. *The Great War and the French People*. Oxford, Providence: Berg, 1993.

Berkovitz, Jay. "Ritual and Emancipation: A Reassessment of Cultural Modernization in France." *Historical Reflections* 32, no. 1 (Winter 2006): 9–38.

Biale, Rachel. *Women and Jewish Law: The Essential Texts, Their History, and Their Relevance for Today.* New York: Schocken Books, 1984.

Bianquis, Marie Merle. *La vocation de la femme d'après la bible: Etudes bibliques dédiées aux Unions Chrétiennes de Jeunes Filles.* Paris: Librairie Fischbacher, 1903.

Birnbaum, Pierre. *Jewish Destinies: Citizenship, State, and Community in Modern France.* Translated by Arthur Goldhammer. New York: Hill and Wang, 2000.

Boulanger, Philippe. "Géographie historique de la conscription et des conscrits en France de 1914 à 1922." PhD diss., Université de Paris-IV, 1998, 2 vols.

Bréjon de Lavergnée, Matthieu. *Histoire des filles de la charité (XVIIe–XVIIIe siècle).* Paris: Fayard, 2011.

———. *La Société de Saint-Vincent-de-Paul au XIXe siècle: Un fleuron du catholicisme sociale.* Paris: Cerf, 2008.

Bristow, Edward. *Prostitution and Prejudice: The Jewish Fight against White Slavery 1870–1939.* New York: Schocken Books, 1983.

Cabanel, Patrick. *Juifs et protestants en France, les affinités électives XVIe–XXIe siècle.* Paris: Fayard, 2004.

———. *Les protestants et la république de 1870 à nos jours.* Paris: Éditions Complexe, 2000.

Canning, Kathleen. "Social Policy, Body Politics: Recasting the Social Question in Germany, 1875–1900." In *Gender and Class in Modern Europe*, edited by Laura Frader and Sonya Rose, 211–38. Ithaca, NY: Cornell Univ. Press, 1996.

Caron, Vicky. *Between France and Germany: The Jews of Alsace-Lorraine, 1871–1918.* Stanford, CA: Stanford Univ. Press, 1988.

Chessel, Marie-Emmanuelle. *Consommateurs engagés à la Belle Époque: La ligue sociale d'acheteurs.* Paris: Presses de Sciences Po, 2012.

Cholvy, Gérard. *La religion en France de la fin du XVIII à nos jours.* Paris: Hachette, 1991.

Cholvy, Gérard, and Yves-Marie Hilaire. *Histoire religieuse de la France contemporaine, 1880–1930.* Toulouse: Éditions Privat, 1985.

Clark, Christopher. "The New Catholicism and the European Culture Wars." In *Culture Wars: Secular-Catholic Conflict in Nineteenth-Century Europe*, edited by Christopher Clark and Wolfram Kaiser, 11–47. Cambridge: Cambridge Univ. Press, 2003.

Clark, Christopher, and Wolfram Kaiser, eds., *Culture Wars: Secular-Catholic Conflict in Nineteenth-Century Europe*. Cambridge: Cambridge Univ. Press, 2003.

Clark, Linda L. "Bringing Feminine Qualities into the Public Sphere: The Third Republic's Appointment of Women Inspectors." In *Gender and the Politics of Social Reform in France, 1870–1914*, edited by Elinor Accampo, Rachel Fuchs, and Mary Lynn Stewart, 128–56. Baltimore, MD: Johns Hopkins Univ. Press, 1995.

Cohen, Yolande. "Protestant and Jewish Philanthropies in France: The Conseil National des Femmes Francaises, (1901–1939)." *French Politics, Culture and Society* 36, no. 3 (2018): 74–92.

Commission exécutive du Synode du Poitou, *Le Synode: Son passé—Son present*. Cahors: Imprimerie Typographique A. Coueslant, 1900.

Corbin, Alain. *Women for Hire: Prostitution and Sexuality in France after 1850*. Translated by Alan Sheridan. Cambridge, MA: Harvard Univ. Press, 1990.

Coubé, Abbé. *Le patriotisme de la femme française*. Paris: Lethielleux, 1916.

Cova, Anne. *Au service de l'église, de la patrie et de la famille: Femmes catholiques et maternité sous la IIIe République*. Paris: L'Harmattan, 2000.

Curtis, Sarah. "Charitable Ladies: Gender, Class and Religion in Mid-Nineteenth Century Paris," *Past & Present* 177, no. 1 (November 2002): 121–57.

———. *Civilizing Habits: Women Missionaries and the Revival of French Empire*. Oxford: Oxford Univ. Press, 2010.

Dalencourt, J. *Mission évangélique aux femmes de la classe ouvrière: Œuvre de Mme Dalencourt*. Paris, 1881.

Darrow, Margaret. *French Women and the First World War: War Stories of the Home Front*. Oxford, New York: Berg, 2000.

———. "French Volunteer Nursing and the Myth of War Experience in World War I," *American Historical Review* (February 1996): 80-106.

Davies, Peter. *The Extreme Right in France, 1789 to the Present: From de Maistre to Le Pen*. London: Routledge, 2002.

Della Sudda, Magali. "La Politique Malgre elles: Mobilisations féminines Catholiques en France et en Italie (1900–1914)." *Revue Française de science politique* 60, no. 1 (2010): 37–60.

———. "Les femmes catholiques à l'épreuve de la laïcité: La Ligue Patriotique des Françaises ou la première mobilization féminine de masse

(1902–1914)." In *Politiques de la laïcité au XXe siècle*, edited by Patrick Weil, 123–47. Paris: Presses Universitaires de France, 2007.

Desan, Suzanne. *Reclaiming the Sacred: Lay Religion and Popular Politics in Revolutionary France*. Ithaca, NY: Cornell Univ. Press, 1990.

Diebolt, Evelyne. "Femmes protestantes face aux politiques de santé publique 1900–1939." *Bulletin de la Société de l'Histoire du Protestantisme Françaises* 146, no. 1 (2000): 91–132.

———. "Women and Philanthropy in France: From the Sixteenth to the Twentieth Centuries." In *Women, Philanthropy, and Civil Society*, edited by Kathleen D. McCarthy, 29–65. Bloomington: Indiana Univ. Press, 2001.

Douen, O. *Histoire de la société biblique protestante de Paris.* Paris: Agence de la Société Biblique Protestant, 1868.

Dreyfuss, J. H. *Sermons de guerre: Troisième s*érie. Paris: Librairie Durlacher. 1921.

Dumons, Bruno. *Les dames de la Ligue des Femmes Françaises (1901–1914).* Paris: Les Éditions du Cerf, 2006.

———. "Resistances des ligues feminines catholiques a l'idee laique." In *Le pouvoir du genre: Laïcités et religions, 1905–2005*, edited by Florence Rochefort, 83–99. Toulouse: Presses Universitaires du Mirail, 2008.

Encrevé, André. *L'expérience et la foi: Pensée et vie religieuse des huguenots au XIXe siècle.* Geneva: Labor et Fides, 2001.

———. *Les protestantes en France de 1800 à nos jours.* Paris: Éditions Stock, 1985.

Eysteinsson, Astradur. *The Concept of Modernism.* Ithaca, NY: Cornell Univ. Press, 1990.

Fayet-Scribe, Sylvie. *Associations féminines et catholicisme XIXe–XXe siècle.* Paris: Éditions Ouvrières, 1990.

Felski, Rita. *The Gender of Modernity.* Cambridge, MA: Harvard Univ. Press, 1995.

Ford, Caroline. *Creating the Nation in Provincial France: Religion and Political Identity in Brittany.* Princeton, NJ: Princeton Univ. Press, 1993.

———. *Divided Houses: Religion and Gender in Modern France.* Ithaca, NY: Cornell Univ. Press, 2005.

Frader, Laura, and Sonya Rose, eds. *Gender and Class in Modern Europe.* Ithaca, NY: Cornell Univ. Press, 1996.

Fuchs, Rachel. "France in a Comparative Perspective." In *Gender and the Politics of Social Reform in France, 1870–1914*, edited by Elinor Accampo,

Rachel Fuchs, and Mary Lynn Stewart, 157–89. Baltimore, MD: Johns Hopkins Univ. Press, 1995.

Fuchs, Rachel G., and Leslie Page Moch, "Pregnant, Single, and Far from Home: Migrant Women in Nineteenth-Century Paris." *The American Historical Review* 95, no. 4 (1990): 1007–31.

Gambarotte, Laurent. *Foi et patrie: La prédication du protestantisme français pendant la Première Guerre Mondiale*. Geneva: Labor et Fides, 1996.

Gibson, Ralph. *A Social History of French Catholicism, 1789–1914*. London, New York: Routledge, 1989.

———. "Le catholicisme et les femmes en France au XIXe siècle," *Revue d'histoire de l'église de France* 79, no. 202 (1993): 63–93.

Graetz, Michael. *The Jews in Nineteenth-Century France: From the French Revolution to the Alliance Israelite Universelle*. Stanford, CA: Stanford Univ. Press, 1996.

Green, Nancy. "The Contradictions of Acculturation: Immigrant Oratories and Yiddish Union Sections in Paris before World War I." In *The Jews in Modern France*, edited by Frances Malino and Bernard Wasserstein, 54-71. Hanover, London: Univ. Press of New England, 1985.

———. "To Give and to Receive." In *The Uses of Charity: The Poor on Relief in the Nineteenth-Century Metropolis*, edited by Peter Mandle. Philadelphia: Univ. of Pennsylvania Press, 1990.

Gubin, Elaine, Catherine Jacques, Florence Rochefort, Brigitte Studer, Françoise Thébaud, and Michelle Zancarini-Fournel, eds. *Le siècle des féminismes*. Paris: Éditions de l'Atelier, 2004.

Haag, Martin. "Statut des femmes dans les organisations religieuses: L'exemple de l'accès au pouvoir clérical." *Archives de Sciences Sociales des Religions* 95 (1996): 48–51.

Harris, Ruth, *Lourdes: Body and Spirit in the Secular Age*. New York: Viking, 1999.

Harrison, Carol. *Romantic Catholics: France's Postrevolutionary Generation in Search of a Modern Faith*. Ithaca, NY: Cornell Univ. Press, 2014.

Hause, Steven. "Anti-Protestant Rhetoric in the Early Third Republic." *French Historical Studies* 16, no. 1 (1989): 183–201.

Hause, Steven, and Anne Kenney. "The Development of the Catholic Women's Suffrage Movement in France, 1896–1922." *Catholic Historical Review* 67, no. 1 (January 1981): 11–30.

———. *Women's Suffrage and Social Politics in the French Third Republic.* Princeton, NJ: Princeton Univ. Press, 1984.

Heitz-Muller, Anne-Marie. "L'ouverture du ministère pastoral aux femmes dans les églises protestantes d'Alsace et de Lorraine." *Revue d'histoire et de philosophie religieuses* 83, no. 3 (2003): 301–23.

Hilden, Patricia. *Working Women and Socialists Politics in France, 1880–1914.* Oxford: Clarendon Press, 1986.

Humbert, Mme Ed. *L'Union Internationale des Amies de la Jeune Fille: Son origine, sa nature, son extension.* Neuchatel: Imprimerie Attinger Frères, 1889.

Hyman, Paula. *From Dreyfus to Vichy: The Remaking of French Jewry, 1906–1939.* New York: Columbia Univ. Press, 1979.

———. "Gender and the Shaping of Modern Jewish Identities." *Jewish Social Studies* 8, nos. 2–3 (Winter/Spring 2002): 153–61.

———. *The Emancipation of Jews of Alsace: Acculturation and Tradition in the Nineteenth Century.* New Haven, CT: Yale Univ. Press, 1984.

———. *The Jews of Modern France.* Berkeley: Univ. of California Press, 1998.

Jordan, Jane. *Josephine Butler.* London: John Murray, 2001.

Kalman, Julie. *Orientalizing the Jew: Religion, Culture and Imperialism in Nineteenth Century France.* Bloomington: Indiana Univ. Press, 2017.

Kaplan, Marion A. *The Making of the Jewish Middle Class: Women, Family, and Identity in Imperial Germany.* Oxford: Oxford Univ. Press, 1991.

Kennedy, Kathleen. *Disloyal Mothers and Scurrilous Citizens: Women and Subversion during World War I.* Bloomington: Indiana Univ. Press, 1999.

Keranflec'h-Kernezne, Comtesse de. *Madame Chenu, 1861–1939.* Paris: Action Sociale de la Femme et le Livre Français, 1940.

Klaus, Alisa. "Women's Organizations and the Infant Health Movement in France and the United States, 1890–1920." In *Lady Bountiful Revisited: Women, Philanthropy and Power,* edited by Kathleen McCarthy, 157–74. New Brunswick, NJ: Rutgers Univ. Press, 1990.

Klejman, Laurence, and Florence Rochefort. *L'égalité en marche: Le féminisme sous la Troisième République.* Paris: Press de la Fondation Nationale des Sciences Politiques, 1989.

Knibiehler, Yvonne, Véronique LeRoux-Hugon, Odile DuPont-Hess, and Yoland Tastayre, *Cornettes et blouses blanches: Les infirmières dans la société française (1880–1980).* Paris: Hachette, 1984.

Koven, Seth. "Borderlands: Women, Voluntary Action, and Child Welfare in Britain 1840–1914." In *Mothers of a New World: Maternalist Politics and the Origins of Welfare States*, edited by Seth Koven and Sonya Michel, 94–136. New York, London: Routledge, 1993.

Koven, Seth, and Sonya Michel. "Womanly Duties: Maternalist Politics and the Origins of Welfare States in France, Germany, Great Britain, and the United States 1880–1920." In *Gender and History in Western Europe*, edited by Robert Shoemaker and Mary Vincent, 319–49. London: Arnold, 1998.

———, eds. *Mothers of a New World: Maternalist Politics and the Origins of Welfare States.* New York, London: Routledge, 1993.

Kselman, Thomas. *Death and the Afterlife in Modern France.* Princeton, NJ: Princeton Univ. Press, 1993.

———. "The Dechristianisation of Death in Modern France." In *The Decline of Christendom in Western Europe*, edited by Hugh McLeod and Werner Ustorf, 145–63. Cambridge: Cambridge Univ. Press, 2003.

LaLouette, Jacqueline. *La séparation des églises et de l'état: Genèse et dévelopment d'une idée (1789–1905).* Paris: Éditions du Seuil, 2005.

Lambert, Yves. "New Christianity, Indifference and Diffused Spirituality." In *The Decline of Christendom in Western Europe, 1750–2000*, edited by Hugh McLeod and Werner Ustorf. Cambridge: Cambridge Univ. Press, 2003.

Landes, David. "Two Cheers for Emancipation." In *The Jews in Modern France*, edited by Frances Malino and Bernard Wasserstein. Hanover, London: Univ. Press of New England, 1985.

Langlois, Claude. "Le catholicisme au féminin." *Archives de sciences sociales des religions* 57, no. 1 (January–March 1984): 29–53.

———. *Le catholicisme au féminin: Les congregations françaises à supérieure générale au XIXe siècle.* Paris: Les Éditions du Cerf, 1984.

Larkin, Maurice. *L'église et l'état en France: 1905: La crise de la séparation.* Toulouse: Éditions Privat, 2004.

Lebovics, Herman. *True France: The Wars over Cultural Identity, 1900–1945.* Ithaca, NY: Cornell Univ. Press, 1992.

Le devoir des femmes françaises par l'une d'elles. Paris: M. J. Caplain, 1902.

Leff, Lisa Moses. *Sacred Bonds of Solidarity: The Rise of Jewish Internationalism in Nineteenth-Century France.* Stanford, CA: Stanford Univ. Press, 2006.

Leglaive-Perani, Céline. "De la charité à la philanthripie: Introduction." *Archives Juives* 1, no. 44 (2011): 4–16.

———. "Donner au Féminin: Juives philanthripes in France (1830–1930)." *Archives juives* 2, no. 48 (2015): 11–24.

———. "Le judaïsme parisien et la Comité de Bienfaisance Israélite (1830–1930)." *Archives juives* 1, no. 44 (2011): 37–53.

———. "Les juifs français dans la lutte contre la traite des blanches (1880–1930)." *Archives juives* 2, no. 44 (2011): 59–76.

Lequin, Yves. *Histoire des étrangers et de l'immigration en France*. Paris: Larousse, 2006.

Lévy, Emile. *La femme juive: Deux sermons*. Imprimerie E. Seitz, 1906.

Machen, Emily. "French Women and the Global Fight for Faith: Catholic International Religious Outreach in Turn-of-the-Century France." *Catholic Historical Review* 100, no. 2 (Spring 2014): 292–318.

Malino, Frances, and Bernard Wasserstein, eds. *The Jews in Modern France*. Hanover, London: Univ. Press of New England, 1985.

Malinovich, Nadia. *French and Jewish: Culture and the Politics of Identity in Early Twentieth-Century France*. Oxford: The Littman Library of Jewish Civilization, 2011.

Mandle, Peter, ed. *The Uses of Charity: The Poor on Relief in the Nineteenth-Century Metropolis*. Philadelphia: Univ. of Pennsylvania Press, 1990.

Mayeur, Jean-Marie. "Le catholicisme français et la Première Guerre Mondiale." *Francia* 2 (1974): 377–97.

Mayeur, Jean-Marie, and Madeleine Rebérioux. *The Third Republic from its Origins to the Great War, 1871–1914*. Translated by J. R. Foster. Cambridge: Cambridge Univ. Press, 1984.

McCarthy, Kathleen. "Parallel Power Structures: Women and the Voluntary Sphere." In *Lady Bountiful Revisited: Women, Philanthropy, and Power*, edited by Kathleen McCarthy, 1–35. New Brunswick, NJ: Rutgers Univ. Press, 1990.

———, ed. *Lady Bountiful Revisited: Women, Philanthropy and Power*. New Brunswick, NJ: Rutgers Univ. Press, 1990.

———, ed. *Women, Philanthropy, and Civil Society*. Bloomington: Indiana Univ. Press, 2001.

McLeod, Hugh. *Secularisation in Western Europe, 1848–1914*. London: Palgrave Macmillan, 2000.

McManners, John. *Church and State in France, 1870–1914.* New York, London: Harper & Row, 1972.

McMillan, James. *France and Women, 1789–1914.* London, New York: Routledge, 2000.

———. *Housewife or Harlot: The Place of Women in French Society, 1870–1940.* New York: St. Martin's Press, 1981.

———. "Religion and Gender in Modern France: Some Reflections." In *Religion, Society and Politics in France since 1789,* edited by Frank Tallett and Nicholas Atkin, 55–67. London: Hambledon Press, 1991.

Mills, Hazel. "Negotiating the Divide: Women, Philanthropy and the 'Public Sphere' in Nineteenth-Century France." In *Religion, Society and Politics in France since 1789,* edited by Frank Tallett and Nicholas Atkin, 29–55. London: Hambledon Press, 1991.

Miniati, Monica. *"Les 'Émancipées': Les femmes juives italiennes aux XIXe et XXe siècles (1848–1924).* Paris: Honoré Champion, 2004.

Moch, Leslie Page. *Moving Europeans: Migration in Western Europe since 1600, 2nd edition.* Bloomington: Indiana Univ. Press, 2003.

Noiriel, Gérard. *The French Melting Pot: Immigration, Citizenship, and National Identity.* Translated by Geoffroy de Laforcade. Minneapolis: Univ. of Minnesota Press, 1996.

Nord, Philip. *The Republican Moment: Struggles for Democracy in Nineteenth Century France.* Cambridge, MA: Harvard Univ. Press, 1995.

Offen, Karen. "Defining Feminism: A Comparative Historical Approach." *Signs: Journal of Women in Contemporary Culture and Society* 14, no. 1 (1988): 119–57.

———. *European Feminisms, 1700–1950.* Stanford, CA: Stanford Univ. Press, 2000.

———. "Intrepid Crusader: Ghénia Avril de Sainte-Croix Takes On the Prostitution Issue." *Proceedings of the Western Society for French History* 33 (2005): 352–74.

———. "Madame Ghénia Avril de Sainte-Croix, the Josephine Butler of France." *Women's History Review* 17, no. 2 (April 2008): 239–55.

O'Sullivan, Michael. "A Feminized Church?: German Catholic Women, Piety, and Domesticity, 1918–1938." In *Beyond the Feminization Thesis: Gender and Christianity in Modern Europe,* edited by Patrick Pasture et al., 191–211. Leuven: Leuven Univ. Press, 2012.

Pasture, Patrick. "Beyond the Feminization Thesis: Gendering the History of Christianity in the Nineteenth and Twentieth Centuries." In *Beyond the Feminization Thesis: Gender and Christianity in Modern Europe*, edited by Patrick Pasture et al., 7-33. Leuven: Leuven Univ. Press, 2012.

Pasture, Patrick, Jan Art, Thomas Buerman, Jan de Maeyer, Leen van Molle, Tine van Osselaer, and Vincent Viaene, eds. *Beyond the Feminization Thesis: Gender and Christianity in Modern Europe*. Leuven: Leuven Univ. Press, 2012.

Perrot, Michelle. "Les femmes et le syndicalisme au temps de la naissance de la CGT." *Cahiers d'histoire de l'Institut de Recherches Marxistes* 61 (1995): 47–53.

Philippe, Bèatrice. *Les juifs à Paris à la Belle Epoque*. Paris: Albin Michel, 1992.

Phillips, C. S. *The Church in France 1848–1907*. London: Society for Promoting Christian Knowledge, 1936.

Pierrard, Pierre. *Juifs et catholiques français: De Drumont à Jules Isaac (1886–1945)*. Paris: Fayard, 1970.

———. *Un siècle de l'église de France, 1900–2000*. Paris: Desclée de Brouwer, 2000.

Poujol, Geneviève. *Un féminisme sous tutelle: Les protestantes françaises—1810–1960*. Paris: Les Éditions de Paris, 2003.

Renan, Ernst, *Souvenirs d'enfance et de jeunesse*. Livre de Poche, 1967.

Robert, Jean-Louis. "The Image of the Profiteer." In *Capital Cities at War: Paris, London, Berlin 1914–1919*, edited by Jay Winter and Jean-Louis Robert, 104–33. Cambridge: Cambridge Univ. Press, 1997.

Roberts, Mary Louise. *Civilization without Sexes: Reconstructing Gender in Postwar France, 1917–1927*. Chicago: Univ. of Chicago Press, 1994.

———. *Disruptive Acts: The New Woman in Fin-de-Siècle France*. Chicago: Univ. of Chicago Press, 2005.

Roblin, Michel. *Les juifs de Paris*. Paris: Éditions A. et J. Picard, 1952.

Rochebillard, Marie-Louise. *Syndicats d'ouvrières lyonnaises*. Paris, Lille: Imprimerie de l'Action Populaire, c. 1904.

Rochefort, Florence. "Ambivalences laïques et critiques féministes." In *Le pouvoir du genre: Laïcités et religions, 1905–2005*, edited by Florence Rochefort, 65–83. Toulouse: Presses Universitaires du Mirail, 2007.

———. "Contrecarrer ou interroger les religions." In *Le siècle des féminismes*, edited by Elaine Gubin et al., 347-64. Paris: Éditions de l'Atelier, 2004.

———. "Féminisme et protestantisme au XIXe siècle, première rencontres, 1830–1900." *Bulletin de la Société de l'Histoire du Protestantisme* 146 (January–March, 2000): 69–87.

———, ed. *Le pouvoir du genre: Laïcités et religions, 1905–2005.* Toulouse: Presses Universitaires du Mirail, 2008.

Rogers, Rebecca. "Retrograde or Modern? Unveiling the Teaching Nun in Nineteenth-Century France." *Social History* 23, no. 2 (May 1998): 146–64.

Rose, Sonya. "Protective Labor Legislation in Nineteenth-Century Britain: Gender, Class and the Liberal State." In *Gender and Class in Modern Europe*, edited by Laura Frader and Sonya Rose, 193–211. Ithaca, NY: Cornell Univ. Press, 1996.

Rothschild, Baronne Thérèse James de. *Souvenirs de la Grande Guerre, 1914–1918.* Protat Frères à Mâcon, 1927.

Rupp, Leila J. *Worlds of Women: The Making of an International Women's Movement.* Princeton, NJ: Princeton Univ. Press, 1997.

Sabatier, Elsia. *Madame Jules Siegfried, 1848–1922.* Privas: Imprimerie Loubarie et Fils, s.d. (1924?).

Samuels, Maurice. *The Right to Difference: French Universalism and the Jews.* Chicago: Univ. of Chicago Press, 2016.

Sarti, Odile. *The Ligue Patriotique des Françaises, 1902–1933: A Feminine Response to the Secularization of French Society.* New York: Garland Publishing, 1992.

Schloesser, Stephen. *Jazz Age Catholicism: Mystic Modernism in Postwar Paris, 1919–1933.* Toronto: Univ. of Toronto Press, 2005.

Schneider, Bernhard. "The Catholic Poor Relief Discourse and the Feminization of the Caritas in Early Nineteenth-Century Germany." In *Beyond the Feminization Thesis: Gender and Christianity in Modern Europe*, edited by Patrick Pasture et al., 35–55. Leuven: Leuven Univ. Press, 2012.

Scott, Anne Firor. "Women's Voluntary Associations: From Charity to Reform." In *Lady Bountiful Revisited: Women, Philanthropy, and Power*, edited by Kathleen McCarthy, 35–55. New Brunswick, NJ: Rutgers Univ. Press, 1990.

Sharp, Lynn. *Secular Spirituality: Reincarnation and Spiritism in Nineteenth-Century France.* Lanham, MD: Lexington Books, 2006.

Shoemaker, Robert, and Mary Vincent, eds. *Gender and History in Western Europe.* London: Arnold, 1998.

Sowerwine, Charles. *France since 1870: Culture, Politics and Society*. New York: Palgrave, 2001.

Steinhoff, Anthony. "A Feminized Church? The Campaign for Women's Suffrage in Alsace-Lorraine's Protestant Churches, 1907–1914." *Central European History* 38, no. 2 (June 2005): 220–21.

———. "Protestants in Strasbourg, 1870–1914: Religion and Society in Late Nineteenth-Century Europe." PhD diss., Univ. of Chicago, 1996.

Stewart, Mary Lynn. "Setting the Standards: Labor and Family Reformers." In *Gender and the Politics of Social Reform in France, 1870–1914*, edited by Elinor Accampo, Rachel Fuchs, and Mary Lynn Stewart, 106–28. Baltimore, MD: Johns Hopkins Univ. Press, 1995.

Stone, Judith. *The Search for Social Peace: Reform Legislation in France, 1890–1914*. Albany: State Univ. of New York Press, 1985.

Stora-Lamarre, Annie. *L'enfer de la IIIe République: Censeurs et pornographes (1881–1914)*. Paris: Editions Imago, 1990.

Summers, Anne. "Work in Progress: Which Women? What Europe? Josephine Butler and the International Abolitionist Federation." *History Workshop Journal* 62 (2006): 214–31.

Swain, Shurlee. "Woman and Philanthropy in Colonial and Post-Colonial Australia." In *Women, Philanthropy, and Civil Society*, edited by Kathleen McCarthy, 153–69. Bloomington: Univ. of Indiana Press, 2001.

Tallett, Frank, and Nicholas Atkin, eds. *Religion, Society and Politics in France since 1789*. London: Hambledon Press, 1991.

Thébaud, Françoise. *La femme au temps de la guerre de 14*. Paris: Editions Stock, 1986.

Vidler, A. R. *A Century of Social Catholicism, 1820–1920*. London: SPCK, 1964.

Wallach Scott, Joan. *The Politics of the Veil*. Princeton, NJ: Princeton Univ. Press, 2007.

Watson, Molly McGregor. "The Trade in Women: 'White Slavery' and the French Nation, 1899–1939." PhD diss., Stanford University, 1999.

Weber, Eugen. *Peasants into Frenchmen: The Modernization of Rural France, 1870–1914*. Stanford, CA: Stanford Univ. Press, 1976.

Weil, Patrick. *Politiques de la laïcité au XXe siècle*. Paris: Presses Universitaires de France, 2007.

Willaime, Jean-Paul. "Les mutations des cadres de la vie ecclésial dans les églises protestantes." In *Histoire du christianisme, v. 13: Crises et renouveau (de 1958 à nos jours)*, edited by Roger Aubert et al., 237-54. Paris: Desclée, 2000.

Winock, Michel. *Nationalism, Anti-Semitism, and Fascism in France.* Stanford, CA: Stanford Univ. Press, 1998.

Winter, Bronwyn. *Hijab & The Republic: Uncovering the French Headscarf Debate.* Syracuse, NY: Syracuse Univ. Press, 2009.

Winter, Jay. "Paris, London, Berlin 1914–1919: Capital Cities at War." In *Capital Cities at War: Paris, London, Berlin 1914–1919*, edited by Jay Winter and Jean-Louis Robert, 3–25. Cambridge: Cambridge Univ. Press, 1997.

Winter, Jay, and Jean-Louis Robert. *Capital Cities at War: Paris, London, Berlin 1914–1919.* Cambridge: Cambridge Univ. Press, 1997.

Witt-Schlumberger, Marguerite de. *Le rôle des femmes de pasteurs en France pendant la guerre.* Paris: Librairie Fischbacher, s.d. probably 1916 or 1917.

Index

211

France (CONTEMPORARY): headscarf
debate in, 151–52, 153–54; identity
crisis in, 151–55; religious upheaval
in, 2
France (FIN-DE-SIÈCLE): Catholic
women as saviors of, 52–54, 58;
demographic decline prior to, 95;
suffragism in, 27, 30; women's associations in, 3–8; women's devotion
to, 137–41; World War I, religion,
and French identity, 148. *See also*
French identity; Third Republic
France juive, La, 45, 136
Franche-Comté, La, 100
Freemasons, 51, 75, 170n8
free milk programs, for infants, 102,
103, 104
French Consumers League, 23
French identity: Catholicism and,
53, 107–8, 151; headscarf debate
and, 151–52, 153–54; immigrant
aid and, 113; Jews and, 28, 87, 123;
laïcité as basis of, 80; Muslims in
contemporary, 151–55; Protestant community and, 28, 64–65;
religious suffrage of women and,
73; secularization and impact on,
91–92; women's ministries and,
64–69, 172n40. *See also* feminism
and religious identity
French League for the Recovery of
Public Morality (Ligue Française
pour le Relèvement de la Moralité
Publique), 114, 186n19
French republicanism. *See* laïcité;
separation of church and state
French Revolution, 13, 171n26
Fridmon, Sophie, 140, 193n38
fronde, La, 133
Frossard, Marie, 4, 7, 142

Gautier-Lacaze, Mme, 43, 98
gay marriage, 2
Goutte de Lait, 102, 103

Haguenauer, M. (Rabbi), 63
Harrison, Carol, 12
headscarf debate, in contemporary
France, 151–52, 153–54
Hebrew Bible, prominent women in, 1
Hoffet, Pastor, 61
Holland, François, 2

immigrants, Muslim, 151–55
immigrant women and women's
organizations, 110–12, 128–29;
ACI (Catholic association), 117–19,
186n24, 187n37; Amies de la Jeune
Fille (Protestant) program for,
115–17, 186n21, 186n24, 186nn27–
28, 187n32; anti-Semitism and, 115,
184n2; Catholic faith and, 118–19;
as domestic workers, 110–11;
French identity and, 113; home
countries of, 184n2; internationalism and, 190n66; Jewish programs
for, 120–24, 188nn47–48, 188nn52–
53, 189n56; numbers of immigrant
men v., 184n4; from Poland, 119;
prostitution and, 113, 114, 122,
186n24, 189n56; reasons for migration of, 184n2; religious aspect of,
111, 113, 115, 116, 118, 186n28;
women's leadership, religion and,
127–28, 191n82
Independent Reformed Evangelical
Church, date of pastorate opening
to women, 178n37
infants, free milk for, 102, 103, 104

Emily Machen is associate professor
of history at the University of Northern
Iowa, Cedar Falls. Her primary research
focus is women and religion in early twentieth-century France. She has published
several articles exploring various aspects
of Catholic, Protestant, and Jewish wom-
en's experiences.